The Battle of Thapsus (46 BC)

Caesar, Metellus Scipio, and the Renewal of the Third Roman Civil War

Gareth C. Sampson

Pen & Sword
MILITARY

First published in Great Britain in 2024 by
Pen & Sword Military
An imprint of Pen & Sword Books Limited
Yorkshire – Philadelphia

Copyright © Gareth C. Sampson 2024

ISBN 978 1 52679 366 9

Typeset by Mac Style
Printed in the UK by CPI Group (UK) Ltd, Croydon, CR0 4YY.

Pen & Sword Books Limited incorporates the imprints of After
the Battle, Atlas, Archaeology, Aviation, Discovery, Family History,
Fiction, History, Maritime, Military, Military Classics, Politics,
Select, Transport, True Crime, Air World, Frontline Publishing, Leo
Cooper, Remember When, Seaforth Publishing, The Praetorian Press,
Wharncliffe Local History, Wharncliffe Transport, Wharncliffe True
Crime and White Owl.

For a complete list of Pen & Sword titles please contact

PEN & SWORD BOOKS LIMITED
47 Church Street, Barnsley, South Yorkshire, S70 2AS, England
E-mail: enquiries@pen-and-sword.co.uk
Website: www.pen-and-sword.co.uk
or
PEN AND SWORD BOOKS
1950 Lawrence Rd, Havertown, PA 19083, USA
E-mail: uspen-and-sword@casematepublishers.com
Website: www.penandswordbooks.com

Dedication

In loving memory of Geoff Sampson (1947–2019)

Contents

Acknowledgements

As always, the first and greatest acknowledgement must go out to my wonderful wife Alex, without whose support and understanding none of this would be possible. Next must come Thomas and Caitlin, who are a constant source of joy and anxiety.

Special thanks go out to my parents who always encouraged a love of books and learning (even if they did regret the house being filled with books). My father Geoff is no longer with us, and his loss is still felt by us all.

There are a number of individuals who through the years have inspired the love of Roman history in me and mentored me along the way; Michael Gracey at William Hulme, David Shotter at Lancaster, and Tim Cornell at Manchester. My heartfelt thanks go out to them all.

A shout goes out to the remaining members of the Manchester diaspora: Gary, Ian, Jason, Sam. Those were good days; we will not see their like again.

As always, my thanks go out to my editor Phil Sidnell, for his patience and understanding.

It must also be said that as an Independent Academic, the job of researching these works is being made easier by the internet, so Alumnus access to JSTOR (Manchester and Lancaster) and Academia.edu must get a round of thanks also.

List of Illustrations

Maps & Diagrams

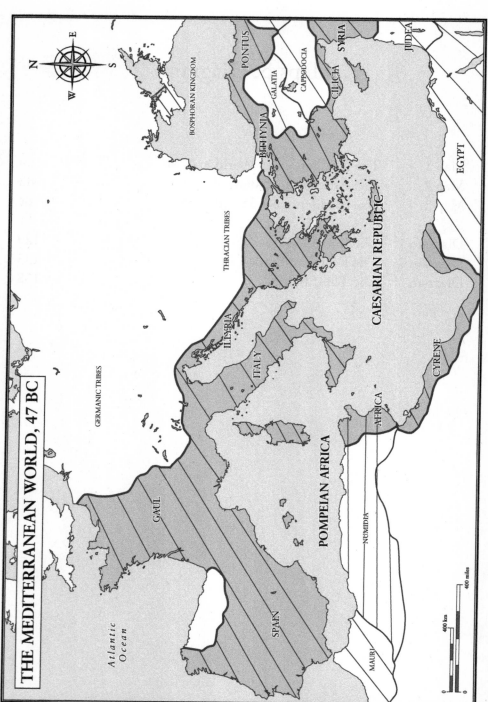

Map 1: The Mediterranean World in 47 BC.

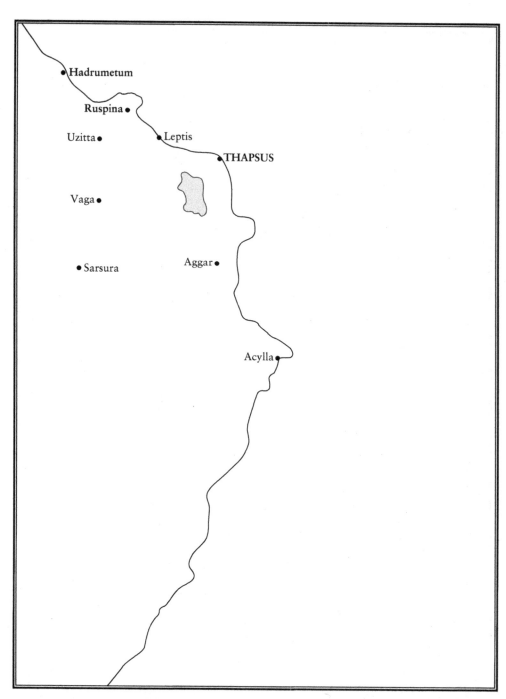

Map 2: The African Campaigns (46 BC).

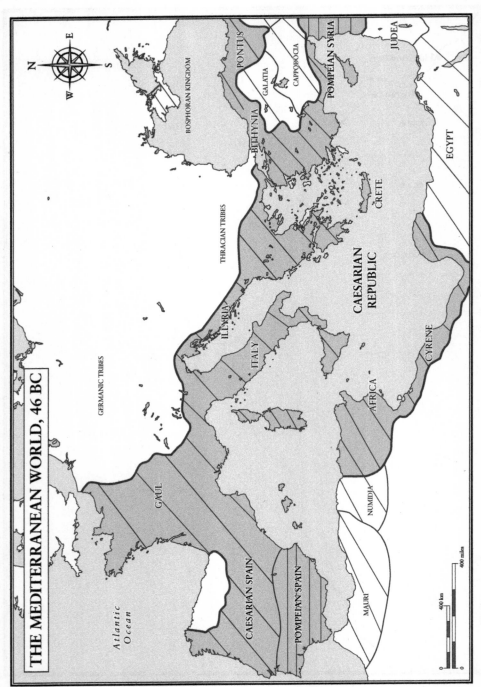

Map 3: The Mediterranean World in 46 BC.

Within the map:

THE MEDITERRANEAN WORLD, 46 BC

N E S W

Atlantic Ocean

GERMANIC TRIBES

GAUL

CAESARIAN SPAIN

POMPEIAN SPAIN

MAURI

NUMIDIA

AFRICA

CYRENE

ITALY

ILLYRIA

THRACIAN TRIBES

CAESARIAN REPUBLIC

BITHYNIA

PONTUS

GALATIA

CAPPODOCIA

POMPEIAN SYRIA

JUDEA

EGYPT

CRETE

BOSPHORAN KINGDOM

400 km
400 miles
0
0

Introduction

The Battle of Thapsus – Scipio vs Caesar, and the Challenge to the Caesarian Narrative

On what now equates to 6 April 46 BC, two great armies met in battle on the coast of North Africa, with control of the Mediterranean world going to the winner. 156 years earlier a similar battle had been fought between two legendary generals: Scipio Africanus of the Roman Republic and Hannibal of the Carthaginian Empire. This earlier battle (Zama) had been won by Scipio and ensured Roman domination of the Western Mediterranean, one of the cornerstones of their rise to control of the Western world. Now another Scipio took up the challenge laid down by his famous ancestor, as he too faced one of the ancient world's greatest generals. On this occasion, however, Scipio was not fighting a foreign threat, but an internal one and his opponent was none other than C. Iulius Caesar himself.

The Battle of Thapsus forms the third great battle of the early period of this Third Roman Civil War (49–44 BC), following those of Dyrrhachium and Pharsalus in Greece, in 48 BC. Scipio had missed the first of these battles, which saw Caesar defeated by his arch rival Pompeius, but was present for the second, which saw Pompeius narrowly defeated by Caesar. The subsequent murder of Pompeius on an Egyptian beach, saw command of the Pompeian faction fall to his father-in-law, the head of the Scipio-Metellan families (two of the Republic's most successful), Q. Caecilius Metellus Pius Scipio Nasica. He now had to take command of the retreating Pompeians and forge them into a new fighting force capable of defeating Caesar and seizing back control of the Republic they had lost at Pharsalus.

Whether by accident or design, Caesar's own account of the civil war finished with the murder of Pompeius Magnus on an Egyptian beach, following his defeat at the Battle of Pharsalus in 48 BC. It may well be that his account would have continued but was cut off by his own murder and the subsequent histories of the Alexandrian, African and Spanish Wars were created by contemporaries and subordinates. However, the suspicion is that this was a deliberate act on Caesar's part as he wanted the death of Pompeius to be seen as the end of the civil war.

For the last two millennia, pro-Caesarian propaganda has followed Caesar's lead and focused on his victory at Pharsalus as the turning point in the Republic's history, portraying the campaigns that followed as mere tidying up exercises. Yet, both Caesar and those who follow his lead overlook the fact that the civil war didn't end in 48 BC, but continued for a number of years; Caesar had to fight two further major campaigns and two further major battles (Thapsus and Munda). Even then the Pompeians continued to fight on, in both Spain and Syria, so that when Caesar met his untimely end in Rome on the Ides of March 44 BC, the civil war was still raging.

It is easy to understand why Caesar would follow such a path and want to gloss over these subsequent campaigns and battles, as both undermined and diminished the victory he had achieved at Pharsalus. If it was such a great victory, then why did the civil war continue? Equally, if the civil war was the fault of Pompeius then why did so many fight on after his death? Both questions undermined Caesar and his grip on the Roman Republic. In the Caesarian (and later Augustan) propaganda and subsequent myth, the great general was forced by the perfidious Pompeius to take up arms against his enemies, and after his brilliant victory in Greece in 48 BC (tactfully ignoring the Battle of Dyrrhachium), both the Senate and People fell over themselves to beg Caesar to restore stability to the Roman Republic and bring them peace.

Yet if the war continued for another four years and even outlasted his death, clearly this propaganda and myth were challenged. Yet whilst few in either Caesarian, or Augustan Rome, could do so publicly, two millennia later, we do not have to be so censorious. One thing is clear, however, notwithstanding Caesar's own attempts to write the history books and despite what he may have hoped, the Roman Civil War (the third by this author's calculations) continued beyond the defeat and subsequent murder of one of its two main protagonists.

As has been argued in the books earlier in this series, the civil war broke out in 49 BC following the political machinations of Pompeius (as repeated in Chapter One), who needed such a crisis to propel him to the role of

Protector/Guardian (or Princeps) of the Republic. Again, as we have seen, this strategy backfired spectacularly in 48 BC when he was unexpectedly defeated in battle and treacherously murdered on an Egyptian beach.

Yet, although the two men had dominated the narrative of the civil war (and some would say still do), as subsequent events proved, this was not simply a civil war between two rival generals, but a war for control of the Republic. The Pompeian faction was composed of two main (and contrasting) sub factions: the family and supporters of Pompeius himself and the 'Republican' faction (for want of a better name), who were opposed to any individual who might dominate the Republic (even Pompeius). In the face of Caesar's attack on his own state, even though many clearly understood that it had been engineered by Pompeius, they had no option but to ally with the 'lesser of two evils' and back Pompeius against Caesar.

As events showed (something which will be analysed later in this work), neither faction collapsed following the death of Pompeius, in fact just the opposite. As Caesar himself must have realized, the death of Pompeius and his 'martyrdom' on an Egyptian beach would ensure that there would be no negotiated end to the civil war. We can easily imagine that Pompeian propaganda painted Caesar as the dark mastermind behind this perfidious act.

For the Pompeian clan, the death of their patron would have to be avenged, and a new figure emerged to head up the faction and soak up the political patronage: Q. Caecilius Metellus Pius Scipio Nasica (Metellus Scipio), Pompeius' father-in-law and head of the two greatest Republican families. For the 'Republican' faction, Caesar's victory and Pompeius' murder made Caesar an even greater threat to the safety of the Republic and one which must be totally opposed and defeated. If anything, the death of Pompeius, made this task easier in spirit, if not in actuality, as they would have been under no illusions that had Pompeius defeated Caesar then he would have been the biggest threat to the Republic. With Pompeius removed, they now had a Republican martyr rather than an enemy. This faction rallied around Caesar's long term political rival, and another scion of a noble Republican house, C. Porcius Cato.

Though both key factions, and as we will see, an emerging third faction, were determined to fight on, determination was clearly not enough. As we have seen the Pompeian grand army had been destroyed at the Battle of Pharsalus, the foreign elements had either been killed or fled back eastwards and the Roman elements surrendered and integrated into Caesar's own army. Furthermore, Pharsalus had been as crushing a psychological blow as a military one and (with one notable exception) Rome's provinces and allies, who had been eager to support Pompeius militarily, were now inclined towards the new favourite, Caesar.

Yet, as we shall see, there were three Caesarian mistakes that gave succour to the Pompeian faction's continued resistance and allowed them to recover and challenge Caesar once more. The first came in 49 BC, when Caesar's forces were defeated and destroyed in their attempt to invade Pompeian North Africa. The next came in 48 BC in the aftermath of Pharsalus when Caesar allowed all the key Pompeian factional leaders (naturally except Pompeius himself) to survive and escape. The final one came in 47 BC, when, rather than immediately seizing the initiative (as had been his preference in the civil war to date) Caesar ignored the civil war for the majority of the year in favour of other enterprises. Thus the Pompeian faction not only had the continued desire to fight, but also the leadership, a secure and wealthy base of operations and time to rebuild.

Thus, Caesar's chance to end this civil war faded and somewhat reduced the impact of his victory at Pharsalus. That victory had made him the leading candidate, but as Pharsalus itself had shown, the front runner in a civil war did not always emerge victorious. The stage was set for another great battle between the two factions and again, the Pompeians ensured that it would be fought on their own ground.

What followed was the Battle of Thapsus in 46 BC, a battle that rivalled Pharsalus in terms of its impact in this Third Roman Civil War, but one that (until now) has always been overshadowed by its predecessor. It was at Thapsus that the fate of the Republic was (temporarily) determined and it can be argued that it had as much impact as Pharsalus in terms of its outcome: the near destruction of the Pompeian faction and its key leaders in the bloody aftermath.

The battle was the culmination of a three month campaign across the sands of North Africa, where time and again the Pompeians faced Caesar in battles and skirmishes, coming close to defeating him and changing the course of Roman and world history. Thus the battle needs to be reviewed in its own right, not merely as an afterthought to its more famous predecessor, but to determine its rightful place in Roman history as one of the key battles in the Republic.

Caesar would have us believe that Pharsalus saw his rise to control the Roman Republic as inevitable from that point on, Thapsus reveals the truth of the matter. Whilst later generations may be awed by Caesar's reputation, his contemporaries were not and his enemies were determined that the last battle was a fluke and that, as seen at Dyrrhachium, Caesar could be defeated.

The following work analyses how close they came to achieving that aim. It does not simply examine the battle itself, but looks at the factors that brought it about and saw the re-emergence of the Pompeian faction, who went from defeat at Pharsalus to forcing Caesar to launch a risky invasion of their North African powerbase to stem their challenge to his flimsy control of the Republic. The work focuses on the key Pompeian leaders, especially Metellus Scipio, who has gone from one of the notable Republican 'martyrs' to that of a minor figure these days.

The critical three month long campaign in the sands of North Africa is analysed, with the two armies playing a cat and mouse game of skirmishes and small scale battles, such as the further Pompeian victory at Ruspina, before moving on to the decisive clash at Thapsus itself. The work also analyses the aftermath of the battle which again saw the Pompeian threat re-emerge and continue to challenge Caesar's control of the Republic.

After which it is hoped that the reader will have a fuller understanding of one of the key battles in the late Republican civil wars and both the factors that led to it and the consequences that stemmed from it. Also an awareness that the Roman civil wars did not end with Pharsalus and that it was wishful thinking on Caesar's part that to assert that it did, thinking (and subsequent propaganda) that must be challenged if we are truly to understand the fall of the Roman Republic.

Timeline

Pre-Third Civil War (70–49 BC)

91–70 First Roman Civil War
72   Pompeius victorious in Spain against Perperna
71   Crassus victorious in Italy against Spartacus
        Formation of the Duumvirate between Pompeius and Crassus
70   Consulship of Pompeius and Crassus – Constitutional Reforms
        Enacted
68   Pompeius is appointed to command the war against the
        Mediterranean Pirates
67   Pompeius is appointed to command the Eastern War against
        Armenia and Pontus
65   Crassus as Censor tries to annex Egypt.
64   Pompeius annexes the remnants of the Seleucid Empire
63–62 Second Civil War
62   Pompeius returns to Italy.
60   Reformation of the Duumvirate between Pompeius and Crassus
59   Consulship of Caesar – passes Duumvirates' legislation.
        Marriage of Pompeius to Caesar's daughter
58   Tribunate of Clodius – street violence in Rome
        Caesar launches the Romano-Gallic War
57   Tribunate of Milo – street violence escalates.
56   Pompeius is appointed to take charge of Rome's grain supply.
        Conference at Lucca – Reformation of the Duumvirate
55   Consulships of Pompeius and Crassus
54   Crassus takes command of the First Romano-Parthian War
53   Battle of Carrhae – Crassus defeated by the Parthian Surenas.
        Killed in the retreat.
        Violence in Rome prevents Curule elections.
52   Murder of Clodius, burning of the Senate House
        Pompeius appointed Sole Consul, conducts judicial purge.

50 Breakdown of the Relationship between Pompeius and Caesar
49 The Senate pass the *senatus consultum ultimum* against Caesar.
   Caesar commits treason by invading Italy across the River Rubicon

The Early Years of the Third Roman Civil War (49 BC)

49 **Italian Campaign**
   Caesar invades Italy.
   Battle of Corfinium
   Pompeius withdraws to Brundisium.
   Battle of Brundisium
   Pompeius withdraws across the Adriatic to Dyrrhachium
   Caesar seizes Rome.
49 **Gallic Campaign**
   Caesarian forces lay siege to Massilia.
   Pompeian-Massilian fleet defeated twice off Massilia.
   Massilia surrenders to Caesar after the Fall of Spain
49 **Spanish Campaign**
   Caesarian forces cross Pyrenees and invade Pompeian Spain
   Battle of Ilerda – Caesar trapped in a deteriorating position.
   Caesar convinces more Spanish tribes to back him.
   Pompeian forces decide to retreat and are routed by Caesar.
   Caesar wins over the Pompeian army and allies in Southern Spain
49 **Western Mediterranean Campaigns**
   Pompeian forces evacuate Sardinia after a local revolt, Caesarian forces occupy island
   Caesarian forces invade Sicily, Cato withdraws without a fight.
   Caesarian forces invade Roman Africa
   Siege of Pompeian-held Utica.
   Caesarian victory at the Battle of Utica
   Caesarian army destroyed at the Battle of Bagradas River by Numidian forces.
   Africa held by the Pompeians.
49 **Adriatic and Illyrian Campaign**
   Pompeian fleet defeat Caesarian fleet and ensure control of the Adriatic.
   Caesarian army starved into surrender; Illyria conquered by Pompeians.

Timeline – The Early Years of the Third Roman Civil War (48 BC)

48   **Epirote / Illyrian Campaign**
Caesar crosses the Adriatic and lands in Epirus, Pompeius moves
to intercept.
Pompeian Fleet cuts Caesar off, skirmishes between Pompeius
and Caesar
Pompeian attack on Brundisium
Political disorder in Italy
Antonius crosses the Adriatic with Caesarian reinforcements.
Caesar marches on the city of Dyrrhachium, Pompeius follows.

Caesar lays siege to Pompeius' army in the Bay of Dyrrhachium
Failed Caesarian attack on the city of Dyrrhachium.
Failed Pompeian attack on Caesar's siege lines.
Pompeius breaks through Caesar's siege lines to the south of the
Bay.
Caesar launches a counterattack on the Pompeian bridgehead.
Pompeius launches a counterattack on Caesar.
Caesarian army is routed, with thousands of casualties.
Caesar regroups his army, breaks off the siege and marches inland
to Macedonia, to join up with his other forces and face Metellus
Scipio
Pompeius harasses Caesar's army south and then breaks off and
marches inland.

48   **Greek / Macedonian / Thessalian campaigns**
Metellus Scipio crosses into Thessaly from Asia Minor
Caesarian forces spread into Greece, Thessaly, and Macedonia
Metellus Scipio defeats Caesarian forces in Thessaly but is slowed
down.
Caesarian forces defeated in Macedonia by Faustus Sulla
Caesarian forces secure Aetolia and Acarnania
Pompeian forces fall back to the Isthmus of Corinth

Two Pompeian and Two Caesarian armies converge on each other.
Domitius' army avoids marching into Pompeian trap and turns
southward.

The two Caesarian armies unite.

Metellus Scipio's army marches to Larissa and is joined by Pompeius.

The two Pompeian armies unite.

Caesar marches towards Pompeius and offers battle on the plain of Pharsalus.

Battle of Pharsalus – Pompeius is defeated.

Pompeius retreats eastwards by ship, followed by Caesar on land.

The bulk of the Pompeians retreat to Dyrrhachium and Corcyra and then try to hold the Peloponnese before retreating across the Mediterranean to Cyrene

Cassius and his fleet fail to attack Caesar at the Bosphorus and defect, giving Caesar the ability to chase Pompeius effectively.

Pompeius choses to land in Ptolemaic Egypt and is murdered on the beach.

Caesar becomes entangled in a Ptolemaic Civil War

The Pompeians retreat to Roman Africa to regroup.

Pharnaces II invades Roman Asia Minor

The Third Roman Civil War (47 BC)

47   **Epirote / Illyrian Campaign**

Octavius continues Pompeian resistance.

Battle of Sunodium – Gabinius defeated, later dies.

Vatinius crosses from Brundisium.

Battle of Tauris – Vatinius defeats Octavius

Greek Campaign

Possible continued Caesarian action against Megara.

Spanish Campaign

Caesarian armies tied down by continued unrest.

Sardinian Campaign

Pompeian fleet based at Sardinia raids Sicily.

Rome
Armed clashes between the supporters of warring Tribunes.
Battle of the Forum – Roman army sent in to suppress violence.

The Third Roman Civil War (47 BC)

46   **North African Campaign – East**
Caesar invade North Africa, fails to take Hadrumetum.
Battle of Ruspina – Pompeian victory.
Sieges of Leptis and Acylla
Second Battle of Ruspina – Caesarian victory.
Battle of Uzitta – Pompeian victory.
Battles of Leptis and Hadrumetum – Caesarian naval victory.
Caesarian retreat to Aggar
Battle of Zeta – stalemate
Battle of Sarsura – Caesarian victory.
Battle of Tegea – Caesarian victory.
Battle of Thapsus – Total Caesarian victory.

Numidian cavalry sack Utica.
Afranius and Faustus Sulla retreat westwards towards the Mauri.
Metellus Scipio takes ship from Utica, Cato commits suicide.
Pompeians surrender Utica.
Battle of Hippo Regius – Metellus Scipio commits suicide.
Juba and Petreius commit suicide.
Numidia surrenders to Caesar, becomes a Roman province.
L. Iulius Caesar is murdered by unknown assassins.
Caesar returns to Rome and is appointed Dictator for ten years.

North African Campaign – West
Pompeius Magnus leads an attack on the Mauri.
Battle of Ascurum – Pompeius defeated.
Maurian invasion of Numidia led by Sittius.
Gaetulian Revolt
Sittius defeats Numidian army of Saburra.
Sittius defeats Sulla and Afranius, who are subsequently murdered.

Spanish Campaign

Pompeius Magnus leads a Pompeian expedition to Spain.

Pompeius seizes the Balearic Islands.

Pompeians inspire revolt in Farther Spain, Caesarian Governor driven out.

Survivors from North Africa arrive.

Pompeius invades Southern Spain raising a new Pompeian army.

Caesar sends general to reinforce Northern Spain.

Caesar leaves Rome for Spain (again).

Syrian Campaign

Sex. Iulius Caesar is murdered by his own men in a Pompeian inspired revolt.

Caecilius Bessus seizes Syria and its legions in the name of Metellus Scipio.

Bessus defeats the Caesarian forces from Asia Minor.

Notes on Roman Names

All Roman names in the following text will be given in their traditional form, including the abbreviated first name. Below is a list of the Roman first names referred to in the text and their abbreviations.

A.	Aulus.
Ap.	Appius
C.	Caius
Cn.	Cnaeus
D.	Decimus
F.	Faustus
K.	Kaeso
L.	Lucius
M.	Marcus
Mam.	Mamercus
P.	Publius
Q.	Quintus
Ser.	Servius
Sex.	Sextus
Sp.	Spurius
T.	Titus
Ti.	Tiberius

Section I

The Architects of the Third Civil War (49–47 BC)

Chapter One

The Roman Evolution – The Road to the Third Civil War (133–50 BC)

To fully understand the events that took place in 46 BC, both leading up to the Battle of Thapsus and its aftermath, the reader needs an awareness of the events that preceded it. Whilst these have been covered in depth in the two previous volumes,[1] an overview can only be of use to the reader, especially given the deep roots of this conflict.

The Senatorial Oligarchy Prior to 133 BC

The key to the Roman political system, which we today label the Republic (from the Latin *res publica*; roughly translated as the public good) lay with the Senatorial oligarchy, an ever expanding group of Roman families who ruled Rome the city and then its ever expanding empire. Starting out as a closed grouping of clans led by warlords, who overthrew the Kings of Rome in the late sixth century BC, they controlled the military and political functions of their city state. The fifth century BC saw the closed nature of this elite challenged by men of wealth, but not birth, who wished to join the ruling clique (the so called 'Struggle of the Orders') which ended in the 360s BC, with the richer families of the Plebeian Order joining with the older Patrician families to forge a new ruling political elite, to exploit the rest of the Plebeian Order and continue their dominance. The main net effect of this being that the new Senatorial elite was open to any family of wealth regardless of their historic or ethnic origins. Thus, as Rome the city state expanded its empire across Italy, so the ruling oligarchy expanded with it.

The key to the success of Rome's political stability lay with the oligarchy itself, both by its constant expansion of new blood and by its ever shifting pattern of family and factional alliances that reshaped with every generation. With the People safely under their control the only threats to the dominance of the oligarchy came from within its own ranks; men whose military success or political machinations threatened the collegiate nature of oligarchy and thus brought the other families or factions together to oppose their dominance. This happened on numerous occasions through the centuries, as can be found throughout Livy's accounts, but was best demonstrated in the 180s BC when none other than Rome's greatest general to date – P. Cornelius Scipio 'Africanus', the conqueror of Hannibal – was brought down (along with his brother) by the combined might of his political opponents. Thus, the system of checks and balances within the ruling oligarchy seemed to be strong enough to deal with internal threats and maintain political stability.

Rome, Blood and Politics (133–91 BC)[2]

Yet, just fifty years later, this stability was shattered by the murder of one of their own number when this process of uniting to bring down a rising politician got seriously out of hand and led to political murder. The victim in question was a junior member of the Roman elite, but one of impeccable background by both bloodline and marriage. The man in question was Ti. Sempronius Gracchus, son of a two-time Consul and whose mother was none other than the daughter of Africanus himself and thus related to Rome's leading family. Over the subsequent millennia Gracchus has frequently been portrayed as a revolutionary figure seeking to overturn the established order. Yet at heart he was a blue-blooded aristocrat serving his political faction and his patron.

Into this space emerges another P. Cornelius Scipio, grandson of Africanus, named Aemilianus, though he too later took the same title as his grandfather. Possessing some of his grandfather's military ability, his greatest gifts seem to have been political ones and seemingly learnt from his grandfather's mistakes. He twice used political emergencies – the Third Romano-Punic War in Africa and then the Romano-Numantine War in Spain – to subvert the unwritten constitution and gain himself extraordinary commands, utilizing the theoretical sovereignty of the People.

In 135 BC, Scipio had the People overturn the law preventing repeat Consulships (brought in by his opponents within the oligarchy) to allow himself to be Consul for a second time for the following year. Given the military disasters in Spain (the Romano-Numantine War) and Sicily (the First Slave War), the People were eager for a dashing Roman general to take charge and restore Roman pride, and who better than a Scipio? With Scipio in Spain, however, his faction needed the usual share of political offices for the next year (to ensure no adverse legislation was passed) and thus young Gracchus took his first steps on the political ladder, holding the junior magistracy of the Tribune of the Plebian Order.

This junior magistracy was something of an anomaly. Having started out as an office purely for the Plebeian Order, it became absorbed into the official body of Roman magistracies, held by both junior aristocrats and leading non-aristocratic Plebeians, yet maintained the power of passing laws (*plebiscita*) in the assemblies. This anomaly had been exploited previously by Tribunes in past centuries, most notably C. Licinius Stolo in the fourth century and C. Flaminius in the third century.

What happened next was an exceptional combination of a stubborn and politically inventive young aristocrat, eager to fulfil his patron's wishes, with a junior magistracy of potentially unlimited power. Just as his patron Aemilianus had utilized the popular sovereignty of the People to his own ends, so Gracchus did, overturning established and widely accepted precedents and showcasing the power of such an approach. In Gracchus' case it benefitted him little as he was lynched by a rival group of the oligarchs who (in their minds at least) could come up with no other way of stopping him. Thus this crucial year in Roman politics had created two major milestones in the political history of the Roman Republic, a clear demonstration of the power of the Tribunate and political murder. The subsequent forty years of Roman politics saw a repeating escalation of both factors, as has been covered elsewhere.[3]

The subsequent aftermath of this episode saw the murders of none other than Scipio Aemilianus himself and Gracchus' own brother, Caius, who had used the same office of Tribune to push a radical reform agenda. A period of uneasy calm fell across the Republic, but this was shattered by another protégé of Aemilianus, C. Marius, who equally exploited another period of military disaster and popular dissatisfaction with the Senatorial oligarchy by the People to utilize both elements of the Aemilianic playbook: popular election to the Consulship and exploitation of the powers of the Tribunate. Again, Marius' exploits and accomplishments are analysed elsewhere,[4] but it led Marius to unprecedented political glory (six Consulships between 107 and 100 BC, including five in a row between 104–100 BC) alongside unprecedented military success: the destruction of the invading Germanic tribes. After disposing of some temporary allies, with whom he had formed a Triumvirate (Saturninus and Glaucia), Marius successfully stepped back from the limelight and returned to the collegiate oligarchy, awaiting another military crisis to exploit.

The First Civil War and the Collapse of the Republic (91–71 BC)[5]

In fact he waited just under a decade for one to appear, as the Republic collapsed in a series of ever increasing disasters. First came the Senatorial oligarchy's disastrous mishandling of the demands of their Italian allies for a greater share in the success of the growth of Rome's empire. Whilst the local elites had been absorbed into the oligarchy there were many more left behind. Given the recent history of political reforms, it is hardly surprising that the oligarchy initially closed ranks and chose to ignore this issue. However, it is equally unsurprising that eventually one of the oligarchic factions made the calculation that it was in their interest to exploit it. Naturally this exploitation was fronted by a young Tribune (M. Livius Drusus), and equally naturally, it ended in bloodshed in Rome, with Drusus' assassination (91 BC). The irony being Drusus was the son of the man who did so much to oppose Ti. Sempronius Gracchus a generation earlier.

This murder set off a chain reaction amongst the already disgruntled Italian allies and saw the formation of a rebel alliance of two major factions, centred on Rome's long standing old Italian enemies (the Samnites and the Marsi), which saw the Republic collapse into civil war between Rome and the rebel alliance of Italians. Two years of hard fighting across Italy, saw Rome emerge victorious in battle, accompanied by the major political concession that the Italians had originally wanted; namely the extension of the Roman franchise and citizenship for all (loyal) Italians.

Despite this victory, the Roman ruling oligarchy collectively managed to snatch defeat from the jaws of victory, with the inevitable political arguments and factional manoeuvrings over the citizenship franchise leading to bloodshed in Rome itself (again centred on a Tribune, P. Sulpicius), and more importantly giving Marius the opportunity he had been patiently waiting for. Exploiting the chaos in Italy, one of

Rome's eastern enemies, Mithridates VI of the Pontic Empire, used the opportunity to attack Rome's eastern territories and expand his own empire, before Rome inevitably attacked him. Now finding an overseas military crisis worthy of him, Marius returned to his tried and tested technique of seizing a military command through the use of a Tribune (Sulpicius). Though he had learnt that tactic from his own mentor, Aemilianus, he too had a protégé, L. Cornelius Sulla, and it was Sulla that Marius betrayed by seizing the Mithridatic command.

Facing both personal humiliation and political ruin, and no doubt stung by Marius lying to his face and betraying him after he left the city, Sulla made use of the one weapon he had: his army, and took the lessons of the previous forty years to their logical conclusion. Along with his Consular colleague and political ally (Q. Pompeius Rufus), they convinced their army that as legally appointed Consuls they had a duty to restore order in Rome, and with the agreement of the rank and file (though not the officers) they attacked their own city, plunging the Republic into a near twenty year cycle of civil war, between various Roman generals drawing in rebel forces from within both Italy and Spain.

Again the events of this First Civil War have been analysed elsewhere,[6] but over the subsequent near two decades, the Republic came close to collapse, with various warlords seizing power at the point of an army or carving out their own fiefdoms from the Republic; men like Marius, Cinna, Sulla, Sertorius, and C. Valerius Flaccus. Both Marius and Sulla seized Rome by force (in 87 and 82 BC respectively) both accompanied by a wholesale slaughter of their enemies. Sulla particularly took this to a logical extreme and had legally drawn up prescription lists; murder by bureaucracy.

It was Sulla who did so much to restore order to the Republic along with two of his own protégés, both sons of civil war generals who had been killed: Cn. Pompeius and M. Licinius Crassus. Both supported Sulla's war across Italy in 83–82 BC, with Crassus being instrumental in the final battle for Rome (Colline Gate). Pompeius then added Sicily and Africa to Sullan control, followed by an agreement between Valerius Flaccus and Sulla which brought Gaul and Spain back to central control. Thus, briefly, the Republic was reunified, with Sulla creating a new blueprint for post-civil war Rome. Despite the bloodshed and mass murder, Sulla clearly realized that the Senatorial oligarchy would not tolerate an obvious ruler, so he publicly stepped down from his 'emergency role' won at the point of a sword but legalized by retrospective legislation. He then 'retired' from all official positions, but with his faction controlling the Senate and his veterans settled throughout Italy in military colonies, settled back to exert the role of 'Princeps' of the Republic and ensure its smooth running by eliminating any internal dangers.

However, this fascinating experiment was cut short by his untimely death (of natural causes ironically) leaving the role vacant and with no one of sufficient power to take his place. Almost immediately civil war broke out in Italy once more, with armies again marching on Rome, followed by the survivors of this campaign and previous campaigns regrouping in Spain and Asia Minor, ensuring the continuation of the First Civil War, exacerbated by the largest slave revolt the Republic ever saw in Italy.

By 71 BC, Sulla's two most enthusiastic protégés, Pompeius and Crassus, sat at the gates of Rome with victorious armies, having defeated their civil war opponents in Spain and the slaves in Italy respectively. Thus, the stage was set for the civil war to continue into a fresh campaign.

The Duumvirate and the New Republic (70–64 BC)[7]

What followed next must have surprised most people, as the two rivals, who had no love for one another, combined forces, forming a Duumvirate and seized control of the Republic, with an unprecedented combination of military might, money and popular acclaim. The wider Sullan faction were displaced, and the two men rammed through a reform programme, restoring much of what Sulla had swept away, including the powers of the Tribunate.

They too then publicly stepped down from power and 'retired' into the collegiate nature of the Roman oligarchy, temporarily filling the role that Sulla had intended as Princeps of the Republic, ensuring that their reforms were not overturned. By 67 BC this partnership was dissolved and both men went back to competing for power and glory in their own unique ways, Pompeius on the battlefield of the East, and Crassus immersing himself in the Machiavellian world of Roman political intrigue. It was during this period that Crassus too picked up a protégé, a man whose obscure ancestral background was vastly overshadowed by his immediate lineage.

Though C. Iulius Caesar played no active part in the First Civil War, he was inexorably linked to the anti-Sullan faction, by both blood and marriage. His aunt was none other than the wife of Marius and it is unknown what level of contact the two men had over the years (Marius died when Caesar was 12). Furthermore, during the 80s BC, Rome was ruled by the Marian-Cinnan faction and Caesar embodied this alliance through marriage to Cinna's daughter. The subsequent slaughter of the Marian faction when Sulla took Rome meant that Caesar was Marius' nearest (and only) surviving relative, with many amazed that such close connections to Sulla's enemies saw him emerge from Sulla's proscriptions unscathed.[8]

With Pompeius conquering a new empire in the east and Crassus engaged in politicking in Rome, new threats to the Republic's stability emerged, but were dealt with. The first came in the form of a move by the Senate to disqualify the two men elected as Consuls for 65 BC. Uncoincidentally one of them was named Sulla (P. Cornelius Sulla, nephew of the deceased Dictator and current head of the family). The men were dismissed on a charge of bribery, the first and only time that such a charge had led to disqualification, as it was a common enough practice.[9] Thus a resurgence of the Sullan faction had been quashed.

In fact it seems that having two leading figures brought balance to the oligarchy in the way that one did not, with the two men cancelling each other out. While Pompeius was distracted in the east, Crassus made a bold bid for glory when he attempted to annex the Ptolemaic Empire using the power of the Censorship, another extraordinary leap of power. Republican stability was restored when his fellow Censor, supported by the non-aligned and Pompeian factions within the Senatorial elite, blocked such a move.

The Second Civil War (63–62 BC)

This Second Civil War is routinely, and in my view erroneously, classed as the 'Catilinarian Conspiracy' one of the many terms conjured up by historians (both ancient and modern) to avoid using the term civil war (see Appendix Four). At its heart lay an attempt by the Sullan faction, both political and military to restore the position they had lost under the New Republic; an aftershock as it were. However, whilst the quick resolution to this latest crisis, one major battle in Italy, showed the strength of the New Republic, the challenge did not have the backing of either of the two oligarchs, though Crassus' role is impossible to determine and the supporters of Pompeius attempted to recall him into a senior position to deal with the crisis, which in itself was defeated by the Crassan and non-aligned factions.

At the heart of this Second Civil War lay the two pillars of the Sullan faction; the faction members within the Senatorial oligarchy and the discharged veterans settled in Italy. These were the two pillars which Sulla was to have relied on to ensure the stability of the New Republic, yet both found themselves swept aside in the Pompeian-Crassan Republic. Those members amongst the Senate now found themselves being prosecuted for their actions during the Sullan peace (despite their legality at the time) with a new generation of untainted young politicians using these prosecutions as a means of gaining political capital. Chief amongst them were M. Porcius Cato and C. Iulius Caesar. This state of affairs, combined with having to compete with the factions of Crassus and Pompeius for magistracies and the disqualification of the young Sulla in 66/65 BC clearly engineered resentment amongst those who had believed that they were now the victorious faction.

On its own, this resentment would not have been a problem, as there was little they could do about it. Unfortunately, it coincided with a similar seething resentment amongst the Sullan veterans in Italy who equally were not reaping the rewards which they felt they deserved. Having been discharged onto the land and set up with farms by Sulla, these men found an Italy that had been devastated by the civil war campaigns of 83–82 BC and then by the massive slave insurrection of the late 70s BC. Thus, Italy was in economic hard times and so were the veterans. Naturally these Sullan veterans turned to their former officers and the Sullan officers turned to their former veterans and a plot was hatched to stage a coup and restore 'Sullan' control of the Republic once more.

However, the coup in Rome was a shambles reflecting the poor quality of the leadership of the Sullan faction. With P. Cornelius Sulla seemingly not playing a leading part, leadership seems to have fallen to P. Cornelius Lentulus Sura, a former Praetor who had fallen foul of the Pompeian-Crassan Censors of 70 BC and been purged from the Senate. Faced against them were the faction of Crassus, who seems to have known about the coup and may well have been stirring it up for his own ends and the faction of the absent Pompeius. The coup was betrayed, and the ring leaders rounded up. Cicero, one of the Consuls of 63 BC, claimed the credit for saving the Republic from his arch nemesis L. Sergius Catilina (one of the conspirators and a rival of his); a boast that few at the time cared for. The revolt of the Sullan veterans was better organized and an army was raised. The threat, however, was ended at the Battle of Pistoria in January 62 BC when Cicero's consular colleague (C. Antonius) defeated the Sullan army.

Thus, there were both positive and negative aspects of the prospects of the New Republic. On the negative side a fresh civil war had broken out with discharged civil war veterans forming a ready-made army for disgruntled members of the oligarchy. On the other hand though, the government was able to see off this threat relatively easily, without having to turn to its two 'guardians'. The positives outweighed the negatives, and the New Republic survived its first challenge.

The Return of the Duumvirate

The strength of the New Republic was soon tested once more, and again, initially, the system responded well, when one of its two 'founders' (Pompeius) returned home from a long Eastern campaign where he had carved out a new empire for Rome in the Near and Middle East. The Pontic and Armenian Empires had been defeated in battle, the Seleucid Empire annexed, the Ptolemaic Empire dominated, and the Parthian Empire humbled.[10] Rome was now the leading power in the Near and Middle East and one man claimed the credit: Cn. Pompeius 'Magnus'. Pompeius returned to Rome (in 62 BC) enjoying the adulation of his victories, but soon needed political validation of them; from the discharge of his men to the ratification of his new political structure in the East.

Naturally, he attempted to convert this military victory into political capital, and equally naturally the rest of the Senatorial oligarchy closed ranks against him, including his old rival Crassus. Thus Pompeius' influence could only secure one Consul each year (61 and 60 BC), leaving the other free to block his proposals. This stalemate continued until later in 60 BC when, in circumstances that are still unclear, Pompeius and Crassus reconciled, an event probably engineered by Caesar, who put himself forward as the next Pompeian candidate for the Consulship. Caesar was consequently elected (for 59 BC), but the two men's influence did not extend to securing both Consulships, again showing the underlying strength of the non-aligned oligarchy.

Yet, whereas in previous years Pompeius had been willing to allow his political proposals to be blocked, now with Crassus onside and Caesar as Consul (59 BC), they drove through his requirements regardless of the constitutional opposition. Thus the inherent weakness of the New Republic was shown, that when the leading oligarchs united in common cause, there was nothing the others could do to stop them. Yet this temporary alliance soon dissolved, with Caesar receiving his pay off: an extraordinary command in Gaul, where he would be safe from his newly acquired political enemies, who would have been eager to hold him to account for his actions as Consul. In political terms this was self-exile, in military terms, however, Caesar harboured what most would have considered a delusion, the ambition of conquering all the tribes of Gaul. With Caesar out of the way, Pompeius and Crassus returned to the longstanding game of political manoeuvrings, usually against each other, whilst ensuring that Caesar's actions as Consul were not overturned.

However, another of their actions of this year came back to haunt them, as they had sponsored the extraordinary move of a Patrician oligarch, P. Claudius Pulcher, to be adopted into the Plebeian Order solely for the purpose of standing for the office of Tribune, a role which he duly won. Having an active Tribune was an essential move to prevent any legislation which overturned the Duumvirs' laws of the previous year. Yet Clodius, as he was now known, seemingly had no wish to be the tool of any patron and soon shrugged off their patronage and launched into a radical political reform programme using a combination of Tribunician power and street gang violence to push his measures through against both the protests of the Duumvirs and the rest of the oligarchy.

Pompeius responded in kind and tried again, with a fresh Tribunician agent, this time using T. Annius Milo (Tr. 58 BC) but armed him with his own street gang. Naturally this made matters worse, as there were now two opposing political street gangs fighting across Rome (a city without a police force or militia). Clodius was now out of office but retained his own street gang to defend his physical and political position. Both Pompeius and Crassus, the two potential 'guardians' of the Republican system seemed content to let the matter worsen rather than intervene, still manoeuvring against each other.

The Duumviral Coup of 55 BC

By 56 BC, however, the situation had worsened to such an extent that it now represented an opportunity and the two men met in the city of Luca, in Cisalpine Gaul, to thrash out a new agreement. Joining them was their former agent, Caesar, who still had no wish to return to the political fray but needed an extension of his initial five year extraordinary command in Gaul, where not only had he avoided getting himself killed, but was actually well on his way to conquering the tribes of Gaul, an act with naturally attracted the attentions of every other would-be conqueror to take up the command themselves, leaving him politically vulnerable.

Thus the three men and their supporters, which are reported to have included over two hundred Senators, plotted what was basically a temporary coup, or in their view, a restoration of proper oversight of the Republic they had helped to re-found. At its heart lay the Duumvirs Pompeius and Crassus ensuring their election as co-Consuls of 55 BC and the subsequent election of their supporters to the lower magistracies. More importantly lay the seizure of the bulk of the Republic's military resources for the next five years with three extraordinary commands.

Caesar retained the Gallic command for another five years (which would, and indeed did, have serious implications if he did not complete its conquest in that time). Crassus was awarded control of the Eastern Republic's Syrian legions for five years, with a plan to invade and conquer the Parthian Empire, Rome's sole remaining rival in the Middle East. Pompeius received command of the two Spanish provinces for five years and the critical dispensation to rule them in absentia through legates, thus remaining at Rome. Between them, the Duumvirs and Caesar gained control of the bulk of the Republican legions. Caesar and Crassus would command their pet projects to vastly increase the size of the Republic's empire (in Gaul and Parthia), whilst Pompeius would take up the reins of 'Princeps' in Rome and guard their collective interests, now backed up by the legions of Spain, a relatively short march away from Italy.

The Rise of the Pompeian Republic (54–52 BC)

Naturally, Pompeius and Crassus maintained Republican precedent when they laid down their Consulships at the end of their year in office. However, whilst Crassus left for his Eastern War, Pompeius remained in Rome, but still in command of legions of Spain, totally against precedent. With Crassus and Caesar both absent, Pompeius was clearly ascendant in Rome, but did not immediately use his power to enhance his position. Quite frankly he allowed the situation in Rome to deteriorate, waiting to exploit the opportunity.

From his point of view, fortune smiled on him, when his long-time rival and sometime ally, M. Licinius Crassus, the only man he judged to be powerful enough to oppose him, was killed in the aftermath of the Battle of Carrhae in Parthia in 53 BC.[11] Thus one rival had been eliminated. Despite the chaos in the Middle East, the very region that Pompeius had conquered for Rome, for him the prize was in Rome, and the Eastern Republic was left to fend for itself.

The opportunity he had been waiting for duly arrived in late 53 BC / early 52 BC with the crisis caused by gang violence at the elections for the magistracies, with both Milo and Clodius standing (for the Consulship and Praetorship respectively). This violence reached a crescendo in January 52 BC when Clodius was murdered and at his subsequent funeral his supporters burnt down the Temple being used as the Senate House. With no magistrates elected, due to the chaos and violence, the Senate had only one option and turned to Pompeius, to 'save' the Republic.

Pompeius naturally played his hand well, refusing the emergency office of Dictator, due to its recent Sullan connotations. A new constitutional solution was found, sole Consul (or temporary Princeps). Having been elevated to this position, Pompeius ruthlessly set about 'saving' the Republic. Order was restored to the streets of Rome with armed veterans, and a juridical purge of all troublemakers was undertaken, with exile as a result; the most notable victim being the Pompeian agent, T. Annius Milo, scapegoated for the murder of Clodius. With order restored, Pompeius again made a show of his Republican credentials by taking a colleague.

The colleague Pompeius chose also made a clear political statement. Pompeius had previously been married to Caesar's daughter (Iulia), an arrangement that came about in 59 BC. In 54 BC, Iulia died, leaving

Pompeius as Rome's most eligible bachelor.[12] In 52 BC, he chose to fill the vacancy, with the daughter of a certain Q. Caecilius Metellus Scipio Nasica, scion of the two most traditional Republican oligarchic families; a Scipio by birth and a Metellus by adoption. Pompeius then made Scipio his consular colleague, thus allying himself with one of Rome's most powerful factions. Furthermore, the lady in question, Cornelia Metella, was the recent widow of P. Licinius Crassus, the youngest son of his old rival Crassus, who had also fallen at Carrhae. As the eldest son (Marcus) was with Caesar in Gaul, Pompeius was thus able to hoover up the old Crassan clients as well, now without a patron.

Thus Pompeius was finally able to become the most dominant oligarch in the Roman Republic and briefly achieved his goal of being called on by the rest of the Senatorial oligarchy to 'save the Republic'. Yet this dominance was temporary and having made an excellent job of restoring the stability of the Republic, he naturally had to stand down as Consul after his year of office. In many ways he did too good a job of restoring stability as, with the Republic at peace, there was no longer a crisis to justify his elevation. Furthermore, whilst he had increased his political dominance by both his actions and his alliance to the Scipio-Metellan faction and the Crassan faction, there were many in the Senatorial oligarchy who clearly did not trust Pompeius in the slightest, an attitude not helped by his legions in Spain.

Yet Pompeius' dominance was not without material opposition. With the elimination of his old rival Crassus, there stood only one man who could challenge him, namely his former agent, Caesar. During 52 BC and Pompeius' rise to dominance, Caesar at this time had suffered a severe reversal in his conquest of Gaul, with the resistance of Vercingetorix, which not only meant that he was not in a position to intervene (not that he would have wanted to), but also that his conquest of Gaul was delayed, with the impending deadline for the expiration of his command in 50 BC (having been renewed for five years by Pompeius and Crassus in 55 BC).

How Do You Solve a Problem like Caesar (51–50 BC)

The study of the final two years between Pompeius' temporary elevation and the outbreak of the Third Civil War can be interpreted in many ways, but two strands of thought emerge in particular. On the one hand, there is the collapse of Republican institutions because the Senatorial oligarchy was not able to control the ambitions of two of its most ambitious members, both of which had permanent legions under arms, with the refusal of Pompeius to accommodate a more recent (though certainly not younger) rival.

On the other hand, there is a more Machiavellian interpretation of these events, that saw Pompeius realize that Caesar was not just a threat, but was actually an opportunity. Though Caesar was a successful general and had actually seemed to have conquered the tribes of Gaul (perhaps temporarily, perhaps permanently, as seen at the time), which brought with it popular adulation and oligarchic respect, he had nowhere near the powerbase in Rome to compete with Pompeius nor the political skill to match him.

If he survived the Gallic campaigns, Caesar would clearly want his victories and conquests acknowledged, and a subsequent command; the most likely being the currently vacant eastern command of the Romano-Parthian War. It was highly unlikely that Caesar would have wanted to return to Rome and challenge Pompeius politically. An eastern command would have offered the possibility that he too would follow Crassus into an untimely demise. However, Pompeius knew both the Parthians and Caesar's abilities well and probably concluded that if he did facilitate such a command then there was every chance that Caesar would succeed or eclipse his own achievements as the 'Roman Alexander'.

Yet, if we work on the principle that Pompeius was a Machiavellian political manipulator then clearly another thought would have entered his mind, one that provided a solution to the conundrum he faced. Pompeius' key problem was how to dominate the Roman Republic, as its Princeps, but doing so by popular acclaim; both within the People and far more importantly within the Senatorial oligarchy. The events of 52 BC had given him a blueprint: engineer a crisis and even his opponents would be forced to give him supreme power. If a domestic crisis within the city of Rome itself had brought about a temporary elevation, a far bigger crisis should lead to permanent elevation. And here we only have to look at the example of both Sulla before him and Octavianus Caesar after him.

If we follow this logic, then a far greater crisis was needed to facilitate his elevation. A war in the east was too remote to be of visceral concern to the oligarchy within Rome, but a direct threat to their position and even lives was another matter. On the one hand, Caesar's attempted conquest of Gaul removed that threat even more, in terms of tribal invasions, but presented a perfect opportunity for another civil war. If Caesar could be manipulated into attacking his own country, examples of which Pompeius had seen first-hand in the First Civil War, then the oligarchy in Rome would have no option but to turn to him and elevate him to the position of Princeps. Clearly there was a risk in this strategy; namely that he would need to defeat Caesar in battle to 'save' the Republic and secure his elevation, but then Pompeius was playing for the leadership of the Roman (Mediterranean and Middle Eastern) World.

If we take this view, then the Republic did not collapse into civil war by accident, but by design, the design of Pompeius. Given his control of the Republican machinery, it was easy for him to prevent Caesar's command from being renewed or to stop him being awarded another one. Pompeius, who knew Caesar well, then began a campaign to ratchet up the pressure on him, with the threat of a return to civilian life, the danger of prosecutions for his various political acts (at Pompeian instigation) and then in January 49 bc, the ultimatum that Caesar lay down his command or be declared an 'enemy of the Republic'.

This act was the culmination of a two year campaign to squeeze Caesar politically and yet make him into a clear danger to the Republic; a vainglorious general who put his own political ambition above the safety of the state; which ironically describes what Pompeius was doing perfectly. Yet Caesar lacked Pompeius' political power or ability and reacted exactly how Pompeius expected him to; invading Italy at the head of an army and thus being the 'official' instigator of the civil war which followed; a war that saw both men briefly achieve supreme power in the Republic before being consumed by the conflict they had started.

Chapter Two

A Clash of Titans: The Battles of Dyrrhachium and Pharsalus (49–48 BC)

W ith the origins of the Third Civil War explored, we next need to understand the course of events over the first two years of the war. Again these have been covered in detail elsewhere,[1] but a brief recap is worthwhile to help understand the events that followed.

The First Year – Civil War by Proxy

The Italian Campaigns

Having been forced to invade Italy, Caesar needed to make sure that it was a short campaign and a quick victory. Holding only Gaul and Illyria, Caesar needed to stop Pompeius from being able to tap the resources of the wider Republic, especially in Spain and the Near and Middle East. Likewise, Pompeius knew that Caesar needed a short sharp victory and took steps to ensure that he was denied one. As discussed, Pompeius' plan to be established as Rome's permanent Princeps required a grave crisis and one that was not over too quickly. If Caesar was expecting Pompeius to face him in Italy and stop him marching on Rome, then he was sorely mistaken, as were the Senate.

Instead Pompeius made token efforts at slowing Caesar down before evacuating his legions and supporters to Greece. There are two schools of thought as to this tactic, determined by how one views Pompeius: as political genius or bungler. If we were to take the view that Pompeius did not realize that Caesar would invade Italy, then he was clearly taken by surprise and did not have enough time to march north to meet him, with the only legionary forces available in Italy being two legions in the south, which had been sent to him by Caesar and thus their loyalty was suspect.

However, if we accept that Pompeius manipulated Caesar into attacking Italy, then he wasn't taken by surprise and deliberately failed to defend

Rome. If Caesar was able to march on Rome, then images of the brutal sack of 87 BC (undertaken by Caesar's uncle Marius) would be conjured up and the Senatorial oligarchy, who were neither pro-Caesar nor pro-Pompeius (which would have been the majority of them) would be forced to come off the fence and chose a side, with the majority likely to side with the 'defender of the Republic' rather than its attacker. Crossing the Rubicon had far more impact today than it would have in 49 BC and the situation could have been defused by negotiations, again which Pompeius indulged in a tokenistic effort. Yet if Caesar took Rome, then there would be no turning back. Thus Pompeius sacrificed Rome to Caesar, but got the backing of the majority of the Senate, who came with him.

Thus Pompeius slowly organized the evacuation of Italy, to ensure it did not look like flight, a task which was easily done with naval control of the Adriatic. There were two minor battles fought in Italy; the first came at Corfinium between the forces of Caesar and those of L. Domitius Ahenobarbus, the man the Senate had appointed to replace Caesar as commander in Gaul. With only a scratch force Ahenobarbus was able to slow Caesar down, but when Pompeius refused to send reinforcements (as it did not suit his masterplan), his army revolted and turned to Caesar.

The second battle came at Brundisium, the embarkation point for travel to Greece and Illyria. When he heard of Pompeius' plan Caesar naturally ignored the undefended Rome and headed directly to Brundisium to try to stop his enemies from escaping, thus ensuring a long civil war. Again Pompeius could have evacuated the city in time but chose to wait until Caesar arrived, showing his defence of the Republic and there was a brief siege, with Pompeius theatrically ensuring he was one of the last to leave.

Thus again Caesar inherited another city, theoretically the embarkation point to Greece, but faced a Pompeian controlled Adriatic. Even though Caesar supposedly had command of Illyria on the far side of the Adriatic, the Pompeian navy held sway between the two. Thus Caesar had control of Rome and what was left of the Senate and the Assemblies to give him tokenistic legitimacy. However, with the bulk of the Roman world controlled by Pompeius and the Original Senate sitting in Thessalonica, Caesar was still a rebel.

Having failed to bring the war to a swift conclusion, Caesar now faced a tactical quandary, and one which was to be repeated in the years which followed; namely which direction to campaign in. His forces only controlled Gaul (recently conquered) to the North and Italy itself. To the West lay the two Spanish provinces, a Pompeian heartland, along with seven legions threatening his flank. To the south lay Sicily and North Africa, Pompeian controlled provinces which were perfect to launch naval assaults on Italy. To the East lay the main prize, Pompeius himself, who would need time to assemble a large army to fight Caesar. Once assembled he could re-invade Italy or let Caesar cross to Greece and use that as a battleground (and thus inflict less damage on Italy).

Though Caesar had a toehold in Greece, the province of Illyria, he did not have the ability to cross the Adriatic unchallenged and his revolt could have ended in such a crossing. The land route to Illyria was not under Roman control and would involve fighting the native tribes of the region first. Thus Caesar faced a dilemma: a quick rash dash across the Adriatic to challenge Pompeius before he had the chance to build his army, or consolidation. Caesar chose consolidation, hoping that Illyria could hold out in his absence whilst he dealt with Pompeian threats to the West and South. Naturally Caesar chose the grander campaign, to defeat the Pompeian threat from Spain, leaving subordinates to handle the southern campaign of Sicily and North Africa.

The Sardinian and Sicilian Campaigns
Initially, the Caesarian force met with success. The inhabitants of Sardinia, having no wish to become a battlefield, revolted against the Pompeian garrison and thus it was evacuated. Sicily should have been a tougher proposition, with heavily defended cities, such as Syracuse, sufficient Pompeian forces and a good food supply, all supported by the Pompeian fleets. Unfortunately for the Pompeians, overall command fell to M. Porcius Cato, whose military ability was of questionable quality and whose Republican 'virtues' apparently did not extend to actually fighting his opponents in a civil war.

Thus Cato ordered the evacuation of Sicily without a shot being fired and retreated to Greece gifting Caesar a major strategic asset and costing the Pompeians an important base to threaten Italy and opening up an attack on North Africa. Such an act quite rightly appalled his Pompeian allies and unsurprisingly Cato saw no further active fighting in the civil war campaigns and can usually be found in charge of garrisoning cities (Dyrrhachium and then Utica).

The North African Campaign

With the swift capture of Sicily, the way was now open for the Caesarians to invade North Africa, with its one Roman province the coastal region that had been the rump of the Carthaginian Empire. The bulk of North Africa was the Kingdom of Numidia, a long standing Roman ally (and occasional enemy). The initial Caesarian assault looked like it, too, would have been a quick success, with the Caesarians defeating the small Pompeian garrison at the Battle of Utica and besieging the capital city.

Unfortunately for the Caesarians, control of the Pompeian garrison had been seized by P. Attius Varus, who had commanded the province before. He used his contacts at the royal Numidian court and convinced the Numidian King (Juba) to intervene on the side of the 'legitimate' Roman government. For a variety of reasons, personal dislike of Caesar, long standing ties with Pompeius dating back to the First Civil War and ambition to be on the winning side, Juba threw the weight of the Numidian Kingdom behind Varus and sent a relief army.

Massively outnumbered, a fact that the Caesarian commander C. Scribonius Curio did not immediately cotton onto, the Caesarians broke off from the siege of Utica to fight the Numidian relief army, but fell for a feint (a retreating Numidian advance guard) and blundered straight into the whole Numidian army with a predictable outcome, a Caesarian massacre. With only a handful of Caesarian survivors making it to their ships and away from Africa, the Pompeians had their first victory and Caesar his first defeat.

Though a small victory at the time, the importance of this win only became apparent after the defeats in Greece in 48 BC allowing the Pompeians not only a safe haven, but one supported by one of the richest kingdoms in the Mediterranean, allowing them the chance to rebuild (see Chapter Three). In the meantime, Varus and Juba ruled North Africa in a Romano-Numidian alliance, with quasi-independence from both warring parties.

The Spanish Campaign

The bulk of the Pompeian forces in the Western Republic, however, lay in Spain, a noted Pompeian stronghold. Not only had Pompeius re-conquered the region during the First Civil War (in the 70s BC), but he had seized military control of the two Roman provinces in 55 BC with a five year military command and the right to govern through legates. Thus the Pompeians had had five years to prepare for any forthcoming civil war. The two main Pompeian commanders were both experienced military men, L. Afranius (Cos. 60 BC), a long standing Pompeian deputy and M. Petreius, and between them they had seven legions.

When Pompeius learnt that Caesar had marched on Spain, he would have been delighted, as he would have believed that it would bring him the time he needed to assemble his grand army, drawing on all the resources of the Eastern Republic. Thus, Afranius and Petreius would have had orders to tie Caesar down in Spain for the rest of the year and into the subsequent one, buying Pompeius the time he needed.

Initially Afranius and Petreius successfully followed this strategy with the fighting between the two armies, consisting of skirmishes and ambushes, centred on the city of Ilerda. At one point they even seemed to have Caesar ripe for defeat but failed to press home their advantage, no doubt aware that their master wanted the right to defeat Caesar reserved for himself, rather than having the civil war end prematurely in Spain. It was a failure that would come back to haunt them, and Caesar used this respite to dig himself out of the situation which his rashness had got him into (another theme that repeats itself over the course of the campaign).

With Caesar's position at Ilerda strengthening, Afranius and Petreius made what was to be a disastrous decision to abandon their position and retreat further into the Spanish interior and thus winter down and drag the campaign into its desired second year. Unfortunately, whilst this plan looked good on paper (papyrus), they failed to account for the fact that Caesar needed the campaign wrapped up that year and would not simply allow them the luxury of a staged withdrawal. Thus the Caesarian army chased down the retreating Pompeian one and an orderly retreat became a rout, with a harried and starving Pompeian army being forced to surrender.

Thus, in just one summer season of campaigning, Caesar had defeated the Pompeian forces in Spain and removed them as a threat. Though again, seen as a prelude to the main event in Greece the following year, this defeat proved to be a hammer blow to the Pompeian strategy as it freed Caesar up to return to Italy that year and then storm a crossing into Greece to challenge Pompeius before he had sufficient time to assemble and train his grand army. This was a key factor behind the subsequent loss at Pharsalus the following year.

Yet, Caesar's victory in Spain also came back to haunt him as defeating the Pompeian army was not the same as securing the Roman provinces in Spain to the Caesarian cause. Naturally with no active Pompeian forces, the cities and tribes of the region paid homage to Caesar, which they promptly cast aside when he left for Italy. As we will see, Pompeian revolts in Spain in 48 BC and again in 46 BC had a major impact on Caesar's tactics and the course of the civil war, which would see Caesar repeating this campaign in 45 BC.

The Gallic Campaign

A side show to the Spanish campaign came in the form of the Gallic campaign, which was nothing more than the siege of Massilia, the oldest and most powerful Greek city in Gaul. Key to the route from Italy to Spain, and a long standing Roman ally, Massilia chose to buck the trend of remaining neutral when faced with a Roman army and declared for Pompeius and the (original) Senate. Unwilling to leave an active opponent cutting off his supplies and communications from Italy, Caesar had no choice but to have his commanders lay the city under siege.

The subsequent siege continued throughout Caesar's Spanish campaigns and even saw Pompeian naval reinforcements being sent from Greece, though they were subsequently defeated by the Caesarians. The siege only ended when news reached the Massiliotes that the Pompeian armies in Spain had surrendered, and thus with no hope of Pompeian relief they agreed to negotiated surrender, giving Caesar nominal control of the whole Western Republic (aside from North Africa).

The Illyrian Campaigns

Yet for Pompeius the campaigns in the Western Republic were a side show, one which would hopefully slow Caesar down but not worth investing any more forces in, hence the scant reinforcement sent west (just a few ships to Massilia). For Pompeius the key strategy objective was the Roman province of Illyria which was controlled by Caesarian forces and clearly needed to be eliminated. It is often overlooked that Caesar's military commands were not just the two Gallic provinces (Cisalpine and Transalpine) but also Illyria. This gave him a crucial bridgehead in the

Pompeian east and one which, if he could overcome the Pompeian navy in between, would act as a staging post for an invasion of the East.

Thus, it was critical for Pompeius' plans that this bridgehead be eliminated before Caesar returned from Spain. Thus the Illyrian campaign was Pompeius' chief concern for 49 BC and the one that saw the bulk of the fighting for the Eastern Pompeian forces. It is worth noting that there are no details of this campaign in Caesar's own commentary of the civil war. Whilst the defeat in North Africa receives a full account, particularly drawing attention to the role of the 'perfidious' Numidians (justifying their later annexation), there is no such account of the Illyrian campaigns. This is clearly due to it being the wrong type of defeat. Africa was a sideshow, and a brave Roman army was wiped out by the treacherous action of a foreign army, thus a heroic defeat. The losses the Caesarians suffered in Illyria were to the Pompeians themselves and were a significant setback to Caesar's plan.

Details are few and have to be compiled from the other surviving sources, but the result was clear, a total Pompeian victory, with the Caesarian land forces under C. Antonius (brother of Marcus) being captured and the only Caesarian fleet in the Adriatic, commanded by P. Cornelius Dolabella being driven out into the Mediterranean. This gave Pompeius uncontested command of the Adriatic and removed the platform for a Caesarian crossing, thus fitting into his masterplan for buying time to assemble and train his new grand army.

Thus, on the face of it, the year ended in a stalemate, with Caesarian victories in Sicily and Spain and Pompeian ones in Africa and Illyria. Caesar had nominal control of the bulk of the Western Republic, Pompeius solid control of the Eastern one, each with a fully functioning Roman Senate electing magistratures and issuing commands to the wider Mediterranean world in the name of Rome. Caesar returned to Rome at the end of 49 BC and had the choice to force a crossing to Greece or defend Italy. Pompeius spent the winter waiting for his eastern reinforcements under Metellus Scipio (his father-in-law) which were wintering in Asia Minor waiting to cross the Bosphorus into Thrace.

The Second Year (48 BC) – The Clash of Titans

The Illyrian / Epirote Campaigns

Caesar too would have spent the winter pondering the problem of Metellus Scipio and his eastern army. Once they reached Pompeius and were integrated with his other legions then Pompeius would have a formidable army and would put his own battle plan into action. Therefore until they did so there was a window of opportunity. His victories in Spain had brought him the time to exploit this opportunity, but it involved a considerable risk. Between him and Pompeius lay the Adriatic, which was now completely controlled by the Pompeians, since the elimination of his garrison in Illyria. Even if he could force his way past or evade the Pompeian navy, there was the considerable risk that he would be trapped in Epirus / Illyria, facing two large Pompeian armies ahead of him and having only the Pompeian controlled Adriatic behind him.

However, equally there was the danger of waiting too long, as Caesar was well aware that time was against him and the longer Pompeius had to receive his eastern reinforcements, then the greater the chances were that Caesar would be defeated. With that in mind, Caesar launched a risky dash across the Adriatic, evaded the Pompeian fleet and successfully landed on the Illyrian coastline. The Pompeians naturally reacted by raising their forces from their winter quarters and set off to pin Caesar down before he broke out of his bridgehead. At the same time, the Pompeian navy received orders to attack Brundisium and, at all costs, prevent any further Caesarian reinforcements from crossing to relieve Caesar.

In this, they failed quite spectacularly, as M. Antonius was able to cross with Caesarian reinforcements and relieve the pressure on Caesar. Skirmishes between Caesar and Pompeius followed, but Pompeius stuck to a strategy of avoiding a set piece battle until he had the eastern army of Metellus Scipio to support him.

The Battle of Dyrrhachium – Caesar Defeated

Caesar clearly needed to force Pompeius out of these 'Fabian tactics'[2] and in an effort to do so moved to attack the Pompeian regional capital of Dyrrhachium (now Durres in Albania). Not only was this city the largest port on the eastern Adriatic, but it was the Pompeian supply base for Epirus and the start of the Via Egnatia, the Roman road that cut across

Greece and Macedonia and connected to the Bosphorus, and thus the road that Metellus Scipio would be taking.

Clearly Pompeius could not allow such a prize to fall into Caesar's hands, but not only did he not fall into Caesar's trap (and give battle) but reached the city first, leaving Caesar to face both the city (with its garrison) and Pompeius' army. Not being able to force a battle, and having dispatched a force to slow down Metellus, Caesar then made a tactical error and sacrificed his speed and mobility by trying to lay siege both to the city and, more importantly, to Pompeius' army now trapped in the bay.

What followed was one of the oddest 'battles' in Roman history, with two Roman armies engaging in what can only be described as several months' worth (April to July) of trench warfare in the hills that surrounded the bay. Each side fought for the high ground and laid down fortifications and strong points and launched sallies against the opposition's defences. Pompeius' forces were technically trapped by the Caesarian army, but they held the city and the bay itself and more importantly had total naval control of the Adriatic, meaning they could be resupplied by sea. Pompeius, waiting for Scipio's eastern army could afford to wait. Caesar could not. Several notable attempts were made to end the stalemate, the most notable being when Caesar launched a sneak attack on the city of Dyrrhachium itself aided by sympathizers within the city. However, these sympathizers were nothing of the sort and Caesar walked into a trap, from which he scarcely escaped with his life. A Pompeian counter attack on the Caesarian lines of defence was then barely repulsed.

The end came, not with the arrival of Metellus Scipio, whose advance had been delayed by the second Caesarian army, but by a successful Pompeian assault on the southernmost point of Caesar's line of defences. A successful Pompeian bridgehead was established, and Caesar rushed to counter attack it with his usual boldness. On this occasion, however, the tactic backfired, as Pompeius reacted swiftly and counterattacked himself, with Caesar cut off from his main army. Overwhelmed, Caesar's forces broke with several thousand casualties and Caesar was forced to retreat.

The outcome of the battle was clear (despite later Caesarian attempts to play it down), Caesar had been defeated, both on the day and in the wider battle. The loss of the south meant that his siege lines had been broken and were now pointless and Caesar was forced to retreat towards Macedonia, shaking off the Pompeian pursuit to link up with his second army and try to defeat Metellus before he could link up with Pompeius.

The Battle of Pharsalus – Pompeius Defeated

Thus the campaign spread into Macedonia and Greece proper, with four different armies searching out for each other, Pompeius and Caesar heading eastwards, and Metellus Scipio and the second Caesarian army marching westwards. It was a strangely balletic period with four armies looking for each other whilst simultaneously avoiding each other. In the end, and with some excellent scouting on the part of all four armies, the two Pompeian and two Caesarian cohorts avoided their opponents and met up with their counterparts, making the possible scenarios and outcomes far easier.

Having failed to prevent the two Pompeian armies from combining (another tactical failure) and being stuck in what was ostensibly Pompeian held territory and facing a far larger Pompeian army, Caesar's options had been reduced to two: fight or flight. Again, Caesar chose to gamble and went on the offensive, judging that Pompeius would now have to give battle, in front of all the Senate and his eastern allies, the moment he had been anticipating for over a year.

Yet Caesar's gamble was based on three solid foundations. Firstly, the two Pompeian armies had only just joined and had not had time to integrate, being of multi-ethnic composition with a huge variety of fighting styles, from legionaries to eastern cavalry, archers, and slingers. This meant that Pompeius would have to rely on sheer weight of numbers and his two clear advantages, cavalry and artillery.

Secondly Caesar had been training a specialist part of his army in a new anti-cavalry fighting style, by combining his own legionaries with cavalry in a mixed unit, designed to fight cavalry. These tactics had been used on several occasions against Pompeius' advance guard and had met with success. The only gamble was whether these tactics would work on a far larger scale? The third factor was location, and Caesar chose his ground well, anchoring his left wing against a large river, meaning Pompeius could only utilize his cavalry on one wing in a flanking move not both and thus Caesar could focus his efforts on just that one wing; his right, Pompeius' left.

The subsequent battle did indeed turn on that right wing and Pompeius followed the logical tactic of deploying his massive cavalry advantage on that area. Caesar however, deployed in the usual three lines, had created a fourth line; his specialist anti-cavalry force. When his wing inevitably buckled under the weight of the Pompeian cavalry onslaught, he unleashed this surprise force on the Pompeian cavalry and at that point the battle turned.

It was not inevitable that the Pompeian cavalry would be defeated, given their weight of numbers, but they were turned and did break. With Caesar victorious on the wing and the Pompeians having lost their decisive advantage and momentum, overall victory would go to the general who was able to react most quickly to these new circumstances. With the smaller and more homogeneous army, and expecting his tactic to work, it was Caesar whose reactions were faster and he disrupted the Pompeian army from that wing. Victory took several hours, but the Pompeian army, though fighting hard, inevitably began to turn and finally break up. Caesar had his victory and the whole course of the civil war was turned on its head.

The Pompeian Withdrawal

Caesar had his victory on the day but not in the war, for that he would need to kill or capture the leading Pompeians, especially Pompeius himself. Pompeian casualties in the battle were not heavy, principally falling on the eastern allied contingents and none of the leading Pompeians were killed or captured in the battle. Furthermore, despite his victory, the Pompeians still held the bulk of the region, including its eastern capital at Thessalonica and western capital at Dyrrhachium, not to mention the island of Corcyra, its main naval base.

Furthermore, the Pompeians still had naval control of the seas around Greece. All this helped the Pompeian faction leaders to escape Caesar and regroup. Key to this retreat was its dual nature, with Pompeius himself heading to Thessalonica before moving eastwards to his powerbase in the Near and Middle East, which he had conquered for Rome, and which had supplied him with his large army. The rest of the Pompeian leadership headed west to Dyrrhachium and Corcyra.

Caesar had two key problems, despite his victory. Firstly he could only focus his attentions in one direction and naturally he had to chase down Pompeius himself, which allowed the rest of the Pompeian leadership to slip away and regroup: first on the Adriatic and then the Peloponnese, before evacuating Greece for Cyrene on the North African cost. Secondly though Caesar was victorious on land with no Pompeian forces to stand up to him, he did not have a fleet, meaning he would have to chase Pompeius, who had taken to the seas, on land and thus march to the Middle East, giving Pompeius a considerable head start.

Cassius, Caesar and the Bosphorus

The turning point of this chase came at the Bosphorus when a Pompeian fleet commanded by C. Cassius Longinus, arrived to find Caesar crossing undefended. Had they attacked then they could have at the very least stopped him from crossing, or even killed him. In the event they did neither and actually turned themselves over to him. Thus, not only did Caesar avoid defeat, but he now had a fleet with which to chase down Pompeius. The tortoise had become the hare.

There is considerable debate about why the fleet turned to Caesar when it had him trapped and especially over who the commander was. Appian is clear that the commander was none other than C. Cassius, who later famously co-led the conspiracy that led to Caesar's assassination. This ties in with earlier evidence that Cassius was in command of a Pompeian fleet off Sicily, who then received orders after Pharsalus to go to the Black Sea and the court of the Pontic King of the Bosphoran Kingdom (Crimea). Modern academia disagrees[3] and states that it must have been another (hitherto unknown Cassius with a hitherto unknown fleet) rather than C. Cassius himself based on a handful of other surviving fragments that have Cassius in the east seeking Caesar's favour.

Thus despite all sources pointing to Cassius being in the East after Pharsalus and thus perfectly capable of being the commander, many feel the need to deny him the role and subsequent understanding of his later actions. These other sources do not preclude Cassius being the commander but can be understood if we argue that Cassius did not intend to surrender to Caesar but was mutinied on by his fleet, who threw in their lot with Caesar, as happened to other Pompeian fleets after Pharsalus. If Cassius opposed this then he may well have initially surrendered to Caesar and then been released (with an eye to rejoining Pompeius), but later had to backtrack and reconsider his position, when faced with the news of Pompeius' murder and thus saw the need to reconcile with Caesar more permanently.

Murder in Egypt

Regardless of the identity of the commander, the outcome was clear, Caesar was not stopped and now had a fleet to transport his legions in pursuit of Pompeius. With his options closing down and many in the east wary of antagonising Caesar and his advancing legions, Pompeius found that past loyalties counted for little when faced with this harsh reality, and he found no welcome in the Middle East. The obvious line of retreat would have been to link up with the rest of the Pompeian army that had been evacuated for Greece and were making for Cyrene, sandwiched between Pompeian North Africa and Ptolemaic Egypt (see Map One).

Pompeius, however, was not willing to give up, and realized that fresh forces and monies were needed and so decided to call upon the loyalty of the Ptolemaic dynasty. However, whilst the previous Pharaoh (Ptolemy XII) had been a Pompeian client and placed back on the Egyptian throne with Roman soldiers (in 55 BC), he had died recently (51 BC) and the Egyptian Pharaoh was his young son Ptolemy XIII (co-ruling, somewhat acrimoniously with his sister, Cleopatra VII). Pompeius should have realized that the boy's loyalty to his father's patron was never going to trump his own fears (Caesar's army) or ambitions (sole rule) and so in an attempt to curry favour with Caesar (and totally misreading the Roman character), he arranged for Pompeius to be murdered (by a Roman legionary) on the beach he landed at.

Thus the Pompeian faction was robbed of its charismatic and talented leader, Caesar robbed of the chance of a negotiated settlement to end the civil war and the Republic gained the first (of many) 'martyrs'.

Section II

Civil War Renewed

Chapter Three

In the Shadow of Pompeius: The Recovery of the Pompeian Faction

Though ultimately Caesar had emerged from 48 BC clearly on top in this Third Roman Civil War, it had been far from the smooth and seemingly inevitable process that he would have liked the Roman world and posterity to have remembered. His characteristic bold thrust across the Adriatic in January 48 BC had petered out into the trench warfare and ultimate defeat at the Battle of Dyrrhachium and his seemingly inevitable destruction had been spectacularly avoided at the Battle of Pharsalus. Yet again, he nearly snatched defeat from the jaws of victory when caught crossing the Bosphorus by Cassius and only avoided destruction when Cassius and / or his fleet defected. He finished the year again in mixed circumstances, when, having seen Pompeius murdered on an Egyptian beach, he got himself mixed up in another civil war, that of the Ptolemies, seeing in the new year besieged in Alexandria.

Thus, the current front runner in this latest civil war saw in what now equates to 47 BC suffering from mixed fortunes. Trapped in Egypt with the bulk of his army marching to his rescue, and his internal and external enemies free, Caesar was far from being the unchallenged master of Rome. His internal enemies, numbered both the obvious (the Pompeians in Africa and Illyria), but also those amongst the ruling oligarchy in Rome who had not declared for his enemies, but who now were faced with Caesar's deputy M. Antonius.

His external enemies included the Egyptian army of Ptolemy XIII who were his most pressing problem, but also the Pontic armies of King Pharnaces II, who had used the chaos of the previous year and the death of his patron Pompeius, to launch an attack on Rome's North Eastern Empire and recover and rebuild his father's Pontic Empire, beginning the Fourth Romano-Pontic War (see Appendix One). Thus the civil war against the Pompeians was just one of four pressing issues that Caesar needed to face in order to cement his mastery of the Roman world.

The Recovery of the Pompeian Faction – The Background Factors

Whilst Caesar was so distracted, the same could not be said of his enemies in the civil war, the Pompeian faction(s). In point of fact, their purpose was now crystal clear and not hampered by any external distractions; recover from the physical and psychological blows that the previous year had brought, notably Pharsalus and the subsequent murder of Pompeius. However, as stated earlier (see the Introduction), this recovery was aided by three factors: leadership, time, and space.

The first of these (leadership) was the most important. Despite the rhetoric of later sources, the casualty rate at Pharsalus was remarkably light, with the bulk of the Pompeian casualties coming from the Eastern allied forces. What was most remarkable, however, was not the casualties suffered by the troops themselves, but the lack of casualties suffered by the leadership of the Pompeian faction. Whilst fresh troops could always be raised, fresh leaders could not. What is often overlooked in the rhetoric of Caesar's victory at Pharsalus is the absence of noble casualties, with none being killed in the battle itself and only one (L. Domitius Ahenobarbus, Cos. 54 BC) killed in the aftermath and even then, we get the feeling that this was more down to his own incompetence. Every other Pompeian commander made it safely from the battlefield and reached safe territory.

There were several reasons for this. Firstly, the battle itself was not the overwhelming rout that later sources liked to portray. As has been detailed in depth elsewhere[1], the Pompeian army was overwhelmed on the far wing but then fought a long rearguard action to stave off the inevitable; clearly it did not suddenly collapse, thus giving everyone time to make their escape. Secondly Caesar's pursuit of the survivors seems to have been half-hearted at best and Caesar appears to have continued to pursue his policy of deliberate clemency to avoid affirming the Pompeian propaganda of being a bloodthirsty tyrant.

In sparing his enemies he hoped to end the civil war and avoid creating the enmity that followed the First Civil War, which had seen his own Marian relations wiped out. The third reason was due to the fact that the battle took place in Pompeian controlled territory, in mainland Greece; the Pompeians controlled the Illyrian and Epirote coastlines, the Peloponnese and Macedon. Thus the survivors had a range of nearby secure locations to retreat to.

Accordingly, all of the key Pompeian faction leadership (with the notable exception of Pompeius himself) survived to fight on. What Caesar must have been hoping for was that though they had survived physically they would have been wounded psychologically and would not continue the fight. At best this must have been a vain hope, especially concerning the 'Republican' faction. Any chance of coming to terms with the hardcore Pompeian faction disappeared on that Egyptian beach, with the murder of Pompeius, again posing another of ancient history's great 'what ifs'.

As has been stated before, it is notable that none of the major figures of the Pompeian faction sought terms with Caesar. The only ones to do so were from the lesser members of oligarchy, the most notable of which are three men, whose reputations are far greater today than they were in 48 BC: Cicero, Brutus, and Cassius. Of those it was Cassius' defection that had the greatest impact on the course of the war, as, even though he was a lesser Pompeian commander, his fleet could have destroyed Caesar when he was crossing the Bosphorus and thus either ended the civil war (with Caesar dead) or if Caesar had survived, then ended his pursuit of Pompeius and thus negated Pompeius' need to land in Egypt without his army. Nevertheless, by the end of 48 BC / beginning of 47 BC, the leadership of the Pompeian faction remained intact and determined to fight.

Yet their survival alone would not have meant anything if they had not been given time to regroup. Whether by chance or by design, the Pompeian faction split in the aftermath of Pharsalus, with Pompeius going eastwards and the other leaders westwards, naturally giving Caesar a choice and a dilemma. Understandably he chose to follow Pompeius eastwards as he was the most dangerous. Far less understandable is Caesar's decision in late 48 BC not to immediately move on the remnants of the Pompeian faction who had travelled from Greece to Cyrene (and thus next to Egypt) to meet up with Pompeius. It was this decision more than anything that allowed the Pompeian faction time to regroup and rebuild.

Ultimately, we will never know why Caesar chose this course of action. It certainly can't have been how few forces he had as that had never stopped him acting swiftly in the past and his opponents were in disarray. We are left with three options: firstly he took an arrogant view and no longer considered them to be a threat (a risky strategy which backfired). The second theory takes the opposite view and is a machiavellian one, namely that he wanted his opponents to recover and thus justify the ongoing crisis and his ongoing supreme power (the Dictatorship). However, this requires a level of political forethought that Caesar seemed to lack. The third is that having gone to Egypt, the resting place of Alexander the Great, a long time idol of his, he became enamoured with the idea of carving out an Egyptian powerbase for himself, which had been a long standing Triumviral aim and a goal of both Pompeius and Crassus (his patrons / partners).

Whatever the motivation, the key outcome was that by ignoring the Pompeians in Cyrene, and focusing on the east, Caesar gave them the time they needed to regroup. Yet time is nothing without the means, and here the third factor came into play; namely location. As Pompeius himself had found, to his ultimate cost, there were few provinces or kingdoms in the Mediterranean that wanted to be seen supporting the losing side, hence the defection of the Pompeian Eastern Republic to nominally supporting Caesar, but actually wanting to be left alone by both sides.

With the east ruled out, and Caesarian forces in Greece, Italy and Spain, there was only one logical destination: Roman North Africa and again we seen the failings of Caesar in this choice of destination. As previously detailed at length[2] Roman North Africa was a Pompeian stronghold due to the failure of the Caesarian sponsored expedition of 49 BC. Furthermore he had deliberately chosen to leave it on his southern flank in his eagerness to attack Pompeius in 48 BC. A further Caesarian scheme to attack Pompeian Africa from Spain using the Maurian Kingdom in 48 BC failed when elements of Caesarian Spain rebelled and actually needed a Maurian army to invade Spain to quell it.

Pompeian North Africa (see Map One) was two-fold; the Roman province of North Africa (formerly the rump of the Carthaginian Empire) and the state of Numidia, the superpower of the region. Though reduced from its heights of the Second Century, after being defeated by Rome in the Romano-Numidian War (by Caesar's uncle Marius),[3] Numidia was still a superpower in its own right, with significant armed forces, treasury, and food production. In short Numidia was the perfect base to support a faction in the civil war.

The kingdom was ruled by King Juba I who stands out in this period as a native ruler who bucked the trend of blowing with the wind and not only firmly came out for Pompeius when he was on top, but continued to oppose Caesar when he became the front runner, an act which was ultimately to cost him both his life and his kingdom's independence. Thus the Pompeian stronghold of North Africa gave them the space they needed to rebuild and attracted the bulk of the Pompeian forces, leaders, and supporters in late 48, early 47 BC, aside from those under Octavius who continued to fight in Illyria (see below).

The Reformation of the Pompeian Faction (Late 48 / Early 47 BC)

Though virtually all of the key Pompeian figures survived the aftermath of Pharsalus and made their way to the safe haven of North Africa, the key questions they faced were firstly, who would replace Pompeius, their lost figurehead, and secondly, could the alliance that Pompeius had forged between the two factions (true Pompeians, and anti-Caesarians) survive, or would they collapse into infighting?

The few surviving sources we have for this key period, all agree that there were dissensions between the leading players, and all ascribe the role of peace maker to Cato (and his army of 10,000 Pompeian soldiers):

'*The Pompeian faction had consolidated its position in Africa and after Cato had declined an offer of joint command, the sole command was given to Publius Scipio.*'[4]

'*Pompeius the man was no more, but his name still lived everywhere. For the strong support his party had in Africa had stirred up in that country a war in which the moving spirits were King Juba and Scipio, a man of consular rank, whom Pompeius had chosen for his father-in-law two years before his death. Their forces were augmented by Marcus Cato, who, in spite of the great difficulty of the march, and the lack of supplies in the regions traversed, succeeded in conducting his legions to them. Cato, although offered the supreme command by the soldiers, preferred to take orders from Scipio, his superior in rank.*'[5]

'*But matters were in a bad way with Scipio and Varus. Their dissension and quarrelling led them to pay court to Juba in efforts to win his favour, and the king was unendurable for the severity of his temper and for the arrogance which his wealth and power gave him. When he was going to have an interview with Cato for the first time, he placed his own seat between that of Scipio and that of Cato. Cato, however, when he saw the arrangement, took up his own seat and moved it over to the other side, thus placing Scipio in the middle, although Scipio was an enemy, and had published a book which contained abuse of Cato.*

But at the time of which I speak, Cato actually put a check upon Juba, who had all but made Scipio and Varus his satraps and reconciled the two Romans. And though all thought it meet that he should have the command, especially Scipio and Varus, who resigned and tendered to him the leadership, he refused to break the laws to support which they were waging war with one who broke them, nor, when a Proconsul was present, would he put himself, who was only a Propraetor, above him. For Scipio had been made Proconsul, and the greater part of the army were emboldened by his name; they thought that they would be successful if a Scipio had command in Africa.'[6]

'At first, they experienced a slight delay, due to a dispute between Varus and Scipio about the leadership, inasmuch as the former had held sway for a longer time in these regions, and Juba also, elated by his victory, demanded that he should have first place because of it. But Scipio and Cato, who far excelled them all in rank and in shrewdness respectively, reached an agreement and won the rest over to it, persuading them to entrust everything to Scipio. For Cato, who might have commanded on equal terms with him, or even alone, refused, first, because he thought it a most injurious course in such circumstances, and second, because he was inferior to the other in official rank. He saw that in military matters even more than elsewhere it was very important that the commander should have some legal precedence over the others, and therefore he willingly yielded him the command and furthermore delivered to him the armies that he had brought there.'[7]

Naturally given his post mortem reputation, the sources are at pains to point out the role of peacemaker that Cato undertook, even going so far as to refuse supreme command as it would breach the 'traditions of the Republic he was fighting for', not that such a consideration had ever slowed Cato down in his political career to date. As detailed below there were three key Roman commanders and four key figures in total. Breaking away from the cult of Cato, Dio ascribes the new governing arrangements as being the result of a compact between the two key Roman faction leaders, Metellus Scipio and Cato, which resulted in Metellus Scipio being acclaimed as the new overall leader of the Pompeian faction, by rank and birth, but in effect the emergence of a new ruling clique or Triumvirate at the head of a tripartite alliance.

The Pompeian Triumvirate (+ Juba)

We can see that by early 47 BC, a new ruling clique had emerged within the Pompeian faction, which was in fact the true Second Triumvirate; Q. Caecilius Metellus Pius Scipio Nasica, M. Porcius Cato, and P. Attius Varus. Each leader represented one key element within the newly constructed alliance: Metellus, leader of the Pompeian faction itself, Cato leader of the Republican faction and Varus, leader of the African forces.

Q. Caecilius Metellus Pius Scipio Nasica (Cos. 52 BC)

As the name suggests, Metellus Scipio was the scion of two of the mid-Republic's leading oligarchic families; born a Scipio and adopted into the Metellan family. By birth, though he was ultimately descended from the great Scipio Africanus, he belonged to a cadet branch of the family, actually only descended from Africanus by his daughter Cornelia. Nevertheless his branch of the family had seen consular success (162 and 155 BC, 138 BC, 111 BC) and counted P. Cornelius Scipio Nasica Serapio (Cos. 138 BC), the instigator of the murder of T. Sempronius Gracchus (see Chapter One) as his great grandfather. His own father was P. Cornelius Scipio Nasica (Pr. c. 96 BC) who only seems to have risen to the Praetorship, with his career (and possibly his life) being cut off by the First Civil War.[8]

Scipio's rise to political prominence lay in two factors: his inheritance, and his daughter (Cornelia). In circumstances that are now lost he became the adopted son of Q. Caecilius Metellus Pius, the leader of the Metellan clan and political faction, son of Metellus Numidicus and the close colleague of Sulla (with the two men holding the Consulship of 80 BC). Thus he now found himself elevated into the top level of the Senatorial oligarchy, though just a teenager.

His date of birth is unknown, but given his subsequent career it is assumed to be in the 90s BC. Where he served his military apprenticeship in his 20s is not recorded, but given his connection to Pompeius, a post in the latter's eastern campaigns is possible. His first recorded office is most often given to be the Tribunate in 59 BC,[9] whether his adoption rendered him a Plebeian is still in question.[10] Nevertheless, if he was an office holder this year, the same year that the Duumvirs sponsored Caesar to the Consulship, he may well have been in their political orbit by then. A subsequent Praetorship is unknown, but most commonly ascribed to 55 BC, when the Duumvirs were Consuls.

It was around this time that his daughter (Cornelia) married into the Duumvirs, marrying P. Licinius Crassus, the youngest son of the Duumvir M. Licinius Crassus. Thus by c.55 BC, Metellus Scipio was a leading supporter of the Duumvirs and a man of clear political tact and influence. He moved on from being the father-in-law of Crassus to being the father-in-law of Pompeius in 53–52 BC, when Cornelia was widowed after the Battle of Carrhae and married the latter. Such astute political manoeuvrings brought Metellus Scipio the Consulship of 52 BC, the chosen partner of Pompeius himself. It also brought him immunity from prosecution under the Pompeian purge of political troublemakers of that year, having played no small part in the violence that surrounded the election in 53 BC for the following year.

Following Pompeius' example, he apparently took no Proconsular province in 51 BC, to stay at the heart of the 'Pompeian' Republic. Following the outbreak of the civil war, he received the key Proconsular command of Syria and orders to assemble a large eastern army to bring to Pompeius in Greece. Having crossed to Greece in 48 BC, he seemingly defeated the Caesarian army of Domitius Calvinus sent to stop him but made slow time crossing Macedonia and Thrace to reach Pompeius, missing the Pompeian victory at the Battle of Dyrrhachium. In the subsequent Battle of Pharsalus, he commanded the centre of the army, acquitting himself well.

Even though he wasn't the senior ex-Consul present (Afranius having been Consul in 60 BC) his connections to Pompeius, political ability and impeccable lineage made him the perfect choice to be the new figurehead of the Republican resistance to Caesar. The fact that a Scipio was commanding in Africa made this irresistible and even forced Caesar to take measures to counter the propaganda / pseudo auspice that no Scipio could be defeated in Africa.

The only obvious question mark to this Republican figurehead was his military ability. We have no surviving record of his military experience in his 20s, though it may well have been with Pompeius in the East. His command of the eastern army in 48 BC was competent, though questions remain over the time it took him to reach Pompeius. Nevertheless, as subsequent events showed, he seemed happy to rely on experienced commanders such as T. Labienus and, until Thapsus itself, showed an understandable tactical caution and ability.

M. Porcius Cato (Pr. 54 BC)

The figurehead for the largest element within the Pompeian faction had many similar traits to Scipio. M. Porcius Cato, was another descendant of a more famous ancestor (and opponent of Scipio Africanus) of the same name (these days labelled Cato the Elder). Cato's subsequent reputation, however, belies what was at best a mediocre political career, having risen no higher than the Praetorship, due to his initial opposition to the Duumvirs. He actually shared a number of traits with Caesar in political terms, namely that their later reputation belies a mediocre political talent, but unlike Caesar his military talent was no better than his political.

Like Caesar, he began his political career attacking the dominant Sullan faction in the 60s, but his career faded in the 50s when he opposed the leading Duumvirs and was notably outmanoeuvred by the Tribune Clodius. His previous military experience was limited to annexing the Kingdom of Cyprus from the Ptolemaic Empire, at the behest of Clodius (and Pompeius).[11] His civil war military record was no better, retreating from Sicily in 49 BC without firing a shot and gifting Caesar a major strategic and economic asset. He was subsequently (and unsurprisingly) left out of the fighting at Dyrrhachium and Pharsalus and sent into the Illyrian hills to suppress the local tribes instead.

Yet, it had been Cato who assumed command of the shattered Pompeian forces in the aftermath of Pharsalus, not Metellus Scipio, and he had transported 10,000 men from Greece to Cyrene and then to North Africa. As the commander of the largest Pompeian military contingent, this gave him a key voice in the negotiations that reforged the Pompeian faction.

Furthermore, he remained (and played up to the image of) a staunch defender of 'traditional' Republican values and a committed anti-Caesarian and was thus the focal point for the Republican element of the Pompeian faction.

P. Attius Varus (Pr. 53. BC)

The third member of the Triumvirate, Varus, is often overlooked by the
sources in favour of his more famous counterparts, but this should not
colour our view of him. In many ways his latter career followed the path
taken by C. Valerius Flaccus and Q. Sertorius, who during the First Civil
War carved out native Roman hybrid kingdoms, free from central Roman
control. This example was soon followed by Caecilius Bassus and Q.
Labienus (son of the Pompeian faction leader), who also carved out their
own domain in the east, the latter being a Parthian client.[12]

Having served there as Praetor in the late 50s and having established
a strong link with King Juba of Numidia, he seized control of Roman
North Africa in 49 BC, from the official appointed Pompeian commander
and then used his connections to bring a Numidian army into the
province to destroy the Caesarian invasion force. He disappears from our
sources during 48 BC, but he still ruled (nominally in Pompeius' name)
Roman North Africa supported (propped up) by the power of King Juba
of Numidia. To maintain constitutional proprieties, he is recorded as
surrendering his Propraetorian command over Roman North Africa to
Metellus Scipio, as the senior Roman commander.

Thus, the ruling Triumvirate of the Pompeian faction clearly had no
military figures equal to that of Pompeius or Caesar, and clearly if they
were to defeat Caesar then they would need to act in concert. Nevertheless,
what they lacked in military ability, they more than made up for in political
capital and represented a clear threat to Caesar's military and political
'control' of the Republic. This was especially the case when we consider
the support they received from the fourth man in this ruling council, who
provided the resources to fuel the recovery of the Pompeian faction.

King Juba I of Numidia

As already stated, Juba of Numidia was an exception when it came to
native rulers in the Mediterranean world, both in his initial zeal for
supporting Pompeius, and destroying the Caesarian army in Roman
North Africa and in maintaining this support in the wake of the result
at Pharsalus. The ties between Juba and Pompeius went back to the First
Roman Civil War when Sulla sent Pompeius to drive the Cinnan faction
survivors out of Roman North Africa and Pompeius restored Juba's father
to the Numidian throne. This loyalty to Pompeius was enhanced when he

personally clashed with Caesar himself in Rome, with the latter insulting him publicly and again in 50 BC, when a pro-Caesarian Tribune proposed annexing his kingdom.

Thus he combined a staunch support for Pompeius with a hatred of Caesar and threw the weight of his whole kingdom, still the strongest in North Africa, behind the Pompeian faction, providing it with men, materials, food, and money. Having so staunchly demonstrated his partisanship he would have been under no illusion that defeat meant death, the end of his dynasty and his kingdom.

Other Leading Pompeians

Aside from the ruling Triumvirate there were still a number of key Roman commanders in North Africa.

T. Labienus (Pr.?)

A military commander of great experience, who had formerly been close to Caesar and fought with him in Gaul. He had defected to the Pompeian / anti-Caesarian faction when Caesar started the civil war by invading Italy, having illegally crossed the Rubicon in early 49 BC.[13] Aside from being an excellent commander in his own right he had closely worked with Caesar in Gaul, and more than any man knew Caesar's military strengths and weaknesses.

L. Afranius (Cos. 60 BC)

A veteran Pompeian general who had fought with him in Spain during the First Civil War and the East during the Great Eastern War. An excellent subordinate commander but one whose weaknesses as well as strengths had been shown in the civil war campaigns of 49 BC in Spain when he initially outmanoeuvred Caesar and had him trapped but allowed himself to be subsequently outmanoeuvred and lost his army without a battle.[14]

M. Petreius (Pr. 64 BC)

Another veteran Pompeian commander, who had served through the First Civil War, commanded the Senatorial forces in the Battle of Pistoria during the Second Civil War and was described by Sallust as 'Being a military man, and having served with great reputation, for more than thirty

years, as Tribune, Prefect, Lieutenant, or Praetor.[15] He too had fought
Caesar in Spain and come off second best.

M. Octavius

An expert naval commander, who led the Pompeian forces in defeating
the Caesarians in Illyria 49 BC and who stayed there during the aftermath
of Pharsalus before being defeated (see below).

The Next Generation of Pompeians

Aside from the veteran commanders, there were three junior officers, all
of whom represented the next generation of the Pompeian faction.

Cn. Pompeius Magnus

He was the eldest son of Pompeius and inherited the title Magnus. Born
in the mid-70s BC, he was too young to officially have held office in the
Republic, but was the same age as his father when he rose to prominence
during the First Civil War. Nevertheless, as the heir of Pompeius Magnus
he could expect a significant amount of personal and political support
from his father's clients across the Mediterranean world but in particular
in Spain and the east. Again he too had limited military experience,
but had commanded a Pompeian fleet during the Dyrrhachium and
Pharsalan campaigns.

Faustus Cornelius Sulla

The only surviving son of the First Civil War general and Dictator, Sulla,
Faustus too was a young man who had inherited significant political and
veteran patronage whilst still a young man. Born in the mid-80s BC, he
has started his political career with a Quaestorship in 54 BC before the
outbreak of the civil war curtailed it. Equally as important as his lineage,
was his marriage, to Pompeia, daughter of Pompeius Magnus, making
him his son-in-law.

Faustus had considerable military experience, having fought with
distinction during the Great Eastern War, under Pompeius, particularly
during the siege of Jerusalem, being noted as the first man to storm the
walls. He had commanded Pompeian forces in Macedonia during 48 BC,
successfully fighting the Caesarians force sent against him.

Sex. Pompeius[16]

He was the second (and youngest son) of Pompeius, only in his 20s. He too could command the loyalty of the Pompeian clients and tap into the *mythos* of his father. He had commanded a Pompeian fleet during the Dyrrhachium campaign with some success, showing a flare for naval warfare.

Thus, whilst the Pompeian faction had no one figure to match the loss of Pompeius himself, between them they posed a formidable coalition: political leaders, veteran military men, and up and coming next generation leaders.

The Rise of the Three Hundred – Economic Power and the Pompeians

The detail held within the Caesarian account of the civil war in Africa allows us an insight into a much overlooked aspect of support for the Pompeian faction and its recovery in Africa, namely economic support. Though the details only emerge at the end of the *De Bello Africo*, the account refers to a group of Pompeian supporters known as the Three Hundred.

> 'together with the Three Hundred, who had contributed money to Scipio for the prosecution of the war'[17]
>
> 'for the Roman citizens who were engaged in trade and those members of the Three Hundred who had contributed sums of money to Varus and Scipio'[18]

This group receive several mentions at the end of this work, and this is the only detailed account of them.[19] As far as we can tell they were an organized cartel of Roman bankers and businessmen (equestrians) who bankrolled the Pompeian faction. As was later demonstrated, the size of their wealth can be seen by the fine of 200,000,000 sesterces they were forced to pay to secure their freedom.

The implications are interesting, as we do not often have an insight into the role of the businessmen and traders during a civil war, apart from when they are suffering the economic consequences. This is different, however, and we can clearly see a substantial cartel backing a Roman faction with large sums of money and basing themselves in North Africa, lending their economic and financial support to the Pompeian faction.

Again, aside from the immediate injection of cash into the Pompeians, it shows the depth of support that they had amongst the business community, seemingly far more than Caesar could muster.

The Caesarian Faction without Caesar – The Vacuum

Much as the Pompeian faction had to regroup without its leader, ironically the Caesarian faction too faced the same issue. At first this may seem strange as, unlike Pompeius, Caesar was still alive and well. Yet in terms of fighting the civil war, Caesar was just as absent as Pompeius in 47 BC, and we need to understand not only why this occurred, but what the impact was. Caesar was effectively absent from the civil war between September 48 BC when he reached Egypt in pursuit of Pompeius, and September 47 BC when he returned to Rome to shore up his faltering political and military position. Throughout this period he remained in the Eastern Mediterranean, firstly in Egypt and then in Asia Minor. Though, after being rescued from being trapped in Alexandria, he was able to send orders to his subordinates throughout the Republic's territories, effectively he was an absentee leader.

As has already been mentioned, his constitutional position was unique. Throughout the First Civil War there had been several men who had occupied the dominant political position that now belonged to Caesar, most notably his uncle Marius, his father-in-law Cinna, and their opponent Sulla. It had been Sulla who had revived the Dictatorship and made it into a supreme post without time limit, but he did so whilst occupying Rome itself and using the Senate as a rubber stamp. Caesar was the first to use the Dictatorship as an overseas command, leaving a vacuum in Roman politics, with no Consuls elected (see below) and M. Antonius as a Master of the Horse (the official deputy of a Dictator) trying to wield power in Rome.

Despite being the victor of Pharsalus and with his main opponent dead, Caesar faced a catalogue of political and military problems, many of which were contradictory and the choices he made were revealing. As stated before, despite his victory at Pharsalus, the civil war was clearly not over, with potential campaigns in Africa and Illyria, yet there were also two potential military campaigns in the east, against Ptolemy XIII and Pharnaces II.

Despite being Dictator, with theoretically unlimited power, his control of the Republic was in fact quite weak in practice, with few genuinely enthusiastic supporters and most (both Roman and native) offering only tokenistic support, based on his (temporary) military superiority. The Senate and Rome's ruling oligarchy was composed of three sections, his own supporters, neutrals and pardoned Pompeians and the latter two factions would not take kindly to being ruled from overseas or by a Caesarian governor.

Despite having nominal control of the Roman world, aside from North Africa, in the west his grip on Spain and Gaul was tenuous at best, and on the edge of revolt, whilst in the mid-Mediterranean his control of Illyria was being contested by the Pompeians and in the east he was losing Asia Minor and had the Parthian Empire poised to resume the Romano-Parthian War which had petered out in 52/51 BC.

At the heart of Caesar's problem, lay two factors. Firstly, he had seized control of the Republic by military victory and was the new front runner, but despite this he actually had a very narrow powerbase; his army, elements of the Roman oligarchy and popularity with the People, everyone else simply tolerated him. The second was that the Caesarian faction was built around him and suffered from a cult of personality that required him to be present. When he was absent, this presence (and the implied threat) was removed, and the spell was broken.

That Caesar chose to ignore the rest of the Roman world and the ongoing civil war to focus on the east is telling. His (typically Roman) obsession with Alexander the Great[20] was well known and can only have been inflamed by his stay in Alexandria and his encounter with the body of the legendary king. The campaigns he chose to focus on were seizing control of Egypt (via a pliant proxy), an essential step for any eastern campaign and defeating the renewed Pontic threat of Pharnaces II (son of another legendary king, Mithridates VI).

One gets the feeling that his return to Rome in September 47 BC was an annoyance and that he would rather have remained in the east to renew the Romano-Parthian War that he had helped (along with his Triumviral colleagues) to foster, leading to an Alexandrian style conquest of the east. It seems that for Caesar himself, the civil war, and politics in Rome (which had never been his forte) were matters that were distractions from his dreams of becoming the new Alexander. Thus the Caesarian faction had to do without its charismatic leader and driving force for the next year, with predictable results.

Chapter Four

The Continuation of the Civil War – The Campaigns of 47 BC

Though the year 47 BC is the only one of the period 49–45 BC that had no major battles between the Pompeian and Caesarian factions, this does not mean (as is often assumed) that there was no fighting between the two groups. Though the surviving sources do not focus on these campaigns, a careful reading of them can uncover passing references from which we can at least recover the outline of the campaigns which were fought.

The Civil War in Illyria (47 BC)

Naturally enough, the surviving sources we have focus on Caesar, first in Egypt and then in Asia Minor. Yet despite their neglect of events in other parts of the Roman world, fragments of narrative do survive. Though with the present fragmentary sources we will never know to what extent armed clashes between the two factions continued to take place, we do know for certain that civil war campaigns continued in Illyria, formerly the heartland of the Pompeian faction, centred on the island of Corcyra (Corfu).

We have been told that, after Pharsalus, the surviving Pompeian land forces evacuated Illyria, first for the Peloponnese and then for the North African province of Cyrene, in an aborted attempt to link up with Pompeius. Yet the sources are silent on the remaining Pompeian navy, which had been heavily diminished in the aftermath of Pharsalus by defections (of allied contingents). Nevertheless, despite these defections, the Pompeian navy was still a force to be reckoned with. Most crucially we are not told whether the Pompeians abandoned their naval headquarters of Corcyra when they evacuated the coastal cities.

Nevertheless, we are informed of at least one Pompeian commander whose fleet remained in Illyrian waters to challenge Caesarian control of the region: namely M. Octavius. Octavius had been the commander who had secured the region for Pompeius in 49 BC, defeating the Caesarian forces in Illyria, a major victory which denied Caesar a bridgehead in the region.[1] Thus he was an experienced commander in fighting in that region and its particular topography.

Initially he was faced by the experienced Caesarian commander (and noted former Pompeian) A. Gabinius. Unfortunately for Gabinius (and Caesar), he was ambushed by the native tribes, who had used the ongoing civil war as an opportunity to divest themselves of Roman control, and who then proceeded to trap his army in a gorge and annihilate it, during the winter of 48 / 47 BC.

Battle of Sunodium (late 48 BC)

'[Gabinius] *was forced to fight an action on the march. In this battle he lost more than two thousand soldiers, thirty-eight Centurions and four Tribunes: with what was left of his forces he retired to Salona, where, under the stress of overwhelming difficulties of every kind, he fell sick and died within a few months.'*[2]

'*Gabinius led fifteen cohorts of foot and 3,000 horse for him by way of Illyria, passing around the Adriatic. The Illyrians, fearing punishment for what they had done to Caesar not long before, and thinking that his victory would be their destruction, attacked and slew the whole army under Gabinius, except Gabinius himself and a few who escaped. Among the spoils captured was a large amount of money and war material.'*[3]

'They took the town of Sunodium at the edge of the forest in which the army of Gabinius had been entrapped by the Dalmatians in a long and deep gorge between two mountains.'[4]

'*and also the Roman standards taken from Gabinius*'[5]

It is interesting to note, that, coming in the midst of a civil war (and after Pharsalus), this total destruction of a Roman army by native tribes, complete with the loss of legionary standards attracts so little attention. The scale of the defeat can be seen by the fact that the author of the pseudo-Caesarian Alexandrian Wars has to acknowledge it,[6] though downplays the number of casualties. Appian's number of just under 7,000 foot soldiers and 3,000 cavalry far outstrips the 2,000 soldiers in the 'Caesarian' account.

Given Octavius' experience and knowledge of the region, and a later statement by the 'Caesarian' account (see below) that Octavius conducted treaties with various native tribes, it is tempting to speculate over whether Octavius was the architect of this Caesarian defeat? Whatever the cause, the effect was that the largest Caesarian military force in Illyria had been removed and that once again we find Pompeian commanders working with native allies (as in Africa and Spain) to face the Caesarians. This would have suited Octavius' strategy, with the Pompeians operating from the sea with their fleet and using the native forces to compensate for a lack of Pompeian land forces.

After the death of Gabinius, command of the Caesarian forces in Illyria fell to Q. Cornificius (Pr. 45 BC), who from the Caesarian accounts was clearly out of his depth, as the following extract attests:

'When Vatinius was at Brundisium he learned of what had been going on in Illyricum; moreover, frequent despatches from Cornificius kept summoning him to bring aid to the province, and he heard that M. Octavius had concluded treaties with the natives and in several places was attacking the garrisons of our troops, in some cases in person with his fleet, in others with land forces, employing native troops. So, although he was afflicted by a serious illness and his bodily strength barely enabled him to obey his will, yet by courage he overcame his physical handicap, as well as the difficulties both of winter and the sudden mobilisation.

Thus, as he himself had few warships in harbour, he sent despatches to Q. Calenus in Achaia, requesting him to send him a fleet; but as this proved too slow a business, our troops were in no position to withstand Octavius' attack, and their critical situation urgently demanded something speedier, he fitted beaks to some fast boats, of which he had a sufficient number, though their size was by no means adequate for fighting purposes.

With these added to his warships, and his fleet thereby numerically increased, he put on board some veteran troops, of which he had an abundant supply from all the legions, they had been on the sick list and had been left behind at Brundisium when the army was being shipped to Greece, and so set out for Illyricum.

Now there were not a few coastal communities there which had revolted and surrendered to Octavius: some of these he recovered, others he by-passed when they remained steadfast to their policy; nor would he allow anything, however pressing, to embarrass or delay him from pursuing Octavius himself with all the speed of which he was capable. While the latter was assaulting Epidaurus by land and sea, where there was a garrison of ours, Vatinius forced him by his approach to abandon his assault, and so relieved our garrison.'[7]

Thus we can see that Octavius was engaging in a process of eliminating the various coastal garrisons that the Caesarians had placed in Illyrian/Epirote cities and trying to secure the eastern flank of the Adriatic for the Pompeians once more. Realizing the danger, this forced the Caesarian commander of Brundisium to create a scratch force from both Caesarian reserve naval and land forces and lead his own expedition, without orders from either Caesar or Antonius. Having learnt of this new arrival, Octavius committed to destroying it.

The Battle of Tauris (47 BC)

Octavius, with what was clearly a far superior knowledge of the region, tracked down Vatinius off the Adriatic Island of Tauris (off the Illyrian coast) and ambushed him, with a full account found in pseudo-Caesarian *De Bello Alexandrino*:

'*The Vatinians being thus suddenly taken unawares proceeded to man ship: the Octavians, their ships already manned, came sailing out of the harbour one after another. Line of battle was formed on either side, that of Octavius being superior in formation, that of Vatinius in the morale of the troops.*

When Vatinius observed that neither in the size nor the number of his ships was he a match for a chance engagement, he chose rather to trust to luck. And so he attacked first, charging with his own quinquereme the quadrireme which was the flagship of Octavius. The latter rowed forward against him with the utmost speed and bravery, and the two ships ran together with their beaks head-on so violently that Octavius' ship had its beak smashed away and was locked to the other by its timbers. Elsewhere a fierce engagement took place, with particularly sharp fighting near the leaders; for with each individual captain trying to support his own leader, a great battle developed at close range in the narrow sea. The more closely interlocked the ships, whenever the opportunity was afforded for such fighting, the more marked was the superiority of the Vatinians; for they displayed admirable courage in leaping without hesitation from their own ships on to those of the enemy, and where the fighting was on equal terms their markedly superior courage brought them success.

Octavius' own quadrireme was sunk, and many besides were either captured or else rammed, holed and sunk, some of his combat troops were cut down on the ships, others dived overboard. Octavius himself took refuge in a pinnace; and when too many others sought safety in it and it capsized, wounded as he was, he swam to his own light galley. There he was taken safely aboard and, when night put an end to the action, took to flight, sailing in a stiff squall. He was followed by not a few of his own ships, which chance had delivered from that hazard.

Vatinius, on the other hand, rounded off this success by sounding the retreat and withdrew triumphantly with his entire force intact to the harbour from which Octavius' fleet had advanced to do battle. As a result of that action he captured one quinquereme, two triremes, eight two-banked galleys and a large number of Octavius' rowers. The next day he spent there in refitting his own and the captured vessels; and on the day following he hastened to the island of Issa, in the belief that Octavius had taken refuge there in the course of his flight. In it there was a town, the best known one in those parts, and one which was on the friendliest terms with Octavius. On the arrival of Vatinius there the townsfolk threw themselves upon his mercy, and he learned that Octavius himself with a few small vessels had set course with a following wind in the direction of Greece, intending to make for Sicily next and then Africa. Thus in a short space of time Vatinius had achieved a most notable success, recovering the province and restoring it to Cornificius, and driving his opponents' fleet away from the whole of that coast. Whereupon he withdrew in triumph to Brundisium with his army and fleet unharmed.'[8]

Thus, despite the edge of experience and the element of surprise, Octavius was defeated by Vatinius and in one battle his whole campaign was ended, nominally securing the province for the Caesarians. Naturally, this account overlooks the fact that the various native tribes were still in revolt, but the province was lost to the Pompeians, as was the threat to the vital shipping route from Brundisium to the east.

Of the two commanders, Caesar clearly recognized the major contribution that Vatinius had played in the civil war campaigns and awarded him with the Consulship later in the year (see below). Octavius by contrast, never reached such heights again: he clearly escaped to Pompeian Africa, where the following year he is to be found once again commanding a naval squadron. However, from that point onwards he disappears from our (fragmentary) records.

The Civil War in Greece (47 BC)

By contrast we have no explicit testimony from our surviving sources on events in Greece and Macedon. The Pompeian forces had all withdrawn, first to the Peloponnese and then evacuated from Greece altogether. We have previously been told that late in 48 BC, the Caesarian commander in Greece, Q. Fufius Calenus, was campaigning against the key cities of Athens and Megara, who had declared for Pompeius:[9]

'*Calenus had been sent by Caesar into Greece before the battle, and he captured among other places the Piraeus, owing to its being unwalled. Athens, he had been unable to take, in spite of a great deal of damage he did to its territory, until the defeat of Pompeius.*'[10]

'*Accordingly Athens and most of the rest of Greece then at once made terms with him; but the Megarians in spite of this resisted and were captured only at a considerably later date, partly by force and partly by treachery. Therefore many of the inhabitants were slain and the survivors sold.*'[11]

Thus the majority of the Greek cities all surrendered to Calenus after the news of Pharsalus reached them. The notable exception was the city of Megara which still held out. The translation of Dio can be 'a considerably later date' which may well infer that the siege lasted throughout late 48 and into 47 BC. We are certainly aware that Calenus was still the Caesarian commander in Greece throughout 47 BC, until he was recalled by Caesar on his return to Italy to become Consul (along with Vatinius – see above).

All we can surmise is that apart from the siege of Megara there was no other fighting in Greece or Macedonia and that Calenus ensured that each Pompeian city now swore allegiance to the Caesarian cause.

The Civil War in Spain and North Africa (47 BC)

There is a similar silence from the sources concerning matters in the two Roman provinces of Spain and North Africa and this in itself is most interesting. Spain had been secured to the Caesarian cause in 49 BC by Caesar himself, in a lightning campaign against the Pompeian generals (see Chapter Two). Yet, as we have been told,[12] Caesar, in 48 BC, intended to use Spain as a launch pad for an invasion of North Africa, crossing the Straits and using the pro-Caesarian Kingdom of the Mauri (see Map One) to attack Numidia on its western flank. As we have also seen, in point of fact the situation was reversed when the Mauri had to cross into Caesarian Spain to assist Caesar's governors in putting down a rebellion, which seems to have been organic, but then claimed they were supporting the Pompeian cause. Using both military force and negotiations the rebellion was quashed and the governor who did much to create the rebellion (Q. Cassius Longinus) was replaced and suspiciously died of drowning when his ship went down on the journey home.

Of the two governors of the Spanish provinces, the most notable was M. Aemilius Lepidus, himself the son of a notorious First Civil War general, who marched his army against Rome (77 BC) and a key Caesarian lieutenant. He had been appointed Governor of Nearer Spain in 48 BC and remained there throughout 47 BC. His colleague was the newly appointed Governor of Farther Spain, C. Trebonius, another key Caesarian supporter, who had served (with mixed success) as the commander of the Caesarian siege of Massilia in 49 BC and who was a Caesarian Praetor in 48 BC, who had opposed his colleague M. Caelius Rufus.

In theory, with the rebellion dealt with, these two commanders, along with the two Maurian kings (Bocchus II and Bogud), should have resurrected their plans to cross to North Africa and engage the Pompeian supporting Numidia on its western flank. Yet all we do know is that this never happened; critically we do not know why. In strategic terms, with Caesar unable (or unwilling) to engage with the Pompeians from the east, it was imperative that the Caesarians apply pressure from other quarters, and without control of the Mediterranean, this meant from the west and the Maurian Kingdom. Interestingly, Dio reports that upon his return to Rome in late 47 BC Lepidus was awarded a Triumph by Caesar, yet he also reports that:

> 'although Lepidus had conquered no foes nor so much as fought with any, the pretext being that he had been present at the exploits of Longinus and of Marcellus.'[13]

Furthermore, Dio has the following passage introducing the section on the subsequent Pompeian invasion of Spain in 46 BC (see Chapter Nine):

> 'The legions in Spain under Longinus and Marcellus had rebelled and some of the cities had revolted. When Longinus had been removed and Trebonius had become his successor, they kept quiet for a few days; then, through fear of vengeance on Caesar's part, they secretly sent ambassadors to Scipio, expressing a desire to transfer their allegiance, and he sent to them Cnaeus Pompeius among others.'[14]

Thus Dio conflates the events of 47 and 46 BC into a few sentences and more importantly into a 'few days'. Yet, despite his inaccuracies in terms of timescale, has Dio identified a key factor when he indicated that Spain was not in a fit state to be left without Caesarian legions, due to its instability? Though the rebellion of 48 BC had been suppressed and battles had been fought (Corduba and Alia), key protagonists (such as the Quaestor M. Claudius Marcellus Aeserninus) had been pardoned. Thus it may well have been the case that the two Governors judged that Spain was barely pacified and that if they did transfer the bulk of their legions to North Africa then the region would rise up again and they would be cut off from the Caesarian controlled areas of the Western Republic.

This caution may well have been fuelled by the lack of direction from Caesar himself, and we have no way of knowing whether he sent instructions to them or received news of the rebellion and had to rely in their judgement as to the wisdom of invading North Africa.

Unlike Vatinius in Illyria (see above), there were seemingly no Caesarian commanders willing to take the initiative and persecute the war in this region. Such inertia would cost them the following year.

Whatever the cause, the outcome was clear. There was no Caesarian invasion of North Africa from Spain and no pressure applied to the Pompeians recovery in Numidia / Roman North Africa, giving them more time to regain the initiative.

The Civil War in Sicily and Sardinia (47 BC)

Both of the strategic islands of Sicily and Sardinia had fallen to the Caesarians in 49 BC without a fight, yet Sicily in particular had suffered from Pompeian naval attacks in 48 BC, in a campaign parallel to that on land, campaigns that had come to an abrupt halt when the news of Pharsalus spread.[15] Yet the Pompeians still had significant naval resources to contest control of the Western Mediterranean, and Sicily was the closest Caesarian controlled region to Pompeian North Africa and would be the key staging post to any invasion of Italy and thus the most logical target for the Pompeians. Again, we must rely on passing references, the first from Dio, which, as usual, has no due concern to precise timings and a second from the *De Bello Africo*:

> '*After this they made common cause in the war, carried on their preparations by land, and also made descents by sea upon Sicily and Sardinia, harrying their cities and taking back their ships, from which they obtained a plentiful supply of arms and of iron in other forms, which alone they lacked.*'[16]
>
> '[Caesar] *arrived two days later at Caralis in Sardinia. There he fined the men of Sulci one hundred thousand sesterces for having harboured Nasidius and his fleet and assisted him by supplying troops.*'[17]

Thus we can see that the Pompeians had a fleet based on Sardinia, despite being evicted from there in 49 BC by the Caesarians. The fleet, commanded by L. Nasidius, had at some point in 47 BC returned to the island and made their based at Caralis, the capital of Sardinia, aided by the locals. Again, a passing reference in a surviving source reveals that the ongoing civil war was of a far larger scope than the main accounts preserve. Furthermore, despite declaring for Caesar in 49 BC and Caesar's victory in 48 BC, the locals turned to the Pompeians once more, yet another example of the 'wafer thin' nature of Caesar's control of the Republic.

With bases in North Africa and Sardinia, the entire Italian and Sicilian coastlines would have been vulnerable to the raids of the Pompeian ships and indicates that, with Caesar in the east, the Pompeians held a degree of naval superiority over the Caesarians.

The Decline of the Antonine Republic

Though there were no civil war campaigns in Italy itself during 47 BC, that did not mean that all was peaceful, and the events of 48 BC (in terms of political violence) soon repeated themselves. Though Caesar had military control of Italy, this did not automatically translate into political control of Rome itself. Despite having a Senate purged of all of his obvious enemies, control of the Assemblies and control over the magisterial elections, this too did not seemingly translate into an uncontested Caesarian control over the running of the Republic, a lesson that Caesar seemed to find hard to learn.

During 48 BC, one of the Praetors (M. Caelius Rufus) a man whose election Caesar had supposedly vetted, used Caesar's absence, and the absence of most of the other key oligarchs, to stir up a political storm, exploiting the economic effects of the civil war on the Roman populace, with proposals on debt relief and rent payments. He was opposed by Caesar's Consular colleague P. Servilius Isauricus. The situation was further enflamed by the arrival (from exile) of a former Pompeian agitator, T. Annius Milo (see Chapter One) and between them, the two men attempted to stir up a rebellion in Italy, which had to be put down by military force.[18]

Needless to say, whilst campaigning far from Rome, Caesar needed two things domestically: a constitutional veneer to his military dominance and political calm throughout Rome and Italy. What Caesar failed to realize, unlike Sulla and Pompeius, is that the Republic now needed the permanent guiding presence of a major political figure in order to keep it under control. However, during his enforced eastern absence, Caesar chose M. Antonius for this role, who unfortunately was a man cut from the same cloth as Caesar politically, and not one of the most talented politicians the Republic had ever produced (as was repeatedly shown in subsequent events).

As has been previously mentioned, Caesar found the office of Dictator the most convenient constitutional mantle to assume, giving his military dominance of the Republic a constitutional veneer. However, as has equally been commented on, whilst practical, this was the most politically tone deaf choice that a Roman politician could make. By the mid-first century BC, the Dictatorship had forever been tainted with the bloody sole rule of L. Cornelius Sulla (83–81 BC), who had seized control of the Republic during the First Civil War, accompanied by a slaughter of his enemies (see Chapter One). This was an association of which Pompeius was well aware and he avoided it at all costs (as seen in 52 BC), a position copied by Caesar's adopted son and successor Octavianus.

Nevertheless, there were some obvious constitutional side effects of holding a Dictatorship, namely that no other Curule magistrates could be elected (so no Consuls, Praetors, or Curule Quaestors). The clear exception to this were the Plebeian offices, most obviously the Plebeian Tribunes, the office which more than any other had come to embody the chaos and bloodshed of the Late Republic (see Chapter One). Thus the only offices senior to the Tribunes in 47 BC were the Dictator and his Deputy, the Master of the Horse. With Caesar choosing to hold the office of Dictator in a unique way – namely elected in absence whilst on the other side of the Mediterranean and staying there all year – power in Rome and Italy fell to his deputy, the Master of the Horse, M. Antonius. Antonius had become de facto, the most powerful man in Rome and the most powerful Master of the Horse ever and was in effect the Dictator of Italy.

The problem that Antonius faced was that he only held this position by virtue of Caesar's military superiority and Caesar was on the other side of the Mediterranean. Furthermore, Antonius had no powerbase of his own and this new (and anomalous) position would have been resented by both the pro-Caesarian and non-Caesarian oligarchs within the Senate.

Thus Antonius was trying to rule the Republic in Caesar's name, but without the military aura and political capital that Caesar himself had.

Furthermore, the Master of the Horse was not meant to be the office of a politician, but that of a military deputy. In the absence of Consuls or Praetors, Antonius had little defined constitutional power. Thus we can see the poor position that Caesar left his deputy in. The only magistrates in Rome, aside from Antonius, were the Tribunes (and Plebeian Aediles) and it does seem that Antonius was politically savvy enough to work with / through them, to avoid looking as if he was ruling by dictat. Furthermore, Dio alerts us to Antonius and the Tribunes agreeing on an age old technique of distracting the People from the disruptions and economic hardships with a supply of public festivals:

> 'Most of these festivals, by the way, Antonius gave at Caesar's expense, although the Tribunes also gave a few.'[19]

Though Rome had a full calendar of festivals, funding these in Caesar's name and making them more lavish was a good way of trying to keep the People quiet. However, there was one key potential flaw in Antonius' policy of ruling with / through the Tribunes; namely the Tribunes themselves, who now had even more power than ever, with no political offices above them, only an ill-defined Master of the Horse. This meant that the vetting of the Tribunes (which probably had fallen to Antonius himself) was all the more crucial. As we shall see below, this vetting process failed spectacularly.

Any discussion of Antonius in the surviving ancient sources is bound to have been tainted by Cicero's later vitriolic speeches, the Philippics, which attempted to tarnish every one of Antonius' actions. Nevertheless, the situation Antonius found himself in, ruling in the name of an absent leader, called for tact and discretion; two characteristics that did not seem to be found within his make-up. Furthermore, we do not know what orders he received from Caesar, so we cannot be clear on what actions were his own.

One of the most obvious deeds for which Antonius receives opprobrium is the confiscation of the Roman property of Pompeius. Yet Dio is clear that Antonius paid for these estates (obviously at a knock down price) and Caesar himself auctioned off Pompeian property when he returned from the east (see Chapter Nine). Thus we can see that Caesar's policy of clemency, which he had operated throughout the civil war period to date, was suspended when it came to matters of raising additional funds and he may well have tasked Antonius with this process. However, despite this, Antonius' lack of political acumen shines through here as he clearly didn't think (or didn't care) how it would look trying to step into the now martyred Pompeius' shoes. Furthermore, it may well have been a case of

Caesar using Antonius as a lightning rod for unpopular policies; to keep his own hands clean.

Again, cutting through the vitriol which Antonius receives in the surviving ancient sources, clearly Caesar would have wanted two major outcomes; maintaining a harmonious status quo in Roman politics and amongst the Caesarian military. On both fronts Antonius failed, but then despite his many faults, the key to the Caesarian factions' success was Caesar himself and his absence created a dangerous vacuum, that manifested itself in political and military disruption.

In political terms, we have already seen in 48 BC that Caesar's absence provided a supposedly 'loyal' Praetor the opportunity to seek popular acclaim and power for himself. Unsurprisingly the situation repeated itself in 47 BC and once again centred upon an ambitious Tribune; a certain P. Cornelius Dolabella, a figure who was to play a brief, but important role in this Third Civil War.

Tribunes at War

Dolabella hailed from a longstanding, but undistinguished Patrician family which had reached the Consulship as early as 283 BC, but had only done so twice since (159 and 81 BC). He seemingly supported Caesar from the start as we find him as a legate operating in the naval campaign off Illyria in 49 BC, which ended in a Caesarian defeat.[20] Back in Rome in 48 BC, and with an undistinguished military record, Dolabella must have sensed the political potential in Caesar's absence as he arranged to be adopted into a Plebeian family, for political purposes, something that only the notorious P. (Claudius) Clodius Pulcher had done.[21] Prior to this, giving up one's Patrician status was seen as dishonourable and sacrilegious. However, it meant that he was now eligible to be elected as Tribune, something he achieved in late 48 BC. With his background as a Caesarian commander in the war, he would have been seen as a safe pair of hands and approved of by the ruling faction. Furthermore, Plutarch states that he was already a friend of Antonius.[22] However, his deliberate transfer to the Plebeian order should have set alarm bells ringing.

At some point early in the new year, Dolabella unveiled his programme of legislation, and it was a classic piece of popular law-making; debt relief, the same contentious subject that Caelius Rufus had stirred up the year before. On the one hand the economic effects of the civil war in Italy and the disruption of land holding, with additional confiscations, would clearly have had a negative impact on the fortunes of many of the voting populace. On the other, however, such legislation usually led to political confrontation, with many standing to lose out in such legislation and others motivated by the worry about the popularity such a move would bring to its author. Thus, such a proposal was the very opposite of maintaining peace and stability and unsurprisingly, Antonius declined to support it. Furthermore, the surviving sources voice the rumour that Dolabella was also conducting an affair with Antonius' wife, who does seem to have been cast out by Antonius during this period.[23]

Given his ill-defined constitutional powers, the safest route for Antonius was to use another Tribune to block Dolabella and according to Dio, one (L. Trebellius) did not need Antonius' prompting to do so. However, the constitutional aspects of one Tribune being able to block another's actions had steadily been abandoned since the time of Ti. Sempronius Gracchus in 133 BC (see Chapter One). Thus, as had continually happened since, the two Tribunes gathered their supporters and armed clashes broke out between the two factions, with Antonius looking on, seemingly helpless.

The chronology of these events is compressed by all the sources who mention it. Dio provides the best account and ties the events in with Caesar's activities in the east, providing a rough chronological framework. What is clear, however, is that these clashes continued for many months.

'The Tribunes who were at variance with each other despised Lucius [Trebellius] *because of his advanced age and inflicted many outrages upon one another and upon the rest, until they learned that Caesar having settled affairs in Egypt, had set out for Rome. For they were carrying on their quarrel upon the assumption that he would never return again but would of course perish there at the hands of the Egyptians, as, indeed, they kept hearing was the case. When, however, his coming was reported, they moderated their conduct for a time; but as soon as he set out against Pharnaces first, they fell to quarrelling once more.*'[24]

Thus Dio clearly sets out the impact that Caesar's absence was having, with both Tribunes only moderating their behaviour when they thought that Caesar himself would be arriving and then continuing their clashes when they realized he wasn't. We can see the impotency of Antonius' constitutional position. In terms of chronology, we have no firm dates for Caesar's departure from Alexandria, having quelled the Egyptian Civil War around March 47 BC.[25] With the Fourth Romano-Pontic War raging in Asia Minor, Caesar was highly unlikely to return to Rome, but would have had an opportunity to do so from April onwards, which gives us a date for the pause of hostilities between Trebellius and Dolabella. With Caesar probably on the march for Asia by May / June 47 BC, this gives us a date for the resumption of the chaos in Rome.

Whilst Dio is clearly making a point here, there may well have been truth in the matter that Caesar (in Egypt) was able to exert more influence over events in Rome than Antonius was in Rome itself. Nevertheless if we are to believe the fairly detailed account in Dio, then Antonius allowed this chaos and violence to escalate with a particularly inept handling of the situation. If we follow Dio's account, then Antonius' first action was to leave the city and hand matters over to a deputy:

'*Meanwhile Antonius learned that the legions which Caesar after the battle had sent ahead into Italy, with the intention of following them later, were engaged in questionable proceedings; and fearing that they might begin some rebellion, he turned over the charge of the city to Lucius Caesar, appointing him city prefect, an office never before conferred by a Master of the Horse, and then set out himself to join the soldiers.*'[26]

With this action having seemingly no impact, upon his return to the city Antonius vacillated between the two sides, first supporting one then the other and ending up only making matters worse:

'*Accordingly Antonius, seeing that he was unable to restrain them and that his opposition to Dolabella was obnoxious to the populace, at first joined himself to that Tribune and brought various charges against Trebellius, among them one to the effect that he was appropriating the soldiers to his own use.*

Later, when he perceived that he himself was not held in any esteem by the multitude, which was attached only to Dolabella, he became vexed and changed sides, the more so because, while not sharing with the Plebeian leader the favour of the People, he nevertheless received the greatest share of blame from the Senators.

So nominally he adopted a neutral attitude toward the two, but in fact secretly preferred the cause of Trebellius, and cooperated with him in various ways, particularly by allowing him to obtain soldiers. Thenceforward he became merely a spectator and director of their contest, while they fought, seized in turn the most advantageous points in the city, and entered upon a career of murder and arson, to such an extent that on one occasion the holy vessels were carried by the virgins out of the Temple of Vesta.'[27]

Thus Antonine (Caesarian) Rome collapsed into the worst excesses of the late Republic with bloodshed and arson across the city, with Rome itself being fought over by the two factions, and Antonius standing about, seemingly helpless. At this juncture Caesar must have been glad that Antonius was acting as a lightning rod and taking the blame for this chaos.

However, with the situation worsening and Caesar engaged in the Fourth Romano-Pontic War (see Appendix One) and not expected back anytime soon, the Senate seemingly forced Antonius to act and do the only thing he could; namely bring in the Caesarian legions, though again we do not know the date (perhaps July or August 47 BC). Whilst this seems to have quelled Trebellius (who disappears from our narrative of events, only later to be possibly found serving under Antonius), Dolabella seems to have doubled down and he and his supporters occupied and fortified the Forum, with Rome now being the scene of a siege.

The Battle of the Forum (47 BC)

'On receipt of these announcements the crowd erected barricades around the Forum, setting up wooden towers at some points, and put itself in readiness to cope with any force that might oppose it. At that, Antonius led down from the Capitol at dawn a large body of soldiers, cut down the tablets containing Dolabella's laws and afterwards hurled some of the disturbers from the very cliffs of the Capitoline.'[28]

'For Dolabella had occupied the Forum in order to force the passage of his law; so Antonius, after the Senate had voted that arms must be

employed against Dolabella, came up against him, joined battle, slew some of his men, and lost some of his own.'[29]

'The Tribune of the Plebs Publius Dolabella caused unrest when he proposed a law to cancel debts, and the plebs started to revolt. However, Marcus Antonius, the Master of Horse, sent soldiers into the city and 800 people were killed.'[30]

Thus Antonius, having been pushed into this action by the Senate sent the troops into the Forum and a subsequent battle was fought at the heart of Rome, with nearly a thousand citizens and soldiers slain. However, Dio further relates that this battle did not seem to end the issue,[31] as Dolabella survived and seemingly continued his struggle. The matter was not ended until Caesar himself returned to Rome (see Chapter Five), whereupon he pardoned many of those involved (showing his customary clemency), amongst whom was Dolabella himself.

Thus we can see that for the second year running, ambitious politicians were using Caesar's absence and the economic hardships caused by the civil war to stir up political controversy leading to violence. All this shows how thin the veneer of Caesarian control over Rome was.

Caesarian Legions in revolt

As Dio has alluded to, however, politics was not the only source of instability in Caesarian Italy, as there were issues with the army as well.

'Meanwhile Antonius learned that the legions which Caesar after the battle had sent ahead into Italy, with the intention of following them later, were engaged in questionable proceedings.'[32]

'and the flattering indulgence shewn to their troops by the Military Tribunes and legionary commanders was giving rise to many practices opposed to military custom and usage which tended to undermine strict discipline.'[33]

Thus we can see dissension amongst the Caesarian army, or at least the portion of which Caesar had sent back to Italy. Here Caesar (and his deputies) faced a number of problems. Firstly these soldiers may well have been aggrieved at not being selected to fight in the east and thus access the rewards of such a campaign. Secondly, they may well have been impatient at not being discharged (with the customary grants of money that accompanied it). Thirdly there will have been many former Pompeian soldiers amongst those sent back to Italy, with the vast bulk having surrendered to Caesar after Pharsalus, leaving Caesar with the headache of whether they would be more trouble with him in the east or back in Italy. Thus, the Caesarians faced a disgruntled and possibly mutinous army in Italy, a situation that was not resolved until Caesar himself returned from the east (see Chapter Five).

In terms of the wider civil war, Cicero reports that Caesar had sent P. Cornelius Sulla to Italy with a view to begin ferrying the legions to Sicily, ready for an invasion of Africa. This can be dated to August:

> '*the 12th legion, which* [P. Cornelius] *Sulla visited first, is said to have driven him off with a shower of stones. It is thought that none of the legions will stir.*'[34]
>
> '*Sulla, I believe, will be here tomorrow with* [M. Valerius] *Messalla. They are hurrying to Caesar after being driven away by the soldiers, who say that they will go nowhere until they have got what was promised them.*'[35]

We can see that that the discord mentioned by Dio had turned into outright mutiny with the Italian legions refusing to be shipped to Sicily for an invasion of Africa and Caesar's legate having to return to tell him the news, all delaying the proposed invasion.

Thus as the year wore on, the Caesarian grip on Rome and Italy was further weakened, with open conflict on the streets of Rome and mutinous legions in Italy. Whilst these were all common enough occurrences in civil wars, they showed the thin level of control that the 'winning' Caesarian faction had on the Republic and more than anything showed the damage being caused by Caesar's absence.

The Planned Pompeian Offensive

The school of Caesarian history would like to paint the Pompeians in 47 BC as being a defeated band of survivors hiding in North Africa, waiting for the imperious Caesar to find the time in his busy schedule to put them out of their misery. As the reader will have noticed, this is not a school to which this present study adheres. As we have seen above, the Pompeians used the absence of Caesar and the inaction of his lieutenants to rebuild their strength and plan their next moves.

Whilst Caesar had spent the year 47 BC gaining control of the Eastern Republic and its allies, as we have seen above, his control of the Western Republic was fragmenting. Although the Caesarians had finally driven the Pompeians out of Illyria, their control of Spain and Italy was loosening, and Sardinia and Sicily were subject to Pompeian raids. Having secured the east, it was clear that Caesar intended to invade Pompeian North Africa, but it was equally clear that the renewed Pompeian faction had no desire to be passive and simply wait for Caesar, but went on the offensive, with a plan detailed by Dio:

> '*Finally they reached a state of preparedness and courage that, when no army opposed them and Caesar delayed in Egypt and the capital, they sent Pompeius to Spain. For on learning that the country was in revolt they thought that the People would readily receive him as the son of Pompeius the Great; and while he was making preparations to occupy Spain in a short time and to set out from there to the capital, the others were getting ready to make the voyage to Italy.*'[36]

Whilst the Pompeian invasion of Spain did not take place until after Caesar had invaded Africa in January 46 BC, it is clear that the Pompeians had clearly laid plans to exploit the chaos in Spain and open up a second front. Thus the scene was set for the renewal of the civil war in earnest for the coming year, with a Pompeian invasion of Spain and a Caesarian invasion of Africa.

Section III

The African Campaign of 46 BC

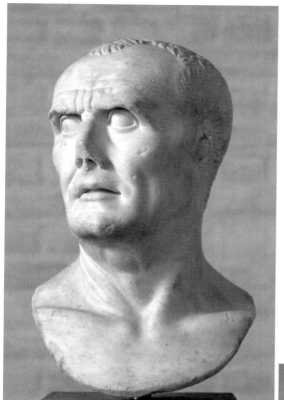

Possible bust of C. Marius.

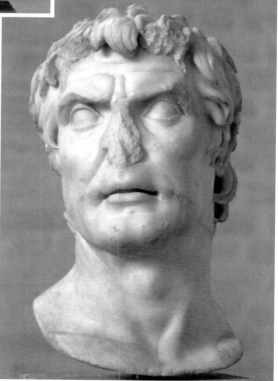

Bust of L. Cornelius Sulla.

Coin of Faustus Sulla. (*CNG Coins*)

Coin of Pharnaces II.

Bust of Juba I of Numidia.

African Interior. (*Adobe Stock*)

Chapter Five

The Caesarian Invasion of North Africa and the Battle of Ruspina

The Return of the King – Regaining Control of the Republic

By September 47 BC, Caesar had completed his eastern campaigns in his usual brisk and efficient manner (see Appendix One) having secured three major outcomes. Firstly (and the original reason for going to the East) he had secured control of the provinces and allied kingdoms of the Eastern Roman Republic, which had previously been loyal to Pompeius. In all fairness they were now as loyal to Caesar as they had been to Pompeius and would change loyalties again with their usual haste if the circumstances required it.

Secondly Caesar had secured a greater control of Egypt (the Mediterranean's richest kingdom) than any previous Roman, including Pompeius and Crassus. He had done so, not only by backing one side of the Ptolemaic civil war and installing a puppet ruler on the throne, but also by choosing as that puppet Cleopatra VII, with whom he shared a close personal relationship (and a son).

Thirdly he had defeated the invasion of the Pontic King Pharnaces II, who had invaded his father's old ancestral kingdom of Pontus, now a Roman province and thus clearly demonstrated to all (especially the Parthians), that Roman territory was not undefended. Caesar had defeated Pharnaces at the Battle of Zela (on what now equates to 2 August 47 BC – see Appendix One) and driven him back across the Black Sea. Caesar had no need to continue the war, as Pharnaces (ironically and perhaps poetically) had to contend with a usurper in his own Bosphoran Kingdom (as he himself had usurped his father) and was conveniently (for Caesar) killed in a battle with the pretender Asander, soon afterwards.

Thus, in little under a year, Caesar had secured the Roman East from both internal and external enemies. The obvious remaining threat, however, was the Parthian Empire, which just six years earlier had defeated

Caesar's old mentor (Crassus) and invaded Roman Syria and which still harboured ambitions of annexing the Roman (and Ptolemaic) East. The First Romano-Parthian War had petered out in 52 BC following the defeat of the invading Parthian force by none other than C. Cassius Longinus. Thus Caesar had to demonstrate to the Parthians that the ongoing civil war did not present them with an opportunity to invade, a point clearly made at the Battle of Zela. Nevertheless, if Caesar left the east, then there would be another opportunity for the Parthians. To that end, Caesar left a cousin, Sex. Iulius Caesar in command of the Roman province of Syria with sufficient forces to defend the province which would take the brunt of any Parthian attack (see Chapter Eight).

We can well imagine that Caesar viewed the resumption of the Parthian War as the major outstanding foreign policy aim for his Republic and a chance to emulate an idol, Alexander the Great. Yet such a campaign could not be undertaken lightly and needed months of preparation. Most importantly he did not have a mandate from the Senate or People for such a campaign and could certainly not undertake it whilst the civil war raged in the Western Republic and his control of the Republic was so perilously thin.

In many ways it is useful to juxtapose Caesar's situation in the Eastern and Western Republics. The east, with its history of dominant warrior rulers had no issue paying (wafer thin) homage to Caesar. He had secured the loyalty of the rulers of the region and replaced any he suspected. He had also secured control of the key region of Egypt in the manner of an absent Pharaoh, with the mother of his son in control. He had defeated an invading enemy and made a clear statement to all that the Eastern Republic and its allies were defended.

Yet by contrast, in the Western Republic his civil war opponents controlled North Africa and were making attacks on Sicily and Sardinia and would soon be in a position to harry Italy itself. His control of Spain was so precarious that his forces had to remain in place to prevent another uprising. In Gaul, the recently conquered Gallic tribes would have been waiting for a similar opportunity to revolt and may already have done so (see Chapter Eight). Rome itself had descended into its usual pre-civil war political chaos, with bloody battles across the centre of Rome itself and the army having to be brought in to quell the fighting. Finally, his legions in Italy were in near open revolt and refusing the commands of his subordinates.

Thus, it was clear that if he did not return to the Western Republic, all of his victories to date could have unravelled and it was not out of the realms of possibility that Metellus and Cato could return to Rome to have him declared an outlaw once more. All of these factors must also have brought home to him that without his physical presence, his faction were not that competent at keeping the Republic under the control he needed to pursue his military ambitions.

Thus, Caesar set off for Italy, returning there by (what now equates to) September 47 BC. Clearly, he had three aims; restore control over his legions, prepare for an invasion of Pompeian North Africa and finally restore control over the Republic. We know that Caesar landed in Tarentum in Italy in late September 47 BC, with Cicero especially scampering to curry favour with Caesar in person. Having dealt with the hangers on, Caesar made straight for Rome, to assess the problems first hand.

Of all the issues he faced, it seems that the political chaos in Rome was the easiest to deal with. As we have already noted (see Chapter Four), two of the main protagonists – the Tribunes Dolabella and Trebellius – had already toned down the fighting simply on a rumour that Caesar was returning home, so when the man himself landed in Italy, the dissensions ceased. This temporary ceasefire was built upon by Caesar, showing a deft political touch (for once) in further defusing the situation:

'And they did not cease until he himself suddenly appeared before them; then they reluctantly quieted down. They were expecting to suffer every conceivable ill fate, and there was talk about them all through the city, some judging one way and others another; but Caesar even at this juncture followed his usual practice. Accepting their attitude of the moment as satisfactory and not concerning himself with their past conduct, he spared them all, and even honoured some of them, including Dolabella. For he owed the latter some kindness, which he did not see fit to forget; in other words, in place of overlooking that favour because he had been wronged, he pardoned him in consideration of the benefit he had received, and besides honouring him in other ways he not long afterward appointed him Consul, though he had not even served as Praetor.'[1]

Thus Dolabella was pardoned and even promoted, perhaps being seen as someone who had the ear of the People far more than Antonius. Furthermore, he would have been useful in passing the domestic legislation Caesar had in mind. Nothing is mentioned of Trebellius, but we find a Trebellius as Aedile in 44 BC and serving M. Antonius in 43 BC. With the immediate dissensions quelled, Caesar set out to restore a veneer of constitutional government. Most obviously Consuls were elected/ appointed for the first time this year; though it is not clear whether Caesar gave up the Dictatorship straight away, but he certainly allowed it to lapse, preferring to stand for Consul for 46 BC, alongside M. Aemilius Lepidus (who had previously been left in charge of Rome in 49 BC and stabilized Spain in 48 BC). Thus Caesar, at least for a short while, reverted to a more standard constitutional position, that of a Consul not a Dictator, at least whilst he faced his 'Republican' enemies in North Africa.

The new Consuls (for what remained of 47 BC) were two staunch Caesarian generals, Q. Fufius Calenus and P. Vatinius,[2] who had both distinguished themselves in combat during the year (in Illyria and Greece respectively – see Chapter Three). If we interpret Dio (see below) then Caesar filled the rest of the offices for 47 BC, as well as those for 46 BC, rewarding his allies.

The most obvious loser in these arrangements was M. Antonius, who lost his role as Master of the Horse, gaining nothing in return; he seems to have entered a period of internal exile, with no further offices and not accompanying Caesar on either his African or Spanish campaigns. Clearly Antonius' star was in the decline in the Caesarian faction, as it was under his watch that Rome fell into bloody chaos and the legions mutinied. Equally clearly Aemilius Lepidus was now the new rising star; awarded a Triumph by Caesar for his campaign in Spain and then chosen as fellow Consul for 46 BC; a dynamic that was to have major implications within the Caesarian faction when Caesar himself was removed from the equation.

It is notable that whilst it was under Antonius' watch that Trebellius and Dolabella were allowed to stand as Tribunes, having supposedly been vetted, nothing is known about the Tribunes elected for 46 BC, under the watchful gaze of Caesar, such was their anonymity in the remaining sources. Only one possible candidate has been put forward and that is Antonius' younger brother Caius.[3] Thus, having seen elected officials in both 48 and 47 BC cause political bloodshed and undermine his control of the Republic, it seems that finally Caesar ensured proper vetting of all magistrates elected for the following year, noted for its political calm (at least in our surviving sources). As well as ensuring compliant magistrates for 46 BC, Dio has the following:

> '*Upon the Senators he bestowed priesthoods and offices, some of them for the rest of that year and some for the next. Indeed, in order to reward a larger number, he appointed ten Praetors for the next year and more than the customary number of priests; for he added one member each to the Pontifices and to the Augurs, of whom he was one, and also to the Quindecemviri, as they were called, although he had desired to take all the priesthoods himself, as had been decreed. The knights in the army and the centurions and subordinate officers he conciliated in various ways, especially by appointing some of them to the Senate to fill the places of those who had perished.*'[4]

Thus Caesar filled up the offices for 47 and 46 BC as well as the Senate, ensuring that all the leading members of his faction received a reward as befitted the ruling clique.

Furthermore, having seen the economic consequences of the civil war being used by both Caelius in 48 BC and Dolabella in 47 BC, Caesar clearly needed to pass some measures to address the issue, or at least to be seen to be addressing the issue. Again Dio preserves the clearest account:

> '*For he made a present to the multitude of all the interest they were owing from the time he had gone to war with Pompeius, and he released them from all rent for one year, up to the sum of two thousand sesterces; furthermore he raised the valuation on the goods, in terms of which it was required by law for loans to be paid to their worth at the time the loan had been made, in view of the fact that everything had become much cheaper as a result of the great amount of confiscated property. By these acts he attached the People to himself.*'[5]

> '*He also remitted a year's rent in Rome to tenants who paid two thousand sesterces or less, and in Italy up to five hundred sesterces.*'[6]

Thus Caesar effectively put into place a version of the Caelian and Dolabellan plan, and paid the rents for the poorest, cut the interest people owed on loans and raised property valuations upon which loans had been made. Thus, as well as controlling the magistrates, he removed the most contentious economic issues that faced the People of Rome and thus (seemingly) removed the root cause of their support for 'rogue' magistrates in an effort to calm the political tensions in Rome.

Furthermore, Caesar also appears to have put the confiscations that Antonius and others had been indulging in on a legal footing with an official auction; thus guaranteeing the property rights of the new owners and a hefty contribution to the official treasury, with Antonius the most notable person being forced to pay for Pompeius' property.

Thus, in short order, Caesar had defused both the current political chaos and had taken measures to prevent its re-occurrence when he next left Rome on campaign. In the short term at least, sound governance had returned, and Rome would (again) be under the control of Lepidus in Caesar's absence, with a full set of (carefully vetted) magistrates to support him and a (voting) populace having been bought off. Having re-secured his (temporary) control of the Republic, the next step was to do the same with the army.

The Return of the King – Regaining Control of the Army

As we have seen, the Caesarian legions in Italy, many of which had been Pompeian soldiers had been mutinying, mostly by refusing to obey orders to transfer to Sicily. However, they were not yet in outright total rebellion, the likes of which had been seen in the past where they elected their own leaders and started taking military action themselves. The most obvious danger to Caesar was not that they refused his orders, but that there was the clear potential for them to defect to the Pompeian cause, as had happened briefly in Spain the previous year, instantly giving the Pompeians a military presence in Italy.

It seems, however, that unlike the political situation, the return of Caesar to Italy merely exacerbated the tensions within the legions, leading to an outbreak of violence. Both Dio and Appian present us with summaries of the events:

'*The legions, however, caused him no slight trouble; for they had expected to receive a great deal, and when they found their rewards inferior to their expectation, though not less, to be sure, than their deserts, they made a disturbance. The most of them were in Campania, being destined to sail on ahead to Africa. These nearly killed Sallustius, who had been appointed Praetor in order to recover his Senatorial rank; and when, after escaping them, he set out for Rome to inform Caesar of what was going on, many followed him, sparing no one on their way, but killing, among others whom they met, two Senators'*[7]

'*They demanded that they should all be dismissed to their homes. Caesar had made them certain indefinite promises at Pharsalus, and others equally indefinite after the war in Africa should be finished. Now he sent them a definite promise of 1,000 drachmas more to each man. They answered him that they did not want any more promises but prompt payment in full, and Sallustius Crispus, who had been sent to them on this business, had a narrow escape, for he would have been killed if he had not fled.'*[8]

The threat to Rome itself was clear enough, with two Senators murdered and the army reaching the Campus Martius itself. Appian and Dio differ on Caesar's next step:

'*When Caesar learned of this, he stationed the legion with which Antony had been guarding the city around his own house and the city gates, as he apprehended attempts at plunder.'*[9]
'*Caesar, as soon as he heard of their approach, wished to send his bodyguard against them, but fearing that it, too, might join in the mutiny, he remained quiet until they reached the suburbs.'*[10]

In both cases it seems that Caesar, naturally, turned to the only armed force he had at his disposal, whether it was Antonius' one legion or his own bodyguard, and tried to secure the city from a potential attack. With the immediate danger to Rome, and himself, prevented, Caesar then used his undoubted personal charisma to go into their midst (no doubt with a bodyguard) to personally address the legions and their demands, which the sources detail at some length.[11] Ultimately, with promises of an immediate payment of monies owed, the promises of riches from the forthcoming African campaign, the offer of public land on discharge and his undoubted connection (or appearance of a connection) to the common soldier, Caesar managed to quell the mutiny and secure enough legions for an attack on Africa.

Thus, upon his return to Italy, Caesar had managed to (temporarily) quell the political and military chaos that had broken out in his absence and could plan for his next move; to crush the Pompeian threat once and for all, restore his control over the Western Republic, and plan for life (and campaigns) after the civil war. Naturally his opponents planned on it being his last campaign and the one that would see this rebellion crushed and the 'true' Republic restored.

The Caesarian Invasion of North Africa – The Crossing

Never one to stand idle, especially when it meant him having to engage in the daily grind of Roman politics, Caesar planned on an immediate attack on North Africa, even though it was winter. Aside from his natural impatience, the political and military situation in the Caesarian Western Republic was not secure enough to be left unattended over the winter months. If they had, then the recently calmed army would have been given time to stew on their situation and the Pompeian naval attacks would have increased, as would the instability in Spain.

Without control of the Mediterranean and with Pompeian fleets an ever present danger, Caesar opted for the shortest route possible, so transferred his army from Italy to Sicily and then marched across Sicily to the embarkation point of the city of Lilybaeum (modern Marsala), the ancient Carthaginian route between North Africa and Sicily.

Naturally such a long preparation meant that his enemies, who still had many friends and allies in Rome, Italy, and Sicily, had plenty of warning of Caesar's approach and the route he would take. Despite their naval strength, the Pompeian battleplan would clearly have called for Caesar to land in North Africa, be cut off from Italy and then defeated without a resource to escape. Thus the Pompeians were in no rush to prevent Caesar from crossing, especially in the depths of winter (as he had done in early 48 BC).[12]

Interestingly there were apparently a number of auspices which advised Caesar against such a winter crossing. Whilst these are usually added by later historians, we do have a first-hand account from Cicero himself, who presents a refreshing take on auspices.

'*Again, when Caesar himself was warned by a most eminent soothsayer not to cross over to Africa before the winter solstice, did he not cross? If he had not done so all the forces opposed to him would have effected a junction. Why need I give instances, and, in fact, I could give countless ones, where the prophecies of soothsayers either were without result or the issue was directly the reverse of the prophecy?*

Ye gods, how many times were they mistaken in the late civil war! What oracular messages the soothsayers sent from Rome to our Pompeian party then in Greece! What assurances they gave to Pompeius! For he placed great reliance in divination by means of entrails and portents. I have no wish to call these instances to mind, and indeed it is unnecessary, especially to you, since you had personal knowledge of them. Still, you are aware that the result was nearly always contrary to the prophecy.'[13]

One point to which Caesar did seem to pay lip service came in the form of the legend of the Scipios, the greatest of which had been Scipio Africanus, who had defeated Hannibal in North Africa. Though Caesar clearly saw himself in the Scipio role, the fact that he was facing the head of the Scipio family (Metellus Scipio) combined with a rumoured prophecy that no Scipio could be defeated in Africa, did force Caesar to pay some heed to this legend. To that end he enlisted the assistance of a minor member of the Scipio clan, P. Cornelius Scipio Pomponianus Sallustio:[14]

'*On learning that the enemy were emboldened by an ancient oracle to the effect that it was always the prerogative of the family of the Scipios to conquer in Africa, he either flouted in pleasantry the Scipio who commanded the enemy, or else tried in good earnest to appropriate to himself the omen, it is hard to say which. He had under him, namely, a man who otherwise was a contemptible nobody, but belonged to the family of the Africani, and was called Scipio Sallustio. This man Caesar put in the forefront of his battles as if commander of the army, being compelled to attack the enemy frequently and to force the fighting.*'[15]

For the campaign which follows we have two excellent sources, the African War (*De Bello Africo*) supposedly written by Caesar, but more likely written by one of his officers as a continuation of Caesar's civil war narrative. This is supplemented by a detailed account in Dio.

According to the *De Bello Africo*, Caesar reached Lilybaeum on 17 December 47 BC, with just one legion. Over the next week a total of six legions (roughly 30,000 men) had been mustered and embarked, along with 6,000 cavalry. We are also told that it was 25 December when Caesar's invasion fleet left Sicily and crossed to Africa taking three days. Unfortunately for him, the fleet was scattered by the winter winds disrupting their crossing.

Though the Pompeians knew that Caesar was coming, the exact point of his landfall was unknown to them, so all they could do was to adopt a flexible defensive position, fortifying the obvious ports and harbours and having cavalry cover the coastline. The largest city on the Roman North African coast at the time was that of Utica, the capital of the Roman province (with Carthage still being a ruin).

It seems that it was here that the Pompeian faction made its official headquarters including hosting the Pompeian Anti-Senate, which had previously been convened in Greece, and the Three Hundred (see Chapter Three).[16] The city had been the target of the Caesarians' first, and ultimately disastrous, invasion of 49 BC and was commanded by M. Porcius Cato, probably more due to the need to keep him away from any major land engagements than any other considerations. Thus Utica would have been the most heavily defended of all the North African coastal cities.

An Aborted Landing – The Battle of Hadrumetum

That being the case, Caesar chose a lesser port as his target and thus chose the city of Hadrumetum, further to the south on the African coastline (see Map Two). As he had done with his bold invasion of Epirus in 48 BC, Caesar needed to deploy his army quickly and secure the port as a base before the Pompeians could deploy in sufficient numbers to drive him back into the sea. The *De Bello Africo* tells us that the town had a Pompeian garrison, which when combined with the locals, amounted to the equivalent of two legions,[17] commanded by a C. Considius Longus. This was supplemented by a force of 3,000 Numidian cavalry commanded by Cn. Calpurnius Piso Frugi, who had been patrolling the coast.

The Pompeians chose not to contest Caesar landing a portion of his army by the city (some 3,000 infantry and 150 cavalry, according to the *De*

Bello Africo[18]) and establish a bridgehead. Again, we will never know why they allowed him to do so, perhaps having orders to let Caesar land and thus trap him on African soil. With the bulk of his army still at sea, Caesar fell back on his usual tactic, namely trying to suborn either the garrison, the populace, or their commander, a tactic that had worked so well upon his initial landings in Epirus in 48 BC. However, unlike, Epirus, the cities of Roman North Africa had had over two years of being governed by the Pompeian faction and were initially not for turning (especially with Numidian contingents so close). Considius too proved to be immune to Caesar's persuasion.

Thus, with insufficient forces to attack the city (the bulk still being at sea) and with the city proving immune to his charms, Caesar was left with the usual three choices; wait, retreat, or march inland. Of the three, waiting would have allowed him the chance to contact and muster the rest of his army, but would equally allow Metellus and the Pompeians the chance to muster against him. Retreat was not only against his nature, but would have undermined the shaky morale of his army. Thus Caesar was left with one option (his favourite), that of striking camp and marching against his opponents at speed, disrupting their plans, as had proved so successful in Greece in 48 BC. The *De Bello Africo* states that he waited only 'a day and a night' before doing so.[19]

It was when he struck camp, however, presumably to march southwards, that Considius and Piso saw their chance and attacked. Though on paper Considius had the greater number of soldiers, we do not know how many of the aforementioned two legions were actually Roman legionaries and how many were local auxiliaries, but we must suspect there were very few actual legionaries in his force. Thus Caesar had the greater number of Roman legionaries. What evened the balance were Piso's 3,000 Numidian cavalry, which compared to Caesar's 150.[20] Furthermore, Caesar's force was on the march and had just struck camp and were not in battle formation. The clash which followed was little more than a skirmish, but given how vulnerable Caesar's position was, it could have ended his campaign there and then:

> 'they seized Caesar's camp, which he had just quitted to begin his march, and began to pursue his rearguard. On seeing this the legionary troops came to an abrupt halt, while the cavalry, few as they were, nevertheless

displayed the utmost gallantry in charging against such vast numbers. An incredible thing took place: less than thirty Gallic cavalry dislodged two thousand Moorish cavalry and drove them to take refuge in the town. After they had been repulsed and hurled back within their fortifications, Caesar made haste to proceed with his projected march. But as the enemy repeated these tactics all too frequently, now following in pursuit, now once again driven back into the town by the cavalry, Caesar posted in the rear of his column a few cohorts of the veteran troops which he had with him, as well as part of his cavalry, and so proceeded to march at a slow pace with the remainder of his force.'[21]

Thus Caesar was able to beat off both the initial attack and subsequent sorties by the Numidian cavalry. The whole clash is resonant of those that took place following Caesar's landing in Illyria when he was pursued by a Pompeian vanguard who were also beaten off by his specialist force of mixed cavalry and infantry that had been specially trained at countering cavalry and that proved to be so influential at Pharsalus itself.

The Caesarian Recovery

Nevertheless, whilst Caesar had been able to extricate himself from Hadrumetum, as was common, his invasion plans were already running out of steam. The bulk of his army was still at sea, and he had been driven from his initial landing zone, and the Pompeians now knew where he was and could direct their forces accordingly. However, if we are to believe the *De Bello Africo*, there were other coastal towns who did throw open their doors to Caesar, including Ruspina and Leptis (Minor), further to the south and further away from the control of Utica (see Map Two). In the case of Leptis, it seems that the city was just beyond the borders of the Roman province of North Africa and thus was technically a free one. Caesar himself reports a story that there was bad blood between Juba and Leptis, no doubt due to Juba's desire to add the city to his empire.[22]

Naturally, the contrast between the welcome Caesar received at Hadrumetum and that of Leptis raises questions again over Caesar's judgement; namely why did he try to force a landing at the first, when he received such a warm welcome at the other? Again this raises questions around Caesar's preparation and the intelligence he used in choosing a landing site. Nonetheless, Caesar now had a port under his command and used the time to try to re-assemble his scattered fleet (and the army onboard). As the *De Bello Africo* reports, this robbed him of the momentum of his invasion:

> *'For the time being Caesar would not leave the sea or strike inland on account of these wayward vessels, and kept all his cavalry aboard ship, his purpose being, I imagine, to prevent their pillaging the countryside; as for water, he ordered it to be carried aboard.'*[23]

A less sympathetic reading would be that whilst Caesar had control of the city, the Numidian cavalry had control of the surrounding countryside, which is why Caesar's limited cavalry were kept on ship, as he could ill afford to lose them. The *De Bello Africo* states as much when it relates a story about Numidian ambushes:

> *'Meanwhile Caesar's troops were taken by surprise when some rowers who had disembarked to fetch water were suddenly set upon by Moorish cavalry, who wounded many with their lances and killed some of them. These Moors in fact lurk in ambush with their horses in the wadis, so as to start up suddenly and not to fight it out hand to hand in the plain.'*[24]

Thus whilst Caesar had his safe port from which he could properly organize his invasion fleet, the Numidians controlled the local watering holes and were keeping Caesar bottled up in the city, whilst the Pompeians mustered their forces. With access to local resources denied him, Caesar took steps to secure his supply route from overseas (the islands of Sardinia and Sicily) from the Pompeian fleet. Having done this he then advanced on the city of Ruspina, another apparently friendly city, garrisoning both it and Leptis. The *De Bello Africo* provides an excellent summary of Caesar's restlessness, rushing hither and thither whilst the rest of his fleet slowly assembled at Ruspina and Leptis and disembarked his main army.[25]

The Pompeian Response and Labienus' 'Grand Army'

Naturally, the clear danger of using a source like the *De Bello Africo* is that it presents a one sided view of affairs, and we can only view the Pompeian response through the eyes of Caesar or one of his officers. Having been given prior warning of the imminent departure of Caesar from Sicily and having a strategy that required Caesar to land and then be defeated, Metellus Scipio and the Pompeians needed to muster their forces inland and prepare for Caesar's arrival at the unknown point.

Thus they garrisoned the major ports (Utica, Hadrumetum) and had Numidian cavalry patrol the coastline in between. Once Caesar's landing point had been identified then word would have been sent to Metellus, so that he could start organizing a counter attack, whilst the cavalry harried Caesar and denied him an uncontested bridgehead. Then sources state that Metellus went to Juba to discuss a joint action.

Thus, within the week, the Pompeian initial response was sent towards Ruspina, commanded by none other than T. Labienus, Caesar's old colleague from the Gallic War, who had famously defected to the Pompeian cause upon Caesar crossing the Rubicon. Though Labienus had been present at the Battles of Dyrrhachium and Pharsalus, this was the first time he had faced Caesar one on one. Following behind Labienus and his force were reinforcements, led by M. Petreius, one of the Pompeian commanders Caesar had faced in Spain in 49 BC, and Cn. Calpurnius Piso Frugi.

Thus the Pompeians swiftly launched a sizeable counter attack, under some of their best commanders, determined either to defeat Caesar in battle or blockade him in a port before he had the chance to fully deploy his army on African soil. Inevitably, Caesar was out on manoeuvres with a force when the Pompeian army was sighted approaching Ruspina. Equally inevitably he chose to face it rather than retreat to the city:

'Meanwhile, when Caesar had now advanced about three miles from his camp, information obtained by his scouts and mounted patrols reached him that the enemy's forces had been sighted by them at no great distance. And indeed simultaneously with that information they began to see a great cloud of dust. On learning this, Caesar promptly gave orders for his entire cavalry force, of which arm he had no great abundance available at the moment, and his small contingent of archers to be summoned from the camp, and for the standards to follow him slowly in their regular order: he himself went on ahead with a small armed party. Now that the enemy could be seen in the distance, he ordered the troops to don their *helmets and prepare for battle in the open plain: their total number comprised thirty cohorts, together with four hundred cavalry and one hundred-and-fifty archers.'*[26]

Thus Caesar faced Labienus with a substantial force of 15,000 legionaries, along with cavalry and archers. The *De Bello Africo* provides an excellent summary of the composition of Labienus' forces which included Roman legionaries, Numidian cavalry and German and Gallic cavalry from the Pompeian 'grand army' of 48 BC.

'[Labienus] *had kept his own troops in Africa for three years: they were acclimatised and he had now secured their loyalty to himself; he had, moreover, very large auxiliary forces composed of Numidian cavalry and light-armed troops and, besides these, the German and Gallic cavalry which, after the defeat and rout of Pompeius, he, Labienus, had brought across with him from Buthrotum, as well as those which he had levied later on in Africa from natives, freedmen and slaves, and had armed and taught to handle a bridled horse: he had in addition royal auxiliary forces, as well as a hundred and twenty elephants and innumerable cavalry; and finally, legions raised from more than twelve thousand men of every type. On such considerations was based the reckless confidence that fired Labienus, with his sixteen hundred Gallic and German cavalry, his eight thousand Numidians who rode without bridles.'*[27]

Thus Labienus' army was composed of at least 20,000 men, with 12,000 legionaries, 8,000 Numidian cavalry, not to mention German and Gallic cavalry, alongside African war elephants. Aside from the size of this force, the aspect which immediately strikes us is the multi-racial composition of the army, blending Roman, African Gallic and German forces. This immediately draws parallels between Labienus' army of 46 BC and that of Pompeius at Pharsalus in 48 BC, which too was multi-ethnic, combined a core of Roman legionaries with cavalry and ballistic forces from the eastern territories. On this occasion for Pompeius' eastern forces we can read Labienus' African contingents.

The major difference between the army of Pompeius and that of Labienus, however, (aside from the size) was that Labienus had had more time to integrate the various elements of his hybrid army and forge them into a new fighting style. Time for training and integration was the one major factor that Caesar had denied Pompeius in 48 BC and which contributed to his defeat at Pharsalus. The resulting clash between the two forces, the first of the African campaign, was the Battle of Ruspina, fought on what now equates to 4 January 46 BC.

The Battle of Ruspina – Echoes of Pharsalus and Carrhae

Naturally the *De Bello Africo* gives a detailed account of the subsequent battle:

> '*Meanwhile the enemy, led by Labienus and the two Pacidei, deployed a straight line of remarkable length and closely packed, not with infantry, but with cavalry, interspersed with light armed Numidians and unmounted archers in such close formation that at a distance Caesar's men supposed them to be infantry: the two wings, to right and left, were reinforced with strong detachments of cavalry. Meanwhile Caesar deployed a single straight line, the most his small numbers allowed; he drew up his archers in front of the line and posted cavalry to cover his right and left wings, with instructions to take care they were not enveloped by the mass of the enemy's cavalry; for he supposed that he would be engaging infantry troops in the set battle line.*
>
> *There was now on either side a growing feeling of expectancy; but Caesar made no move and saw that the smallness of his own forces called for the use of strategy rather than a trial of strength against the vast numbers of the enemy; when suddenly his opponents' cavalry began to deploy, extending towards the flanks and enveloping the high ground, causing Caesar's cavalry to lengthen and weaken their formation, and preparing simultaneously for an encircling movement. Caesar's cavalry found it difficult to bear up against their vast numbers. Meanwhile as the two centres were proceeding to charge one another, suddenly from out of the closely packed squadrons the light-armed Numidian infantry doubled forward alongside the cavalry and hurled their javelins among the infantry of the legions. Hereupon Caesar's men launched an attack upon them, and their cavalry took to flight; but the infantry stood their ground meantime, until the cavalry should renew their charge and return to succour their own infantry.*

Caesar was now confronted with novel tactics and observed that his men's formation was becoming disorganised as they ran forward to attack, the infantry in fact, exposing their flank as they advanced in pursuit of the cavalry too far from the standards, were suffering casualties from the javelins of the nearest Numidians, whereas the enemy cavalry easily eluded by their speed the heavy infantry javelin.

Accordingly, he had the order passed down the ranks that no soldier should advance more than four feet from the standards. Meanwhile, the cavalry of Labienus, relying on the large numbers on their own side, endeavoured to surround Caesar's scanty force; and the mere handful of Iulian cavalry, worn out by the enemy hordes, their horses wounded, gave ground little by little, while the enemy pressed on them more and more. Thus in a moment all the legionaries were surrounded by the enemy cavalry; and Caesar's forces were compressed into a circle; and so they were all compelled to fight penned behind bars as it were.[28]

In many ways this description owes much to the Battle of Carrhae (53 BC) when Crassus' superior infantry forces were pinned down by range weapons and cavalry attacks. Labienus, it seems, had learnt from the Roman defeats at Carrhae and Pharsalus and, like his former mentor before him, had crafted a force created to deny Caesar his strengths (infantry power) and play to his forces own speciality, speed, and distance.

According to the *De Bello Africo*, sensing the danger, and having recalled the experience of Pharsalus, Caesar gave orders to his army to change their formation to avoid encirclement and annihilation:

'Meanwhile Caesar, aware of the enemy's tactics, gave orders for the line to be extended to its maximum length, and for every other cohort to turn about, so that one was facing to the rear of the standards, while the next one faced to their front. By this means with his right and left wing he split in half the encircling enemy force; and having isolated one half from the other with his cavalry, proceeded to attack it from inside with his infantry, turning it to flight with volleys of missiles: then, after advancing no great distance for fear of ambush, he retired to his own lines. The other half of Caesar's cavalry and infantry carried out the same tactics. This task accomplished and the enemy being driven far back with heavy casualties, Caesar began to retire to his own defence positions, maintaining battle formation.'[29]

Thus Caesar was able to break the encirclement and begin an orderly retreat, only to find the arrival of the Pompeian reinforcements gave his opponents fresh impetus:

'Meanwhile M. Petreius and Cn. [Calpurnius] Piso arrived with Numidian troops, sixteen hundred picked cavalry and a fairly considerable force of infantry, and immediately on arrival hastened straight to the aid of their comrades. And so the enemy, putting their fears aside and taking fresh heart and courage, wheeled their cavalry round and began to attack the rear of the retreating legionaries and to hinder their withdrawal to camp. Observing this, Caesar ordered to turn about and renew the battle in the middle of the plain. As the enemy repeated the same manoeuvre, but without any return to hand-to-hand fighting, and as Caesar's cavalry found that their horses, worn out with the effects of recent sea-sickness, thirst and the fatigue and wounds sustained in their unequal contest, were now more reluctant to keep doggedly on the move in pursuit of the enemy, and as there was now but a little daylight left, Caesar urged his encircled cohorts and cavalry to make one vigorous thrust and not give up until they had driven the enemy back beyond the furthest high ground and gained possession of the latter. And so, waiting to give the signal until the enemy's volleys of missiles were half-hearted and inaccurate, he suddenly let loose some cohorts and squadrons of his own troops upon them. In a moment the enemy were driven without trouble off the plain and thrown back behind the high ground, and Caesar's men had gained the position; then, after a brief pause there, they retired slowly in battle formation to their own fortifications. Their opponents, likewise, after this warm reception, then at length withdrew to their own positions.'[30]

Thus Caesar was forced to break off his retreat and launch a counter attack to drive off this renewed onslaught. If we are to believe the De Bello Africo, then this battle ended in a stalemate, with Caesar able to fight off the two waves of Pompeian attacks and retreat safely to his camp at the end of the day. However, if we turn to the other surviving sources then we find a different tale:

'Labienus and Petreius, Scipio's lieutenants, attacked him [Caesar], defeated him badly, and pursued him in a haughty and disdainful *manner until Labienus' horse was wounded in the belly and threw him, and his attendants carried him off, and Petreius, thinking that he had made a thorough test of the army and that he could conquer whenever he liked, drew off his forces, saying to those around him, 'Let us not deprive our general, Scipio, of the victory.' In the rest of the battle it appeared to be a matter of Caesar's luck that the victorious enemy abandoned the field when they might have won; but it is said that in the flight Caesar dashed up to his whole line and turned it back and seizing one of those who carried the principal standards (the eagles) dragged him to the front. Finally, Petreius retired, and Caesar was glad to do the same.'[31]*

'In Africa, Petreius and Labienus, after waiting until Caesar had gone out to villages after grain, drove his cavalry, which had not yet thoroughly recovered its strength after the sea-voyage, back upon the infantry with the aid of the Numidians; and while the latter as a result was in great confusion, they killed many of the soldiers in hand-to-hand fighting. Indeed, they would also have cut down all the others, who had crowded together on some high ground, had they not received grievous wounds themselves.'[32]

'On one occasion, too, in another battle, the enemy got the advantage in the encounter, and here it is said that Caesar seized by the neck the fugitive standard-bearer, faced him about, and said: "Yonder is the enemy."'[33]

Thus, in the other sources, Ruspina is presented as a Caesarian defeat, only saved when Labienus was carried from the field and Petreius retired, though the *De Bello Africo* has Petreius carried wounded from the battle.[34] None of these sources provide casualty figures for either side. As always, the truth will lie somewhere in-between. If Ruspina was a stalemate, then Caesar certainly came off the worst; unable to defeat Labienus' army and forced to retire from the battlefield. The result left him pinned down at the city of Ruspina, whose fortifications were hastily reinforced:

'Meanwhile Caesar fortified his camp with greater care, strengthened its defences by manning them with larger forces, and carried an entrenchment from the town of Ruspina right to the sea, and a second from his camp likewise to the sea: his purpose was to ensure safer communication in both directions and to enable his reinforcements to come up to his support without danger. He brought missiles and artillery from the ships into his

camp, and armed some of the Gallic and Rhodian rowers and marines from the fleet and summoned them to camp, in order that, if possible, on the same principle which his opponents had employed, light-armed troops should be interspersed at intervals among his cavalry. From all his ships he brought archers into camp, Ituraeans, Syrians and men of diverse races, and thronged his forces with numerous drafts of them.[35]

Despite these precautions, Caesar was now pinned down at Ruspina, just six days after his invasion of North Africa, with the Pompeians controlling the hinterland. Labienus was able to use Hadrumetum (further up the coast) as a supply base and sent his wounded there, establishing a clear line of supply.

Furthermore, Caesar now faced two further waves of Pompeians: the first commanded by Metellus Scipio (with a further eight legions and 3,000 cavalry) was en-route to Ruspina, via Utica and Hadrumetum. This would place the total Pompeian force at well over 60,000. A fourth wave came in the form of the Numidian army, commanded by King Juba, that set off from Numidia proper, having been called on by Metellus (an additional 30,000 infantry and 20,000 cavalry). Thus we can see that the Pompeians had not been idle during late 47 BC and once they knew that Caesar was in Italy preparing to attack Africa, they assembled their armies in readiness. Clearly none of them wished to repeat the circumstances of two years previously, when Caesar's dash across the Adriatic at the height of winter caught them off guard, disrupting their plans.

Thus within just six days, the Pompeians had been able to counter the momentum of Caesar's invasion and bottle him up in a coastal city and proved the effectiveness of their new hybrid armies, not to mention the damage they had done to Caesar's reputation of military invincibility. They now awaited the arrival of two further armies to bolster their forces further and deliver the 'knock out' blow to Caesar.

The Civil War in North West Africa I – The Pompeian Invasion of the Maurian Kingdom

The North African coast was not the only ongoing campaign which would affect the civil war as there were two others that were to have an ultimate bearing on the course of the conflict. The first concerned none other than

Cn. Pompeius Magnus, the eldest son of the late great Pompeius, who had received his father's cognomen of Magnus by inheritance. At some point in either late 46 or early 47 BC (the *De Bello Africo* places it after Ruspina), Pompeius set out to invade the region held by the Kingdom of the Mauri, to the west of Numidia (see Map One) and the long standing enemy of the Numidians, whose kings (Bocchus II and Bogud) had thrown in their lot with Caesar.

As we shall see shortly, with the pro-Caesarian Mauri on his western flank, Juba of Numidia could not commit wholeheartedly to the campaign against Caesar, and therefore an attack on them would tie them down. As early as late 48 BC Caesar had conceived of the obvious tactic of tying down Numidia by a Maurian invasion, a tactic which had to be abandoned when the Caesarian legions in Spain mutinied (see Chapter Two) requiring the Maurians to cross into Spain to assist in their suppression.

Thus Pompeius was given his first proper military command, with orders to invade the Maurian Kingdom and tie them down, so denying them the opportunity of helping Caesar. There is also the sense that the senior Pompeian commanders did not want Pompeius jnr near the real campaign, as he was untested in battle (having only held naval commands in 48 BC).

The Battle of Ascurum (Jan 47 BC)

The only source for this abortive campaign is the *De Bello Africo*, which was never going to portray Pompeius in a positive light:

'Taking with him thirty small ships of every type, including a few equipped with beaks, he set out from Utica and invaded the Kingdom of the Mauri and the Kingdom of Bogud. With an army in light order comprising two thousand slaves and freedmen, some with arms, some without, he proceeded to approach the town of Ascurum, where there was a royal garrison. As Pompeius drew near, the townsfolk allowed him to come closer and closer until he was actually approaching the very gates and the town wall: then suddenly they made a sally and drove the crushed and panic-stricken Pompeians back wholesale to the sea and their ships. After this reverse Cn. Pompeius, the son, withdrew his fleet from there and without touching land again set course with his fleet towards the Balearic Islands.'[36]

Thus, Pompeius' first major campaign ended in failure, not that he had been well resourced in the first place, which demonstrates the low priority the Pompeians gave it, an action that was to come back and haunt them.[37] Nevertheless, whoever had agreed to the campaign, had identified a key Pompeian vulnerability, the danger on Numidia's western flank. However, there were two significant consequences to this failure: firstly, it did not keep the Maurians tied down, and may well have spurred them to action and secondly, Pompeius withdrew from the African campaign and chose to open up a new front, in a more familiar region; namely that of Spain, barely held by the Caesarian Governors, with a disgruntled army (see Chapter Nine). This Spanish campaign was also to have a major impact on the subsequent civil war.

The Civil War in North West Africa II – Sittius and the Maurian Counter Attack

The second campaign was also in northwest Africa and represented the opposite of Pompeius' campaign, namely a Maurian attack on Numidia. As you would expect in our surviving Roman sources, events in northwest Africa seldom impinged on their consciousness and we have no evidence for the preparation for this invasion. We know that the Maurian kings (Bocchus II and Bogud) were in Spain in early 47 BC, helping to keep the mutinous Caesarian legions quiet. We must also assume that Caesar had not overlooked the key role that the Numidian army had played in his defeat in 49 BC and that they represented a major danger to his invasion plans. That being the case it seems that the Maurian kings returned to their home in late 47 BC and prepared a second Caesarian front, to keep Juba and the Numidians tied down and divert them from helping the Pompeians.

It is at this point that a previously obscure Roman figure enters the centre stage. His name was P. Sittius, and by late 47 / early 46 BC he was a key commander in the Maurian army, commanding either a portion of the royal army or his own mercenary force. Sittius is an intriguing figure who first comes to our attention during the Second Civil War (63–62 BC), when he is named by Sallust as a supporter of the pro-Sullan faction that tried to seize control of Rome in the coup (see Chapter One).

'*He added that Piso was in Hither Spain, Publius Sittius of Nuceria in the Maurian Kingdom with an army, both of whom were partners in his plot.*'[38]

Thus, to Sallust at least (a contemporary) he was already linked to the Mauri as far back as 63 BC. He was also a friend of Cicero and one of Cicero's letters to him (tentatively dated to c.52 BC) still survives.[39] In it we find out that Sittius was prosecuted, but was successfully defended by Cicero and later we find that he sold off his Roman property to pay his debts and lived abroad, firstly in Spain and later in North Africa.[40] In the intervening period he seems to have risen in the Maurian army and become a noted military commander in the region.[41]

Having waited for Juba of Numidia to march his royal army to the east to support Metellus, Sittius then launched an invasion of Western Numidia, now underdefended. He launched a lightning raid on Juba's Numidia capital city Cirta:

'*Sittius then attacked Cirta, the richest town of that kingdom, and after a few days' fighting captured it, as well as two Gaetulian towns. When he offered them terms, proposing that they should evacuate the town and surrender it unoccupied to him, they refused the terms and were subsequently captured by Sittius, and all put to death. Thereupon he advanced, ravaging both countryside and towns without ceasing.*'[42]

The Sittian invasion worked, not only in its short term military objectives, but it also forced Juba to turn back to defend his kingdom and thus prevented him from bringing the 50,000 strong royal army to assist the Pompeians.

'*Juba got to know of this when he was now not far away from Scipio and his lieutenants and came to the conclusion that it was better to go to the aid of himself and his own kingdom, rather than that, in the course of setting out to help others, he should himself be driven out of his own kingdom, and perhaps be thwarted in both fields. Accordingly, he marched back again, withdrawing his auxiliary forces too from Scipio, in his alarm on account of himself and his own interests; and leaving thirty elephants behind with Scipio, he set forth to the relief of his own territory and towns.'[43]*

Dio himself points out, ultimately, what a turning point this decision was:

'[Caesar] *He was still in this position when one Publius Sittius (if, indeed, we ought to say it was he, and not rather Providence) brought to him at one stroke salvation and victory.'[44]*
    'This fact made it very clear that if Juba had also come up, Caesar could never have withstood the two.'[45]

Thus Caesar, beleaguered in Ruspina, received a massive boost and the royal army of Numidia (some 50,000 strong, including a large contingent of war elephants), which had done so much damage in 49 BC, turned back to the east to face Sittius, drastically reducing the numbers that Caesar would face in what both sides hoped would be the final battle.

Chapter Six

Stalemate in the Desert:
The African Campaigns to the
Battle of Tegea (Jan-March 46 BC)

Caesar Trapped at Ruspina

Though Juba had turned back from advancing on Ruspina, Metellus Scipio soon arrived there, bringing considerable reinforcements:

> 'eight legions of foot, 20,000 horse, of which most were Africans, and a large number of light-armed troops, and thirty elephants.'[1]

We have no casualty figures for the Battle of Ruspina, but we are told that Labienus had 12,000 men, 8,000 African cavalry, 1,600 Gallo-Germanic cavalry, whilst Petreius had a sizeable number of infantry (the figure is not given) and 1,600 cavalry. Thus, if we are to believe the figures quoted, the total Pompeian force was around 50–60,000 infantry, 30,000 cavalry, and 150 elephants, making it larger than the Pompeian grand army that had faced Caesar at Pharsalus. Had Juba not turned back then this would have been inflated by a further 50,000.

Thus we can see that this was no Pompeian remnant, but a new and formidable Pompeian army that had had a whole year to rebuild itself, and the resources of Numidia (Africa's most powerful kingdom) to support it. A Caesarian victory was not only far from inevitable in this war, but looked highly unlikely. The arrival of Metellus' third wave only increased the pressure on Caesar and his army at Ruspina and the *De Bello Africo* has the following to demonstrate the pressure they were under:

> 'Meanwhile Scipio set out with the forces we enumerated a little earlier, leaving a considerable garrison behind at Utica, and pitched camp first at

Hadrumetum. Then, after staying there a few days, he made a night march and joined up with the forces of Labienus and Petreius; whereupon they established themselves in a single camp three miles distant from Caesar. Meanwhile their cavalry went roving round Caesar's entrenchments, intercepting all such troops as had advanced beyond the rampart to forage or fetch water; and this had the effect of keeping all their opponents confined within their defences. By these tactics Caesar's men were afflicted with a severe scarcity of corn, for this reason that supplies had not so far been conveyed to him either from Sicily or Sardinia, and, on account of the season of the year, fleets could not move freely about the seas without risk; moreover, they occupied no more than six miles of African soil in any direction and were hard put to it for lack of fodder. The urgency of this situation drove the veteran troops infantry and cavalry, men who had gone through many campaigns by land and sea and had often been afflicted by hazards and similar privation, to collect seaweed from the beach, cleanse it in fresh water, and give it in this state to their famished beasts, thereby prolonging their lives.'[2]

Appian adds the following:

'Caesar's army began to be alarmed and a tumult broke out among them on account of the disaster they had already experienced and of the reputation of the forces advancing against them, and especially of the numbers and bravery of the Numidian cavalry. War with elephants, to which they were unaccustomed, also frightened them.'[3]

Thus, within ten days of landing in North Africa, Caesar was outnumbered and shut up in Ruspina. Once again his boldness had led him into a dangerous situation. His enemies outnumbered him significantly, especially in cavalry (and elephants) and the terrain suited them perfectly (wide open plains). Unlike at Pharsalus he had no river to anchor one wing on and so he could be surrounded. Furthermore, the enemy he faced this time had had a whole year to integrate the various disparate elements of their army into a cohesive fighting force, unlike Pompeius at Pharsalus. To make matters worse his opponents (again) controlled the countryside, cutting him off from local food sources, requiring supplies from overseas.

Caesar wisely chose not to fight under such circumstances and, clearly requiring reinforcements, sent for them from Sicily. Nevertheless, he needed to break out of the trap he found himself in, before the morale of his army (which had been shaky) started to be tested once more. For the Pompeians also, it was a matter of waiting; their army was designed to fight in open battle and not perform a siege, so they needed to keep ratchetting up the pressure to force Caesar to make a break for it and then confront him in battle on open territory where they could then (hopefully) annihilate him. Nevertheless, the *De Bello Africo* reports daily skirmishes between the two sets of cavalry:

> '*Meanwhile the squadrons of cavalry whose regular duty it was to be on guard in front of the rampart were engaging daily in incessant skirmishes with one another; and there were also times when Labienus' Germans and Gauls and Caesar's cavalry exchanged pledges of good faith and conversed with one another.*'[4]

The Sieges of Leptis and Acylla

With a stalemate at Ruspina, the two sides continued to probe at each other in different ways. Labienus initially made an attack on the only other town under Caesarian control: Leptis, controlled by a Caesarian garrison commanded by C. Hostilius Saserna:

> '*Meantime Labienus with part of his cavalry was endeavouring to assault and force his way into the town of Leptis, which was under command of Saserna with six cohorts; but its defenders, thanks to the excellent fortifications of the town and the large number of their engines of war, defended it easily and without danger. But Labienus' cavalry repeated these tactics fairly frequently and gave them no respite.*'[5]

When that came to nought, attention shifted to another coastal town, Acylla, further to the south of Thapsus, which had declared for Caesar.

> '*This request Caesar gladly granted and gave them a garrison, ordering C. Messius, who had once held the office of Aedile, to set out for Acylla. On learning this, [C.] Considius Longus, who was in command at*

Hadrumetum with two legions and seven hundred cavalry, left part of his garrison force behind and, taking eight cohorts with him, promptly hastened off to Acylla. Messius completed his march more rapidly and was the first to arrive at Acylla with his cohorts. Whereupon Considius approached the city with his forces and venturing to jeopardise his troops, retired back again to Hadrumetum without having achieved anything to warrant so large a force. Subsequently, when a few days later he had procured a contingent of cavalry from Labienus, he returned, pitched his camp, and proceeded to lay siege to Acylla.'

The *De Bello Africo* also gives examples of Pompeian naval forces stationed at Thapsus attacking passing Caesarian naval forces and capturing them.[6]

Caesarian Reinforcements

Whilst the Pompeians held the advantage on land, it appears that they were no longer dominant at sea, as they had been in 49–48 BC. The primary evidence for this is the apparent ease with which Caesarian supplies and reinforcements were able to reach Ruspina. Certainly Pompeian ships were able to harass the Caesarian navy, but not stop them. The *De Bello Africo* reports that two separate supply convoys were able to reach Ruspina: the first coming from the African island of Cercina, full of grain, and the second coming from Sicily and holding military reinforcements:

'*Meanwhile at Lilybaeum the Proconsul Allienus embarked in transports the Thirteenth and Fourteenth legions, eight hundred Gallic cavalry and one thousand slingers and archers and sent to Caesar in Africa his second convoy. With the wind behind them these ships arrived safely three days later at the harbour of Ruspina.'*[7]

Therefore we can see that the Pompeian stranglehold on Ruspina was lessened, with Caesar receiving fresh supplies and military forces. As January progressed, Caesar played a waiting game, trusting that the morale of his men would hold, whilst taking the impetus out of the Pompeian attack. The clear danger here would be that Juba would defeat Sittius and be able to march east once more, to further reinforce the Pompeians. As we would expect, we are woefully ill-informed by our surviving sources of the war being fought between the Numidians and the Mauri, other than the occasional snippet:

'*Meanwhile P. Sittius invaded the territory of Numidia with his forces and forcibly took by storm a stronghold, situated on a well-defended mountain height, in which Juba had collected both corn and all other regular munitions of war, for the sake of prosecuting his campaign.*'[8]

Thus we can see that Juba had been unable to contain the Maurian army of Sittius and was still tied down in Numidia. How well Caesar was aware of this situation remains unknown.

The Caesarian Breakout – 25 January 46 BC

Having received his reinforcements, Caesar now felt strong enough to break out from the encirclement and take the fight to the Pompeians. To that end he led his legions from their camp and took up a new position near Ruspina, occupying the heights overlooking Scipio's army:

'*he ordered all his legions to be led outside the camp and follow him in the direction of the town of Ruspina, where he had a garrison; it was also the first place to have joined his side. He then descended a gentle slope and, keeping to the left side of the plain, led his legions along close to the sea. This plain is remarkably level and extends for twelve miles; and the chain of not so very lofty downs which encircles it right from the very sea gives it the appearance of a kind of amphitheatre. This chain includes a few high hills, on each of which were situated some very ancient turrets and watchtowers; and in the last of these Scipio had a defence-post and picket.*'[9]

In what must have been reminiscent of the Battle of Dyrrhachium, some two years earlier, Caesar then ordered the construction of redoubts on the unoccupied hilltops. Not only had Caesar broken free from the Pompeian encirclement but he had chosen a much better position from which to defend himself against the Pompeian army and its cavalry superiority. Here we must question two apparent Pompeian weaknesses. The first is that they did not seem to notice Caesar marching multiple legions away from his camp; thus allowing them to change position unmolested. The second is that they only had a token force on the heights that overlooked their camp. These two mistakes ceded Caesar the initiative.

The Second Battle of Ruspina – 25 January 46 BC

Whilst the first battle took place on territory favourable to a large cavalry army, the second would now take place on hilly terrain, thus negating some of the Pompeian advantage. Naturally enough, when Scipio and Labienus were informed of the movement of Caesar's army, they deployed their forces in an attempt to dislodge Caesar from the heights.

> *'When Scipio and Labienus observed this, they led their entire cavalry force out of camp and deploying it in battle line, advanced about a mile from their fortified positions and drew up their infantry forces in a second battle line less than four hundred paces from their camp.'*[10]

With the deployment of the Pompeian army, Caesar set about consolidating his grip on the heights and sent a force of Spanish auxiliaries to dislodge the Numidian position on the adjacent hilltop:

> *'he ordered a squadron of Spaniards to launch a speedy attack upon the adjacent hill, dislodge its enemy defenders, and capture the position; and he also instructed a small detachment of light-armed troops to follow them in support to the same objective. Thus despatched they speedily attacked the Numidians, capturing some of them alive and seriously wounding others of their troopers as they sought to escape, and so won the position.'*[11]

It was at this point that Labienus decided to enter the fray and led the right wing of the Pompeian cavalry against this Caesarian force, thus exposing himself to a Caesarian counter. Why he did this remains unknown; perhaps frustration with Caesar being allowed to outmanoeuvre them was a factor. Never one to fail to exploit an enemy's mistake, Caesar inevitably launched a counter attack at the now exposed Labienus.

> *'But when Caesar saw that Labienus had now withdrawn some distance from his forces, he launched the left wing of his own cavalry, so as to cut*

the enemy off. Now in the area where this action was going on there was a very large farm building, constructed with four lofty towers; and this impeded Labienus' field of view and prevented his observing that he was being cut off by Caesar's cavalry. Consequently it was only when he realised that his men were being cut down from the rear that he actually saw the Iulian squadrons.'[12]

When he finally spotted Caesar's trap, Labienus had no option but to retreat or be caught between the two Caesarian forces. Whilst he, and the bulk of the Numidian cavalry, successfully escaped the trap, his 1,600 Gallic and Germanic cavalry were apparently not so lucky:

'As a result, triumph suddenly gave place to panic among the Numidian cavalry, and Labienus made haste to flee straight back to camp. As for the Gauls and Germans, they stood their ground; but hemmed in between the enemy on the higher ground and those in their rear, despite a gallant resistance they were slaughtered to a man.'[13]

Thus the Caesarians emerged victorious from this second clash, brought about by Caesar's exploitation of Pompeian mistakes. The postscript to this battle in the *De Bello Africo*, however, does not ring true:

'On observing this, Scipio's legions, which were drawn up in front of his camp, were seized with a blind panic and began to flee by every gate into their camp. Now that Scipio and his forces had been swept in disorder from plain and hills and driven wholesale into their camp, Caesar ordered the retreat to be sounded and withdrew all his cavalry inside his own fortifications.'[14]

Thus, if we are to believe this, Scipio's army broke at the sight of retreating Numidian cavalry, despite the fact that they were not under attack. Furthermore, we are asked to believe that with Scipio's army and Labienus' cavalry retreating, Caesar failed to exploit this and merely ordered his troops to stand down and retreat to their fortifications. This does not ring true on either point; Caesar would seldom pass up an opportunity to exploit a retreating enemy. What is more likely is that both Scipio and Labienus regrouped in good order to avoid presenting Caesar with further opportunity to exploit their weaknesses. Therefore, after the cavalry clash, both sides quit the battlefield. Nevertheless Caesar now had the momentum, even if Scipio and Labienus still had the numbers.

Showdown at Uzitta

Clearly sensing this momentum, Caesar led his army down from the heights and onto the plain, albeit with the hills behind him. Clearly spooked by the disaster the day before, Scipio and Labienus remained in their fortifications, hoping to take the momentum out of Caesar's advance. However, Caesar then made to move on the town of Uzitta, which was the local Pompeian supply base, forcing them to come to its defence:

> 'fearing that he [Scipio] would lose the town, on which his army had been accustomed to rely for its water supply and all other means of support, led out all his forces. These forces were drawn up, according to his custom, in four lines, the first consisting of cavalry deployed in line of squadrons, interspersed with elephants equipped with towers and armour. Thus deployed, Scipio marched to the relief of the town, while Caesar, observing this move and supposing that Scipio was advancing towards him prepared and fully resolved to fight, accordingly halted before the town in the position I described a little earlier. With his own centre covered by the town, Scipio drew up his right and left wings, where his elephants were, in full view of his opponents.'[15]

Thus, having been forced into the field, Scipio wisely avoided facing Caesar directly and moved to anchor his army against the town, using it and the garrison within to cover his centre. The De Bello Africo begrudgingly admits that this tactic outfoxed Caesar and shifted the momentum once more.

> 'Caesar had now waited till nearly sunset without observing any signs of Scipio's leaving the position in which he had halted and advancing towards him; and his impression was that Scipio would rather remain on the defensive, utilising his position, if the circumstances demanded it, than venture to come to close grips on the plain. Accordingly, there seemed no sense in approaching closer to the town that day. For he was aware

that it contained a large garrison force of Numidians, and he realised that the enemy had used the town to screen his centre, and that he himself was faced with a difficult task in simultaneously attacking the town and at the same time engaging in battle on his right and left wing from a disadvantageous position, the more especially so since his troops had been standing to since early morning without a bite of food and were quite exhausted. Accordingly, he led his forces back to camp, deciding to wait till the following day and then extend his fortifications nearer the enemy's line.'[16]

Thus Scipio met Caesar's challenge and marched to the defence of his supply base at Uzitta, taking up a strong defensive position with his army being supported by the town and its garrison. Realizing Caesar was eager for battle, to build on the momentum of the previous day, Scipio (no doubt advised by Labienus) chose not to oblige by attacking him, but sat and waited it out with his army supplied by the city, whilst Caesar's sat there in the open. Thus Caesar was forced to retreat and Scipio and Labienus salvaged the situation that they had got themselves into.

The Failed Pompeian Siege of Acylla

The *De Bello Africo* confirms the loss of Caesar's momentum as it chooses this point of its narrative to break off and survey the other theatres of conflict. Throughout these clashes, the Pompeian commander C. Considius Longus (the Governor of Hadrumetum) had been besieging the town of Acylla which had declared for Caesar and had a small (three cohorts) Caesarian garrison. In the last few weeks Considius had seemingly made little progress in the siege and broke it off when news of the Second Battle of Ruspina reached him, marching his forces to Scipio at Uzitta and then resuming his control of Hadrumetum.

The War at Sea

Again, whilst Caesar, Scipio, and Labienus were coming to blows on land, there was a continuing clash at sea, as the Pompeian navy continued in its attempts to prevent fresh Caesarian forces crossing to Africa. The *De Bello Africo* reports clashes off Thapsus and Aegimurus, with the

Pompeian navy being commanded by P. Attius Varus and M. Octavius. Caesarian propaganda then kicks in with the Caesarian captives being taken to Scipio, who then apparently tortures and executes the veterans who won't change sides, whilst drafting the new recruits into his own legions.[17] Aside from the propaganda element, this episode does tell us that the Pompeians were at least partially successful in intercepting Caesarian reinforcements.

Stalemate – Waiting for Juba

Having allowed Caesar to escape Ruspina and inflict a defeat on his cavalry, Scipio was wisely able to avoid facing him in the field and took the momentum out of the Caesarian campaign, thus plunging both sides into stalemate once more. However, Caesar was not the only commander waiting on reinforcements. As we noted earlier, the largest contingent of the Pompeian force was the Numidian army commanded by its king, Juba, who had been marching towards Ruspina to reinforce Scipio, when news of the Maurian invasion of Western Numidia, led by the Roman mercenary commander P. Sittius, reached him. This forced him to break off and march to defend his kingdom, rather than fight Caesar.

Realizing the need for reinforcements both to face Caesar, and to boost the morale of his forces, Scipio sent urgent word to the king, detailing the Second Battle of Ruspina, and stressing the need for all available men:

> 'Meanwhile King Juba had been informed of Scipio's cavalry battle; and in response to a written summons from the latter he left behind his general, Saburra, with part of his army, to keep Sittius in check, and quitting his kingdom set off to join Scipio. With him he took three legions, eight hundred bridled cavalry, a numerous contingent of Numidians who rode without bridles, and of light-armed infantry troops, and thirty elephants. His purpose in so doing was to add a certain prestige to Scipio's army by his personal appearance, and the more to intimidate Caesar's.'[18]

Stalemate – Low Level Warfare

While the Pompeians were still not committed to a battle, the stalemate came to resemble that of Dyrrhachium, with both sides moving to secure the various high points of the region:

'[Caesar] *began to advance with his troops along the crest of the ridge, carrying forward his lines of fortification and building strong points. He also made strenuous efforts to seize the high ground closer to Scipio and, by capturing it, to forestall his opponents, lest, relying on their superiority in numbers, they should seize the nearby hill and so deprive him of the opportunity of advancing farther. But Labienus too had made up his mind to seize this hill; and his closer proximity to it had enabled him to achieve the objective more rapidly.*'[19]

It was during one of these proxy clashes that Labienus set a trap for Caesar:

'*There was a ravine, of a fair width and with high, precipitous sides, and honeycombed at many points with cave-like hollows; and Caesar had to cross it before he could reach the hill he wished to take. On the far side of this ravine there was an ancient olive grove, dense and thickly planted with trees.*

It was here that Labienus, perceiving that Caesar must first cross the ravine and olive grove if he wanted to seize that position, and availing himself of his local knowledge, took his stand in ambush with a detachment of cavalry and some light-armed troops. In addition he had posted some cavalry out of sight behind the range of hills, in order that, when he himself unexpectedly launched his attack upon the legionaries, this cavalry might make its appearance from behind the hill; thereby Caesar and his army were to be thrown into utter confusion by this double attack and, denied the opportunity either of retiring or advancing, were to be surrounded and cut to pieces.

When Caesar, in ignorance of the ambush, but with a screen of cavalry thrown out in front, came up to this position, the troops of Labienus either misinterpreted or forgot his instructions, or maybe they were afraid of being caught in the trap by Caesar's cavalry; anyway, they came out from behind the rocks in small groups or singly, and made for the crest of the hill. Caesar's cavalry pursued them, killing some and capturing others alive, and then forthwith made all haste towards the hill, which they speedily seized after dislodging Labienus' holding force. Labienus and part of his cavalry barely managed to escape with their lives.'[20]

Naturally the pro-Caesarian source emphasises the weakness of the Pompeian forces and the brilliance of Caesar, when compared to Labienus, but the incident illustrates the situation that this stalemate had brought about; the decision of both armies to send raiding parties into the hills, looking to seize high points and ambush their opponents, is again reminiscent of the Battle of Dyrrhachium some two years earlier. Just like then, with his opponents refusing to give battle, Caesar settled down to a war of attrition and started to construct more elaborate fortifications:

> 'After this action fought by the cavalry Caesar fortified a camp on the hill of which he had gained possession, assigning each legion its share of the work. He then began to carry two fortified lines from his own principal camp across the centre of the plain in the direction of the town of Uzitta, which was situated on flat ground between his camp and Scipio's and was occupied by the latter, their direction being such as to make them converge upon the right and left corners of the town. His purpose in constructing this fieldwork was as follows: when he advanced his forces closer to the town and proceeded to attack it, he should have his flanks covered by these fortifications of his and not be enveloped by the swarms of enemy cavalry and so be deterred from attacking.'[21]

Thus Caesar's army set about advancing on the Pompeian supply base of Uzitta, once again, this time in a slow and deliberate manner, inching his fortifications nearer to the town to neutralize his opponents' superior cavalry. As had happened in Greece two years earlier, once Caesar's momentum had been cancelled, he seemed to retreat into the opposite tactic of digging his army in, building defensive works and fortifications.

The Battle of Uzitta

With Caesar's momentum checked, and having been bolstered by the arrival of Juba and a portion of his army, the Pompeians now chose to go on the offensive, clearly not wanting Caesar to put their supply base of Uzitta under further pressure and aware of the need to keep their own army's morale up. Thus they launched a surprise attack on the Caesarian army at dusk, having waited for them to exhaust themselves with a full day's work on their fortifications:

'*It was now nearly dusk, and Caesar was withdrawing his troops from this work to camp, when Juba, Scipio and Labienus launched a violent attack upon his legionaries, employing all their cavalry and light-armed forces. Caesar's cavalry reeled and gave ground momentarily under the sudden and violent impact of the massed swarms of the enemy. But the latter found that this manoeuvre did not go according to plan; for Caesar halted in his tracks and led his forces back to the assistance of his cavalry.*

*The arrival of the legions put fresh heart into the cavalry, who wheeled round, charged the Numidians in the middle of their eager, but scattered pursuit, and drove them right back into the royal camp, with heavy casualties and many of their number killed. And had not nightfall speedily overtaken this action, and a cloud of dust raised up by the wind hampered everyone's vision, Juba and Labienus would have been captured and have fallen into Caesar's hands, and their cavalry and light-armed troops would have been utterly and entirely annihilated. Whereupon an incredible number of Scipio's troops deserted from the Fourth and Sixth legion, some to Caesar's camp, others to various places wherever each individual managed to find refuge. The cavalry who were once under Curio's command likewise lost confidence in Scipio and his forces, and many of them took refuge with the other*s.'[22]

Even allowing for Caesarian propaganda, the battle seems to have been a disaster for the Pompeians, and the Numidians in particular, who seemed to have folded when confronted with Caesar's legions. That being said, it seems that it was only Caesar's quick thinking in bringing his legions to reinforce his cavalry which saved the day. Nonetheless, the much vaunted Numidian reinforcements which Scipio had been relying on seemed to be far less a military threat than they had first appeared; a point which was seemingly not lost on Scipio's Roman contingents.

Thus for the second time in a row, a Pompeian attack on Caesar had been defeated, and, moreover, had been seen to be defeated, with the superior allied cavalry numbers not only taking the brunt of the casualties, but being seen to be no match for Caesar's legions. As we saw during the fighting in Greece in 48 BC, most notably at the Battle of Pharsalus itself, Caesar's legions were again adept at dealing with cavalry, which suggests an intensive training programme by Caesar. Caesar's position was further strengthened in the aftermath of the battle, when two fresh legions from

Sicily (the Ninth and the Tenth) evaded the Pompeian navy and landed on the coast and made it successfully to Caesar's camp.

A Numidian War on Three Fronts – The Gaetulian Revolt

For King Juba of Numidia, a bad situation became a worse one. Not only had his cavalry been soundly defeated by Caesar and the bulk of his army been tied down in the west of his kingdom facing a Maurian invasion, but a third front now opened up with the revolt of the Gaetulian tribe in the south of his kingdom. The Gaetuli were another native tribe, but one who inhabited the interior of North Africa, south of the Mauri and Numidians. The rise of the (Roman sponsored) Numidian Empire had seen the Gaetulians become vassals of their larger neighbour, with Gaetulian forces being seen during the Romano-Numidian War (112–106 BC). With Juba tied down fighting Caesar and the royal army tied down fighting the Mauri, they saw the opportunity to revolt against their Numidian overlords, seemingly encouraged by Caesar himself, perhaps utilising the connection between them and his uncle, C. Marius.[23]

This now opened up a southern front for the Numidian Empire, which forced Juba to split his already diminished force once again, and dispatch six cohorts (roughly 3,000 men) to the region to deal with the rebellion. Thus the Numidian allied contingent, which Metellus Scipio must have been relying on, was diminished further.

The Second Battle of Uzitta

With the failure of the Pompeian attack, Caesar took the opportunity to finish extending his lines of fortification to the very walls of Uzitta and placed the city under siege. This seemed to have had the desired effect, as the Pompeians left their camp and finally offered battle, unwilling to allow Caesar to capture the city, which would have forced them to withdraw from their position and thus end the deadlock. There would also have been the question of the deteriorating morale of the Pompeian forces given their previous losses. Thus it appeared that Juba, Scipio and Labienus came to a 'now or never' moment and determined that it was time to give full battle. The *De Bello Africo* gives a full description of the formations (if not numbers):

'Scipio's order of battle was as follows. In front he placed his own and Juba's legions: behind these, in a support line, the Numidians, drawn out in so thin and long a formation as to give the impression at a distance that the centre was a single line composed of legionary troops. His elephants he had placed at regular intervals on his right and left wings, and behind the elephants his light-armed troops and Numidian auxiliaries were stationed in support. On his right wing he had posted his entire force of bridled cavalry; for his left wing was covered by the town of Uzitta, and there was no room to deploy cavalry. In addition he had posted some Numidians and a vast multitude of light-armed troops to cover the right flank of his line at a distance of at least a mile or so, pushing them more towards the foothills and so withdrawing them farther away both from the enemy and his own forces. His purpose in doing this was that when the two battle lines charged one another, his cavalry would only have to continue their outflanking movement a little farther in the early stages of the action, and then by sheer weight of numbers they could surprise and envelop Caesar's army, throw it into disorder, and riddle it with lances. Such was Scipio's plan of battle that day.'[24]

'Caesar's battle line, on the other hand, was disposed as follows, my description beginning with his left wing and working round to his right. On his left wing he had the Tenth and Ninth legions: in the centre the Twenty-Fifth, Twenty-Ninth, Thirteenth, Fourteenth, Twenty-Eighth and Twenty-Sixth. As for the actual right wing, he had posted there some of the cohorts of his veteran legions as well as a few cohorts from the legions of recruits besides. His third line he had concentrated on his left wing, extending it right up to the central legion of his line, and had arranged it in such a formation that his left wing was composed of three lines. His motive for doing this was the fact that, whereas his right flank was supported by his fortifications, he was hard put to it to know how his left flank could bear up under the hordes of enemy cavalry; and it was on this same left flank that he had concentrated the whole of his own cavalry and, not feeling too confident in it, had detached the Fifth legion to support this cavalry, and drafted light-armed troops at intervals among the horse. As for his archers, he had posted them in various formations at definite points throughout the line, but chiefly on the wings.'[25]

Yet, despite this confrontation being much anticipated and manoeuvred towards, battle did not immediately take place and in fact was delayed for some hours, with both sides seemingly waiting for the other to attack, with Caesar's natural exuberance apparently curbed. This unnatural reticence could only have been down to his worry about the size of the Pompeian cavalry contingent and the position of Uzitta and its garrison worrying him, as it had previously done (see above). As the *De Bello Africo* comments, the two armies faced each other (only 300 paces apart) for several hours.[26] It was only when Caesar turned his army to return to his fortifications at the end of the day that the Pompeians attacked. We must assume that this was a deliberate ploy on Caesar's part to force his opponents' hand. Despite this ploy, however, on this occasion Caesar came off second best and lost the resulting cavalry battle:

> 'suddenly the entire force of cavalry, the more distant one comprising Numidians and Gaetulians riding without bridles, began a movement on the right and to advance closer to Caesar's camp on the high ground, while Labienus' bridled cavalry maintained their positions and distracted the attention of the legions. Whereupon part of Caesar's cavalry together with the light-armed troops, acting without orders and without discretion, suddenly advanced too far, crossed a marshy tract and found themselves too far outnumbered to be able to contain the enemy. Abandoning the light-armed troops, the cavalry were driven back and fled to their own lines not without casualties; one horseman missing, many horses wounded, and twenty-seven light-armed soldiers killed.'[27]

Again, we must allow for Caesarian propaganda in the number of causalities sustained, but it is clear that, for once, ill-discipline, on the part of the Caesarian forces brought them a loss, with an African cavalry force finally defeating its Roman counterpart (again formed of cavalry and lightly armed infantry). Thus Caesar had been handed a defeat, albeit one in a cavalry skirmish, but again this allowed the Pompeians to claim the momentum and demonstrated to all, especially their own troops, that Caesar could actually be defeated. The end of the day seemingly prevented a wider escalation of this skirmish, with the Pompeians withdrawing to camp and the Caesarians regrouping.

The Anti-Climax – The Return of Low Level Warfare

Despite this appetiser, Metellus, having achieved a very obvious victory (albeit in a skirmish), seemingly had no wish to engage in a full battle and did not present his army in battle formation again. Thus Caesar continued with his fortifications, matched by counter fortifications being dug by the Pompeians, accompanied by cavalry sorties from both sides:

> 'Meanwhile Caesar made it his constant and daily practice to lead his legions down into the plain, proceed with his fieldworks, carried his ramparts and trenches across the middle of the plain, and thereby hinder his opponents' sallies. Scipio likewise built counter-defences, pushing them forward in haste to prevent Caesar from barring him access to the ridge. Thus the generals on both sides were occupied with fieldworks, but none the less engaged one another daily in cavalry actions.'[28]

The War at Sea – The Battles of Leptis and Hadrumetum

With the land campaign once again at a stalemate, it was the war at sea which reached its climax with the balance of power finally swinging decisively in favour of the Caesarians. As detailed above, unlike in 49–48 BC, the two sides were far more evenly matched, with the principal aim of the Pompeian fleet still being to cut Caesar off from his base in Sicily, from which he could receive more men and supplies. Equally, to date, the Caesarian fleet's principal aim had been to ensure that this did not happen and to keep this vital supply line open.

Thus far there had been skirmishes between the two fleets, but nothing decisive. Certainly the Pompeian fleet had not attacked the Caesarian ports, nor vice versa. The battles that broke this deadlock were initiated by P. Attius Varus, one of the key Pompeian leaders (as detailed above). The *De Bello Africo* contains a (naturally) one sided account of this turning point, which began with Varus planning on intercepting the latest Caesarian reinforcement convoy.

> 'Meanwhile Varus, who had previously beached his flotilla at Utica for the winter, learned that the Seventh and Eighth legions were on the way from Sicily. Thereupon he promptly launched his flotilla, manned it on the

spot with Gaetulian oarsmen and marines and, setting sail from Utica, arrived at Hadrumetum with fifty-five ships with the object of setting a trap for them. Caesar, who was unaware of his arrival, despatched L. Cispius with a squadron of twenty-seven ships to the area of Thapsus to patrol there and give cover to his convoy; and he also sent Q. Aquila with thirteen warships to Hadrumetum for the same purpose. Cispius speedily reached his destination, whereas Aquila, lashed by a storm and unable to double the headland, gained a certain cove which was sheltered from the storm and afforded him and his squadron a fairly inconspicuous retreat. The rest of the fleet stood at anchor out at sea off Leptis; and as the crews had disembarked and were roaming here and there about the beach, some of them having gone off to the town to buy themselves food, the fleet had no one to defend it. Learning of this situation from a deserter, Varus seized his opportunity: at the second watch he came out of the inner harbour of Hadrumetum and arrived off Leptis in the early morning with his entire squadron; and there he set fire to the defenceless transports which were anchored out at sea at some distance from the port, and captured two five-banked warships, which offered no resistance.'[29]

Thus, whilst the Pompeian fleet was not able to prevent the Caesarian forces crossing from Sicily, they were able to ambush the fleet off the city of Leptis, catching them unawares. The account that follows naturally ensures that it is Caesar himself who was responsible for the turning point of the naval campaign:

'Meanwhile a message speedily acquainted Caesar with the news as he was touring the defence works in his camp, which was six miles distant from the harbour. Putting everything else on one side and giving his horse its head he speedily reached Leptis, where he insisted that all the ships should follow his lead: he himself then went aboard a small cutter. As he sailed on, he came up with Aquila, who was filled with panic and confusion at the large number of the enemy ships, and then set off in pursuit of the enemy squadron. Meanwhile Varus, disconcerted by Caesar's promptitude and boldness, had turned about with his entire squadron and was now beating a hasty retreat to Hadrumetum. In four miles' sail Caesar overhauled him, recovered one of his quinqueremes, complete with all its crew, and capturing in addition the enemy prize-

crew aboard her, one hundred-and-thirty strong, and then captured the
nearest enemy trireme, which in the course of the action had lagged behind
the rest, with its full complement of rowers and marines. The rest of the
enemy fleet doubled the headland, and one and all sought refuge in the
inner harbour of Hadrumetum. But the wind did not hold for Caesar
also to be able to double the headland; so after riding out that night at
anchor in deep water he approached Hadrumetum at dawn. There he set
fire to the transports which were outside the inner harbour and then, as
all the others had either been beached by the enemy or massed inside the
inner harbour, he waited a little while to see if by chance the enemy were
disposed to fight a naval action and then withdraw back to his camp.'[30]

Though the story is clearly written to portray Caesar as the heroic general, there are some interesting points. Once again, the Pompeian fleet was unable to prevent fresh legions from landing in North Africa to reinforce Caesar. Furthermore, it seemed that whilst it was able to ambush a Caesarian fleet, the Pompeian fleet was no match for the Caesarian one in a straight fight, hence them retreating when the Caesarians were able to get their act together. Though Caesar's role has clearly been embellished, it does again raise the issue of the competence of the Caesarian captains in his absence. Furthermore the whole ambush at Leptis was facilitated by a deserter from the Caesarian side, showing that desertions were not all one way and that there were still Pompeian sympathisers amongst the Caesarians.

However, aside from the immediate outcome, these two naval battles swung the balance of the naval war in favour of the Caesarian side, with the Caesarians no longer willing to tolerate the constant raids of the Pompeian navy and now finally placing the two nearest Pompeian ports (Hadrumetum and Thapsus) under naval blockade. Caesar himself swiftly returned to the armies at Uzitta, whilst the blockades were left under the command of the aforementioned Q. Aquila (Hadrumetum) and L. Cispius (Thapsus).

Low Level Warfare – Caesar vs Labienus Once More

With the Pompeians clearly unaware that Caesar had left the region to take (temporary) command of the naval war, an opportunity was lost and the stalemate at Uzitta resumed. The *De Bello Africo* provides details of another clash between Caesar and Labienus, which again (unsurprisingly) flatters Caesar, but unwittingly reveals details of a major weakness: his lack of supplies.

Though he had finally secured a clear supply route from overseas (Sicily), this did not make up for the lack of resources available locally. To date the Caesarian bridgehead formed only a strip of the North African coastline (Leptis, Ruspina and Acylla – see Map Two), penetrating no more than six miles into the African interior (see above). Thus the Caesarians needed to spend time sending scouting parties throughout the locale in search of food and that gave the Pompeians (and Labienus in particular) an opportunity:

> '*When Labienus learned of this, he advanced seven miles from his camp across the hilly plateau across which Caesar had marched the day before, encamped two legions there and, supposing that Caesar would frequently pass along that same route for foraging purposes, established himself daily at suitable points to lie in wait for him along with a force of cavalry and light-armed troops.*
>
> *In the meantime information reached Caesar from deserters about Labienus' trap. He waited in camp there a few days for the constant repetition of the same daily routine to lead the enemy into carelessness and then, early one morning, he suddenly gave the order that three veteran legions and a detachment of cavalry should follow him by way of the rear gate. Then, sending on the cavalry ahead, he suddenly surprised the enemy ambush lurking in the ravines, killing some five hundred of their light-armed troops and throwing the rest into a very unseemly rout.*
>
> *Whereupon Labienus dashed up with his entire cavalry force to the relief of his routed troops; and as the odds were now too great for the Caesarian horse to contain their powerful onslaught, Caesar displayed to the enemy forces his legions in battle formation. This action utterly daunted and checked Labienus, and Caesar thereupon withdrew his own cavalry without loss. On the following day Juba crucified those Numidians who had left their post and fled back to their camp.*'[31]

Thus, once again, one of Labienus' traps failed and the Numidian forces crumbled when faced with Caesar's legionaries. Yet as the extract points out, when faced with Labienus' superior cavalry numbers Caesar, again, had to withdraw.

The Caesarian Retreat

It seems that despite the endless stream of positive news in the *De Bello Africo*, Caesar's position was deteriorating. Though time and again Caesar had reportedly defeated the Pompeians in skirmishes, the two sides were evenly matched and in a stalemate. The Pompeians were in a strong offensive position, centred on the city of Uzitta, with superior numbers (if not quality) and, more importantly, they had control of the North African interior from which supplies could be regularly drawn.

With the current surviving sources we will never know the true situation that faced Caesar; all we can do is speculate from the actions with which we are presented. Yet there is a clear dichotomy in Caesar's actions. To date, he had invested heavily in the stalemate at Uzitta, curbing his natural impatience and having his army digging fortifications and again engaging in 'trench warfare' with the nearby Pompeians. Yet despite this, he was unable to place Uzitta itself in an effective siege. However, despite having invested all this time and effort, we are next told that Caesar suddenly upped and left, and are presented with the following:

> '*Caesar meanwhile was impoverished by lack of corn; for which reason he mustered all his forces in camp and, leaving troops to garrison Leptis, Ruspina and Acylla, and assigning his fleet to Cispius and Aquila to maintain the naval blockade, the one of Hadrumetum and the other of Thapsus, he himself set fire to his camp and at the fourth watch of the night in battle formation with his baggage concentrated on the left wing evacuated that position and came to the town of Aggar.*'[32]

Thus Caesar retreated from Uzitta at night, burning his camp and abandoning the fortifications he had invested so much time and effort in. Whilst this could have been Caesar changing his mind and abandoning the 'slow and steady' tactics that were really not his forte, we need look no further than the statement in *De Bello Africo* that Caesar was impoverished (*inopia*) by the lack of corn.

Thus, in short, Caesar's army was starving and his choice of sitting and waiting it out at Uzitta had backfired. Unable to maintain his position, Caesar took the only option available: he retreated from the position and sought to inject some fresh momentum back into his campaign (as he had done in 48 BC). The Caesarian army retreated southwards from Uzitta, past the Pompeian-held Thapsus, towards the interior town of Aggar (see Map Two) set between Thapsus and Caesarian held Acylla.

> 'Here in the plain he [Caesar] pitched a single camp and then set off in person with part of his army on a foraging mission round the farmsteads; and finding a large quantity of barley, oil, wine and figs, and a little wheat, he returned to camp with his army duly re-supplied.'[33]

Thus Caesar, having retreated at night, had bought himself some time, which he used to good effect, in finding additional resources to feed his suffering army. Naturally enough when the Pompeians discovered that Caesar had departed in the night, Metellus gave chase, easily locating him on the plain around Aggar:

> 'Meanwhile Scipio, who had got to know of Caesar's departure, proceeded to follow him across the plateau with his entire forces and established himself six miles away from Caesar's camp, with his forces divided among three separate camps.'[34]

The game of cat and mouse between the two armies continued. With Scipio's arrival, Caesar moved his camp from the plain to higher ground but was seemingly determined to regain the initiative. To that end he took a portion of his army past Scipio's camp (seemingly undetected) and attacked the Pompeian held town of Zeta, capturing the garrison and the commander. Having achieved little else of note, Caesar marched his army back towards his own camp, passing Scipio's, when he was again ambushed by Scipio and Labienus, suggesting that his previous march past was not as undetected as he had hoped.

The Battle of Zeta

> 'When he was now not far away from Scipio's camp, which of necessity
> he had to pass, Labienus and Afranius with all their cavalry and light-
> armed troops sprang up and revealed themselves from behind the nearby
> hills where they had been lurking in ambush and flung themselves upon
> his rearguard. Seeing himself thus attacked, Caesar deployed his cavalry
> to bear the brunt of the enemy onslaught and ordered his legionaries to pile
> their packs and promptly deliver a counterattack. As soon as this was under
> way the enemy cavalry and light-armed troops were without difficulty
> driven back and dislodged from the hill directly the legions charged.'[35]

Thus Caesar beat back the initial Pompeian attack and resumed his
march, only to be assailed again:

> 'No sooner had Caesar come to the conclusion that the enemy, beaten back
> and demoralised as they were, would now stop their harrying, and no
> sooner had he begun to resume his march, than once again they promptly
> flung themselves from the cover of the nearby hills and attacked Caesar's
> legionaries, employing the same tactics as described above; Numidians
> and light-armed troops they were, possessed of a marvellous turn of speed,
> fighting in the ranks of the cavalry and used to keeping pace with the
> horsemen and doubling forward or retreating at their side.
>
> As they repeated this manoeuvre quite frequently, chasing the
> Caesarians as they marched and taking to flight when their opponents
> turned to attack them, and as they would not approach at all close, but
> employed peculiar tactics and were content with wounding the horses
> with their javelins, Caesar realised that what they were trying to do was
> no less than force him to pitch camp at a spot where there was not a drop
> of water, so that his famished army, which had tasted nothing at all from
> the fourth watch of the night right up till the tenth hour of the day, should
> die of thirst both men and beasts.'[36]

Once again, a bold Caesarian manoeuvre had led him to be ambushed
and pushed him onto the back foot. Caesar had to change tactics and
formation to prevent his army being becalmed in the middle of the
Numidian plains.

'Caesar withdrew his cavalry, in view of the casualties among their horses, from the rearguard, and called on the legions to replace them. By employing the legionary troops in this manner and advancing calmly and at a gentle pace he found it less awkward to contain the enemy's violent onslaught.'[37]

Thus Caesar was able to extricate his army from the Pompeian harrying and return to camp. Naturally *De Bello Africo* makes light of the situation with unrealistic casualty figures:

'Caesar completed his march, albeit somewhat slowly; for it was the first hour of the night when he brought all his men back to camp, with not a single man lost and ten wounded. Labienus retired to his lines with roughly three hundred men missing, many wounded, and all his troops exhausted by their continuous offensive.'[38]

Nevertheless, Caesar was still clearly on the backfoot and his attack on Zeta had backfired, walking into another ambush, which was always going to be a possibility having marched past the Pompeian camp. The author of *De Bello Africo* points out that the Pompeian harrying tactics, utilizing the Numidian light cavalry, were causing serious issues for the Caesarians:

'For it was surprising the amount of worry and anxiety the enemy's light-armed troops were causing our army, what with their making the cavalry chary of engaging for fear of losing their mounts, since the light-armed troops kept killing them with their javelins, and with their wearing the legionaries out by their speediness; for no sooner had a heavy-armed soldier, when pursued by them, halted and then made an attack on them than their speed of movement enabled them easily to avoid the danger.'[39]

Here we have the key to the Pompeian tactics; to utilize their speed advantage over the more heavily armoured legionaries and Caesarian cavalry, without engaging face to face. Thus the Pompeians, and we can see the influence of Labienus here, were making use of harrying tactics to wear the Caesarians down. Caesar was kept from a set piece battle; where he could deploy his stronger infantry and kept on the move, to resolve his supply issues, with his opponents trying to force him into making rash decisions, for which he had a clear record. The only downside to this tactic was the question of how long they could keep it up; perhaps until Juba dealt with the Maurian invasion and Gaetulian rebellion and marched eastwards to support them?

The *De Bello Africo* certainly reports that Juba was back in the region, engaged on a programme of attacking rebellious towns, the nearest being that of Vaga (see Map Two) which was in the vicinity of Zeta. The town was sacked by the Royal Numidian forces before Caesar could send a garrison.[40] Thus Caesar had a second Numidian army in the vicinity to deal with. The *De Bello Africo* further dates this to 21 March.[41] These cat and mouse campaigns had been going on for nearly three months and Caesar was no closer to achieving any of his campaign goals. We are told that again, Caesar marched his army to Scipio's camp in battle array, but that offer was once more refused.

Frustrated, Caesar again fell back on the tactic of attacking Pompeian held towns, a tactic which would potentially offer three advantages. Firstly, there was the grain held in each town (essential for an army with supply issues), next came the clear statement that the Pompeians could not ensure the safety of the local towns and finally came the hope that it would force Scipio to abandon his harrying tactics and give battle.

Yet, equally, in each case there was a downside. These small towns hardly held enough grain to feed an army of his size, and to defend them would require a garrison, further reducing his force and leaving them open to attack by Juba and his Numidian army. Finally Scipio and Labienus had no need to give open battle, but with clear supply lines and access to reinforcements, they could afford to wait, especially given the clear warning of Pharsalus.

The Battle of Sarsura – More of the Same

Thus, once again, the pattern was repeated, this time with Caesar moving to attack the Pompeian held town of Sarsura (see Map Two). Once again Labienus chose to attack Caesar's rear guard with a force of Numidian light cavalry and this time met with some initial success.

'*When Labienus perceived this, he proceeded to harry Caesar's rear-guard with his cavalry and light-armed troops; and having by this means cut off the baggage trains of the sutlers and merchants who were carrying their wares in carts, he was thereby the more encouraged to grow bolder and come closer to the legions, since he supposed that the soldiers were worn out with carrying their heavy packs and so in no condition to fight.*

But this contingency had not escaped Caesar's attention: he had in fact given instruction that three hundred men out of each legion should be in light order; and these he accordingly disestablished against Labienus' cavalry to give support to his own squadrons. Whereupon Labienus, dismayed at the sight of the standards, wheeled round his horses and beat a hasty and highly undignified retreat. The legionary troops, having killed many of his men and wounded not a few, retired to their standards and proceeded to resume their march. Labienus still kept up his pursuit at a distance, moving along the crest of the ridge of hills upon the right.'[42]

Thus Caesar beat off yet another attack by Labienus and reached Sarsura, which he attacked and sacked, distributing the grain to his men as a reward. The *De Bello Africo* records the last stand of the Pompeian garrison:

'*When Caesar came to the town of Sarsura he massacred Scipio's garrison while his opponents looked on, not daring to assist their friends. Its commander, however, P. Cornelius, a reservist recalled by Scipio, offered a gallant resistance, but was surrounded by overwhelming numbers and killed.'*[43]

Next in Caesar's sights lay the town of Thysdra, but that was considered to be too heavily defended (by C. Considius Longus), and Caesar abandoned the attack and was forced by the lack of water to return to his original base at Aggar, again shadowed by Scipio. Thus another town had been assaulted, another Pompeian strike had been beaten off and again the two armies returned to their stalemate.

Again Caesar took the initiative to try to break this ongoing stalemate, buoyed up by the arrival of additional forces, though only 4,000 infantry, 400 cavalry and 1,000 slingers and archers.[44] Once again Caesar marched on Scipio's camp in battle formation.

Battle of Tegea – A Caesarian victory borne of Frustration (March 46 BC)

Once more Scipio chose to acknowledge Caesar's advance by deploying in battle formation and again chose to secure his army on a town (as he had done previously, see above). The town in question was named Tegea. Again Scipio chose not to engage Caesar but held his position. On this occasion, however, Caesar's impatience got the better of him and despite the strong Pompeian position, he attacked anyway.

'Below Scipio's camp there was a town called Tegea, where he kept a standing garrison force of cavalry numbering some two thousand men. This cavalry he now deployed in line on the right- and left-hand flanks of the town, while he himself led his legions out of camp and after advancing not much more than about a mile from his defences drew them up arrayed in battle formation on the lower slopes of a ridge.

After some little time had elapsed without Scipio's shifting his position, and as the daylight hours were being frittered away in inaction, Caesar ordered some squadrons of his own horse to make a charge against the enemy cavalry which were posted on guard near the town, and despatched some light-armed units, archers, and slingers to the same objective in support. When this manoeuvre was under way and the Caesarians had delivered their attack at full gallop, Pacideius began to deploy his horsemen on a broader front, to enable them to swarm round the flanks of the Caesarian cavalry and still fight with the utmost gallantry and spirit. When Caesar observed these tactics, he instructed the three hundred men in light order, it was his normal practice that this number of men in each of his legions should be in light order, from the legion which was posted in the line nearest the scene of this action to hasten to the assistance of the cavalry.

Meanwhile Labienus sent cavalry reinforcements to support his own horsemen, furnishing unscathed troopers and those whose strength was relatively unspent to take the place of their wounded or exhausted comrades. Now that the four hundred Caesarian cavalry were finding it impossible to contain the violent onslaught of an enemy some four thousand strong and were suffering casualties at the hands of the light armed Numidians and giving ground very slightly, Caesar despatched a second wing of cavalry to dash speedily to the help of his hard-pressed men.

This action raised the spirits of his troops, who delivered a massed charge against the enemy and turned their opponents to flight; and after killing many and wounding not a few and chasing the enemy for three miles and driving them right up to the high ground they retired to their lines. Caesar waited till the tenth hour and then withdrew to his camp in battle order without any losses. In this engagement Pacideius was seriously wounded in the head by a heavy javelin which pierced his helmet; and several of the enemy leaders and all their bravest men were either killed or wounded.'[45]

Thus once more Caesar turned a near defeat into a victory. On this occasion, Caesar gave up waiting for Scipio to engage and launched his own lightning fast attack, with cavalry, archers, and slingers to engage the Pompeians before they could retire. Again, this was a highly risky strategy given that he was vastly outnumbered by the Numidian cavalry and that the Pompeians had a garrisoned town at the centre of their line, showing Caesar's desperation. However, as was often the case, Caesar's recklessness proved to be decisive, as was his decision to commit the rest of his cavalry in a second wave. As had happened before when put under pressure the Numidians broke and were routed.

Yet, despite the tone of the *De Bello Africo*, no Pompeian leaders of note were killed, and the main army retreated back to the safety of its camp. The town remained in Pompeian hands and Caesar, for all of his victory returned to his camp, buoyed up by the success, but still in the same position as that in which he had started the day.

However, this clash proved to be the last of the small battles in the African campaign, with both sides moving to the nearby city of Thapsus, then under naval siege by the Caesarian forces. What followed proved to be one of the most decisive battles in the civil war and the late Republic.

The Battle of Thapsus and its Bloody Aftermath

Chapter Seven

The Battle of Thapsus (46 BC) – History Repeating

Caesar: A Change of Tactics (April 46 BC)

Despite the victory at Tegea, Caesar found himself in the same position he had been for nearly three months; namely chasing Metellus (and Labienus) around the North African interior in a game of 'cat and mouse'. There had certainly been minor Caesarian victories but also a number of 'near misses' when his tactics had backfired, and he had found himself in difficult military positions that he had barely extricated himself from. Furthermore, his army was suffering from a lack of supplies (both food and water) as much as from Pompeian ambushes.

Then there was the question of King Juba and the Royal Numidian army which was being distracted by the Maurian invasion to the east and the Gaetulian revolt to the south. Dio has a passage which shows the Pompeian desperation for the Numidian reinforcements:

'*For Scipio, fearing his own power might be spent too soon, would no longer risk a battle with Caesar, but kept sending for Juba; when the latter would not obey his summons, Scipio promised to make him a present of all the territory that the Romans had in Africa. Juba then appointed others to take charge of the operations against Sittius and in person once more set out against Caesar.*'[1]

This appeal had brought Juba to Metellus, as we have seen from his proximity to Caesar at the town of Vaga (see Chapter Six). This does not mean that Juba had the full Numidian army with him, but as time passed then Juba may well have brought up further reinforcements for the Pompeians.

Thus Caesar realized that his initial tactics had failed (much as in Greece in 48 BC) and that he needed something to inject impetus into the campaign. He clearly decided to double down on his initial tactics, but instead of attacking low level Numidian cities of the interior, focused on capturing Thapsus, the largest port in the region and one which had been under Caesarian naval blockade for some months (since the victories at Leptis and Hadrumetum – see Chapter Six).

The question in Caesar's mind, as well as that of Metellus, must have been that whilst the Pompeians could afford to lose unimportant interior Numidian towns, could they sit back and afford the loss of a key port? Since the battles of Leptis and Hadrumetum, the Caesarians had control of the seas, and certainly the corridor from Sicily to North Africa, which, as we have seen, translated into more men and supplies reaching Caesar. Yet these supplies were rendered less effective by them having to be transported to Caesar in the interior, challenged by the highly mobile Numidian cavalry. Caesar now changed that equation by moving to the coast and thus ensuring a steady supply of food and water for his army, a situation that would only be increased by the capture of Thapsus. Thus Caesar abandoned his failing tactics and changed course:

> 'Finding it impossible on any terms to induce his opponents to come down to level ground and risk their legions and realising that it was equally impossible for him to pitch his own camp closer to the enemy owing to the poor supply of water, and perceiving that his opponents, so far from having any confidence in their own valour, were led to hold him in contempt by their reliance on the dearth of water, Caesar left Aggar on April 4th at the third watch. Then, after advancing sixteen miles by night, he pitched camp near Thapsus, where Vergilius was in command with a considerable garrison.'[2]
>
> 'Accordingly, when Caesar perceived that because of the nature of the land he could not force them to engage in conflict unless they chose, he set out for Thapsus, in order that he might either engage them, if they came to the help of the city, or might at least capture the place, if they left it to its fate.'[3]

The key question, however, was whether Metellus (and Labienus) would rise to this bait or continue to utilize the 'hit and run tactics', which had so far rendered Caesar's campaign ineffective?

The Siege of Thapsus (4–5 April 46 BC)

Thus we have confirmation that after nearly three months, Caesar realized that his initial tactics had failed and accordingly changed the course of the campaign. Now came the focus on the city of Thapsus, which is described accordingly (see battleplan below):

> *Thapsus is situated on a type of peninsula, with the sea stretching along on one side and a lake on the other; the isthmus between them is so narrow and marshy that one reaches the town by two roads, only a little way apart, running along either side of the marsh close to the shore.*[4]

Thus the main approach to the city was a narrow one (between sea and marsh) from the south and one that could easily be blockaded. There was a further northern route around the marsh. The clear danger, however, would be that (as at Dyrrhachium) the besieger could easily become the besieged, if Metellus (and Juba) blockaded Caesar between the city and the marsh. On this occasion, however, the Caesarians had control of the sea. Making use of the time advantage, we are told that Caesar made an immediate start to his siege works:

> *That same day he began to invest the town, seizing and manning several suitable strategic points to prevent the enemy's being able to infiltrate and approach him, or capture any inner positions.*[5]

The city was held by a Pompeian garrison commanded by C. Vergilius, who had been under Caesarian naval blockade for over a month now. Clearly the Pompeians faced a choice, and on this occasion a threefold one; firstly, to ignore Caesar's siege and allow Thapsus to fall (of relative unimportance in itself) and regroup in the interior. Secondly to follow Caesar and try to trap him between themselves and the city, but otherwise not engage and thirdly to follow Caesar and try to dislodge him by force.

As detailed by the *De Bello Africo*, Metellus ignored the first option and (keeping his options open) followed Caesar to Thapsus. In itself this was not a mistake, but Metellus was merely maintaining the strategy he had followed to date, namely, to shadow Caesar and harry him. Yet the Pompeians had now lost the advantage of fighting in the Numidian interior where Caesar had limited access to supplies. Furthermore, Caesar was now committed to staying at Thapsus, and not darting about hither and thither and thus reducing the opportunities for harrying him on the march, which had produced some positive results in the previous months. Thus the Pompeians were now playing more of Caesar's game than they had to date. Yet, Metellus' initial move was a cautious one:

'[Metellus] *forthwith followed Caesar along the high ground and established himself in two camps at a distance of eight miles from Thapsus.*'[6]

Metellus' Choice – The Pompeian Plan

As can be seen below, there were two routes available to reach Thapsus, the widest of which lay to the south, between the marshes and the sea, with another route available to the north. Caesar we are told had invested the city itself and so only had two routes to withdraw from the siege. Thus the Pompeians and Caesarians both faced the same essential issue, there were only two narrow routes either out or in, both bottlenecks. If the Pompeians wanted to reach Caesar, then they had to take one or both of these. Likewise, however, if the Caesarians wanted to retreat, they would have to secure one or both bottlenecks.

Thus the Pompeians (and Metellus in particular) faced a choice and the same three options as before, albeit with caveats. Option One, which they seem to have discarded was to ignore the siege (and Caesar) and wait in the interior. Option Two was now to trap Caesar at Thapsus by cutting off both bottlenecks (north and south) and thus leave Caesar trapped between the marshes, the city, and the sea. Even if Caesar took Thapsus, he would still need to break out from the bottlenecks. The third option would be to relieve the city by forcing the bottlenecks and confronting Caesar there.

Option Three was by far the riskiest, as it placed the Pompeian army on ground that was less than ideal for its strengths – narrow and marshy, rather than a wide open plain to deploy their superior cavalry and elephants. Option Two was the low risk one, bottling Caesar up behind the Thapsan marshes and with the Pompeian-held city at his back. Understanding these options is critical in any attempt to make sense of the various accounts we find in the sources for how the subsequent battle came about.

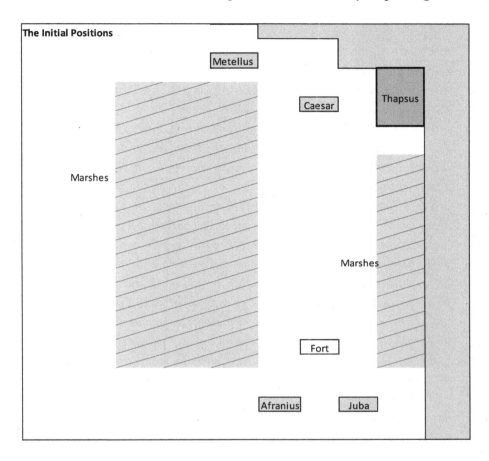

The Initial Positions

Metellus

Caesar

Thapsus

Marshes

Marshes

Fort

Afranius

Juba

We are fortunate that the account in the *De Bello Africo* is supplemented by other accounts, in Dio, Appian and Plutarch, as the Caesarian account is limited to the build-up of the battle, though excellent for its subsequent narrative of the battle itself.

> '*There was a lagoon of salt water, separated from the sea by a certain narrow strip of land not more than a mile and a half wide; and this corridor Scipio now attempted to enter to bring help to the men of Thapsus. The likelihood of such a move had not escaped Caesar's attention: in fact, the day before he had built a fort at this spot and left behind a force of three cohorts to hold it, while he himself with the rest of his forces established a crescent-shaped camp and invested Thapsus with a ring of siege works.*

Meanwhile Scipio, foiled in his undertaking, bypassed the lagoon to the north by a march which he completed in the ensuing day and night, and then, at the first pale light of dawn, took up a position not far from the camp and the defence area I mentioned above, and a mile and a half from the sea coast; and then he began to fortify a camp.

When this was reported to Caesar, the latter withdrew his troops from their work of fortification, left behind the Proconsul Asprenas to guard the camp with two legions, and hurriedly marched to that location with a force in light order.'[7]

'Now Thapsus is situated on a kind of peninsula, with the sea stretching along on one side and a lake on the other; the isthmus between them is so narrow and marshy that one reaches the town by two roads, only a little way apart, running along either side of the marsh close to the shore. On his way toward this city Caesar, when he had got inside the narrowest point, proceeded to dig a ditch and to erect a palisade. The townspeople caused him no trouble, as they were no match for him; but Scipio and Juba undertook in their turn to wall off the neck of the isthmus, where it comes to an end at the mainland, by running palisades and ditches across from both sides.

They were engaged in this work and were making great progress every day (for in order that they might build the walls across more quietly they had stationed the elephants along the portion not yet protected by a ditch and hence easy for the enemy to attack, while on the remaining portions all were working.'[8]

'However, Scipio was encouraged by these advantages to hazard a decisive battle: so, leaving Afranius and Juba encamped separately at a short distance apart, he himself began fortifying a camp beyond a lake near the city of Thapsus, that it might serve the whole army as a place from which to sally out to the battle, and as a place of refuge.'[9]

Thus we are able to piece together the strategy that Metellus implemented. The *De Bello Africo* has the highly dubious statement that the Pompeians advanced towards Thapsus via the southern route (see above), yet an army of allegedly 80,000 men were foiled by Caesar's fort, held by only three cohorts (roughly 1,500 men). This then forced Metellus to take the northern route and make camp there. Yet far more logical statements can be found in both Dio and Plutarch.

Metellus, it seems, had decided (wisely in theory) to trap Caesar on the Thapsan side of the marshes and thus bottle him up. To that end the army initially approached Thapsus via the south, where Metellus left Afranius and Juba to create a siege line from the marshes to the coast (see battleplan above). Thus the Pompeians had no wish to force Caesar's fort to gain entry towards Thapsus, but were walling him in. With Afranius and Juba covering the south, Metellus himself took the northern route and did the same. Though not mentioned until later, Metellus it seems was accompanied by a sizeable naval contingent, perhaps from Thapsus itself, to cover his coastal flank.

There are obvious benefits and dangers to this Pompeian tactic. This strategy was the continuation of the policy started at Ilerda in 49 BC and continued at Dyrrhachium in 48 BC, namely, to wall Caesar in and wear him down, rather than face him in open combat. In theory Caesar was now trapped on the Thapsan side of the marshes, with both exits blocked by the developing Pompeian siege lines, with the Pompeian-held city on his flank.

Yet, as was aptly demonstrated, there were clear dangers to this tactic. Firstly the Pompeian army was split into two sections (north and south) separated by the Thapsan marches. Secondly the key strength of the Pompeian army in Africa had been its mobility, with their hit and run tactics, and superior cavalry, and now they were bedding down for a siege, negating these advantages. Thirdly Caesar still had naval superiority (unlike at Dyrrhachium) and could be supplied from the sea, even without control of the port of Thapsus.

Caesar Trapped (Again)?

Thus, once again, Caesar found himself trapped in the siege of a city (as at Dyrrhachium in 48 BC), caught between the Thapsan marshes and the city itself and facing developing Pompeian siege lines blocking off both his land exits. Yet, the Pompeians had effectively forced Caesar into a corner, with only two options. On the one hand, he could wait it out (as he had at Dyrrhachium) and counter the Pompeian siege lines with those of his own. On the other hand, however, he could force his way out before these siege works had time to be completed and actually force Metellus into a set piece confrontation. Given both his temperament and the experience of Dyrrhachium, no one would be surprised to learn that Caesar chose the second option, deciding to force his way out.

The Battle of Thapsus (6 April 46 BC)

Technically Caesar faced three separate Pompeian forces: Metellus to the north, Juba and Afranius to the south and the Pompeian garrison of Vergilius to the east. Yet the danger in the Pompeian dispositions was that all three forces were cut off from each other, either by Caesar's army or the very marshes they planned to trap him behind. Thus Caesar determined to attack the greatest of these Pompeian forces, that of Metellus, first. The clear danger to Caesar was that the other two forces would attack his flank. To reduce this risk a force was left behind at the city of Thapsus to deal with the garrison and the Caesarian fort to the south was relied on to defend his southern flank, as was the speed of his attack and the lack of Pompeian co-ordination. The *De Bello Africo* presents a detailed account of the dispositions of the two sides (though not the numbers):

> '*When Caesar arrived there and observed Scipio's battle line arrayed in front of the rampart, with the elephants posted on the right and left wings, while none the less part of his troops were busily engaged in fortifying the camp, he himself disposed his army in three lines: the Tenth and Seventh legions he posted on the right wing, the Eighth and Ninth on the left, while five cohorts of the Fifth legion were stationed on each of the actual wings, forming a fourth line to contain the elephants; and his archers and slingers were deployed on either wing, and the light-armed units interspersed among the cavalry.*'[10]

Thus again we see shades of Pharsalus here, with a Caesarian fourth line designed to counter the enemies' superior cavalry (and in this case elephants). With a typical bold movement, Caesar had exploited the division in the Pompeian forces and faced Metellus without the totality of his army (no numbers are given) and in a position where he could not utilize his greater element of mobility. Again this is reminiscent of Pharsalus, where the Pompeian army was limited by having a river on one wing. Here, at Thapsus, there were marshes to one side and coast on the other. Caesar's attack seems to have caught Metellus completely off guard. Certainly, Plutarch's account of the battle emphasises the elements of speed and surprise (as does that of Dio[11]):

> '*But while he* [Metellus] *was busy with the project, Caesar made his way with inconceivable speed through woody regions which afforded unknown access to the spot, outflanked some of the enemy, and attacked others in front.*'[12]

Plutarch's account earlier stated that Metellus had determined on a battle (above), but this is highly unlikely. His army was building a camp and major siege lines to block Caesar's exit and starve him out. The last thing on his mind would have been a set piece battle with Caesar, especially with only a portion of his army. Yet that is exactly the circumstances he now faced and whilst the benefit of hindsight would have warned him of the risks, he now faced a stark choice. We will never know how long

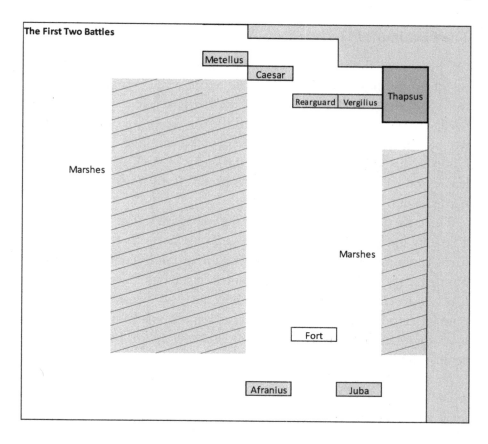

Metellus had to make his decision, when the army of Caesar was spotted advancing on his position. In theory he had the same two options of fight or flight, but flight would have lost him the whole Thapsan position without a fight and could have seriously doomed his whole campaign. Thus in reality, Metellus had to stand and fight.

Nevertheless, the position was far from hopeless, and defeat was not inevitable. In fact Metellus didn't need to win, merely to withstand and repulse the Caesarian attack and force Caesar back towards his own Thapsan siege works. He had a solid position, reinforced with elephants on both wings and would have signalled to the two other Pompeian forces to come to his aid. All he had to do was to hold his position.

In reality the Battle of Thapsus was three separate conflicts: Caesar vs Metellus on the north coast, the Caesarian rearguard vs the Pompeian garrison at Thapsus itself and Caesar vs Juba and Afranius on the south-eastern coast.

The First Battle (The Northern Approach) – Caesar vs Metellus

Of these three clashes, it was clearly the one on the northern coast that was the most important. Caesar needed to break the Pompeian siege and force Metellus' army from the narrow northern passage. Equally Metellus needed to remain in place and fight off the Caesarian attack. If this attack was beaten off, then Caesar's entrapment could continue. In wider terms, however, this was the clash between the leader of the Caesarians and the leader of the Pompeians and the results would clearly impact on the whole narrative of the war.

There are no accurate numbers for the respective size of the two forces. The only figure we have is from Appian, who states that Metellus' total force (presumably counting Juba's Numidian contingent) was 80,000, but then they would have been split between the two Pompeian armies.[13] Caesar's force must have been smaller, not only because of his total numbers, but because we are told that he *hurriedly marched to that location with a force in light order*[14] and having left two legions behind to guard against the Pompeian garrison in Thapsus itself (see below).

Naturally the *De Bello Africo* emphasises the disorganized nature of the Metellan army, though given Caesar's sudden assault this may well been an accurate representation of the situation they faced:

'*Now in the course of making these rounds of his army he* [Caesar] *observed that the enemy in neighbourhood of their rampart were excited, rushing hither and thither in alarm, now retiring inside the gates, now trooping out in a spasmodic and undisciplined fashion. Several others were beginning to observe the same symptoms when without more ado his lieutenants and reservists implored Caesar not to hesitate to give the signal.*'[15]

As with Pharsalus, Caesar clearly identified that the wings of the Metellan army, where their elephants were stationed, were the key to his victory and thus engaged them first. We only have three accounts that provide any details as to the direction of the battle:

'*when Caesar suddenly attacked the men who were with Scipio, and by using slings and arrows from a distance threw the elephants into great confusion. Then as they retreated, he not only followed them up, but fell upon the workers unexpectedly and routed them, too; and when they fled into their camp, he dashed in with them and captured it without a blow.*'[16]

'*Meanwhile on the right wing the slingers and archers in crowds launched rapid volleys of missiles against the elephants. Whereupon the beasts, terrified by the whizzing sound of the slings and by the stones and leaden bullets launched against them, speedily wheeled round, trampled underfoot the massed and serried ranks of their own supporting troops behind them, and rushed towards the half-completed gates of the rampart. The Numidian cavalry, who were posted on the same wing as the elephants, followed suit and abandoned by their protective screen, started the rout. Having thus speedily got round the elephants, the legions gained possession of the enemy's rampart; and when the few defenders who offered a spirited resistance had been killed, the remainder precipitately sought refuge in the camp from which they had issued the day before.*'[17]

'*The defeat began with Juba, whose elephants, unaccustomed to war and only recently brought from the woods, panic-stricken at the sudden noise of the trumpets, wheeled round and charged their own side. The army immediately turned to flight, nor were the generals too brave to flee; the deaths, however, of all of them were remarkable.*'[18]

We can clearly see an echo of Pharsalus here, with Caesar determined to attack the Pompeian wings and their greatest asset, their elephants and cavalry. On this occasion, the Caesarians engaged them at distance (to negate their size advantage) using archers and slingers, which is in fact a reversal of the situation at Pharsalus where the Pompeians had the advantage in using slingers and archers. Thus, not only was the Pompeian advantage in elephants negated, but it was turned to Caesar's advantage, when they were turned and charged through the Pompeian ranks. Thus, one disaster for the Pompeians was compounded by a second when the Numidian cavalry, who had shown over the previous months their lack of resilience in close quarters (see Chapters Five and Six), turned and fled.

Faced with these two blows, the Metellan army unsurprisingly collapsed, their retreat compounded by the very siege works they had built to blockade Caesar. Caesar naturally exploited this rout to ensure that the Pompeians were not able to use these fortifications to regroup:

> 'Meanwhile Scipio's forces, now thrown into utter confusion, were in wholesale retreat in every sector of the field, and Caesar's legions promptly pursued them without giving them any respite in which to pull themselves together. When the fugitives reached the camp they were making for, with the object of making a recovery there and defending themselves once more, and of trying to find someone to lead them, someone to look up to, under whose authority and command they could carry on the fight; when they got there and perceived that there was nobody guarding it, they forthwith discarded their armour and beat a hasty retreat to the royal camp. This too on their arrival they saw to be in the hands of the Caesarians.'[19]

Thus, the Pompeians were routed from the northern battlefield and many seemingly retreated to Juba's camp in the south, which had also fallen to the Caesarians (see below). What followed was a massacre of the survivors by the Caesarians, but again, as at Pharsalus, no major figures were involved:

> 'Abandoning all hope of salvation, they now stopped on a hill and gave the military salute by lowering their arms. This gesture, unhappily for them, stood them in but little stead. For Caesar's veterans were filled with such burning indignation and resentment that, so far from any possibility of inducing them to spare the enemy, they actually wounded or killed several men of culture and distinction among the ranks of their

own side, calling them ringleaders. Among these was Tullius Rufus, an ex-quaestor, who was mortally wounded by a soldier who deliberately ran him through with a heavy javelin; and similarly Pompeius Rufus was stabbed in the arm with a sword and would have been done to death, had he not promptly rushed to Caesar's side.

This behaviour caused grave alarm among quite a number of Roman Knights and Senators, who retired from the battle lest they themselves should also be massacred by the soldiers, who after so resounding a victory had apparently taken it for granted that they were free to perpetrate any excesses, on the assumption that they would go unpunished in view of their magnificent achievements. Accordingly, although all these troops of Scipio implored Caesar's protection, they were massacred to a man, despite the fact that Caesar himself was looking on and entreating his troops to spare them.'[20]

Thus Scipio's army was destroyed, though there were a number of notable survivors (see Chapter Eight), and Caesar had a comprehensive victory, his first of three that day.

The Second Battle (Thapsus) – Rearguard vs Garrison

The second battle came at Thapsus itself, when, unsurprisingly the Pompeian garrison, under C. Vergilius, showed that they would not stand by and allow Caesar to attack Metellus unchallenged. Furthermore, had they been able to overcome the Caesarian rearguard then they would have had Caesar trapped between the two Pompeian forces. This second clash is only recorded in the *De Bello Africo*:

'Meanwhile the members of the garrison of Thapsus made a sortie from the town by way of the seaward gate and, whether their object was to hasten to the aid of their fellows, or to abandon the town and secure their own safety by flight, out they came and accordingly, wading waist-high into the sea, made for the land. They were, however, prevented from reaching land by stones and heavy javelins hurled by the slaves and lackeys in the camp; and so they returned back into the town.'[21]

As we can see, the *De Bello Africo* was dismissive of this clash, yet it earlier stated that Caesar was so concerned about this possibility that he left behind two legions under the command of L. Nonius Asprenas. Given this, it is likely that there was a battle between the garrison of Vergilius and the rearguard of Asprenas, with the Pompeian garrison being driven back into the city. Though overlooked by the sources, this battle would have played a critical role in safeguarding Caesar's attack on Metellus.

The Third Battle (The Southern Approach) Caesar vs Juba and Afranius

Interestingly there is no direct account of this clash in the *De Bello Africo*, other than the reference to Caesar '*having made himself master of three camps*'[22] (see below). This ties in with the earlier assumption that Metellus was forced away from the southern coastal entrance with no mention of

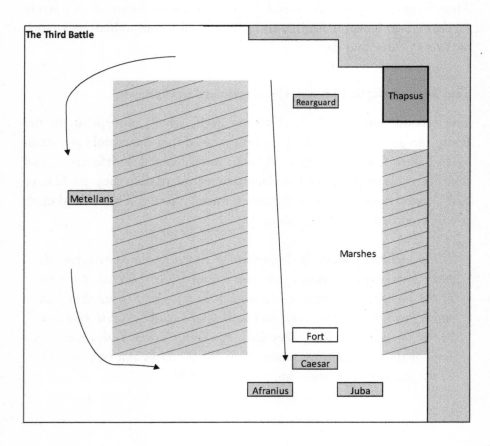

him leaving any forces there. Nevertheless we do find references in other works, many of whom are equally confused as to where Juba was during the fighting.[23]

> '*Juba, upon seeing this, was so startled and terrified that he ventured neither to come to close quarters with any one nor even to keep the camp under guard; so he fled and hastened homeward.*'[24]
>
> '*Caesar, immediately after Juba's flight, captured the palisade and caused great slaughter among all who came in the way of his troops, sparing not even those who came over to his side.*'[25]
>
> '*Then, after routing these, he took advantage of the favourable instant and of the impetus of fortune, and thereby captured the camp of Afranius at the first onset, and at the first onset sacked the camp of the Numidians, from which Juba fled.*'[26]

Thus it seems that Juba and Afranius were camped separately around the southern approach to Thapsus, and neither was able to send help to Metellus, indicating the swiftness of Caesar's attack. It is also clear that Caesar, upon routing Metellus immediately swung around and attacked the southern Pompeian forces, perhaps using the shorter route on the 'inside' of the Thapsan marshes. It seems that neither Juba nor Afranius were able to muster a solid defence, with the sources reporting that Juba fled without a fight. We know that Afranius survived the battle, but not what resistance he put up before he retreated.

Caesar Triumphant

Thus, as he had a habit of doing, Caesar completely turned the campaign on its head and in one afternoon destroyed the Pompeian 'grand army'. There are two sources which report the casualty figures:

> '*Having made himself master of three camps and killed ten thousand of the enemy and routed a large number, Caesar retired to camp with fifty soldiers missing and a few wounded.*'[27]
>
> '*Thus in a brief portion of one day he made himself master of three camps and slew fifty thousand of the enemy, without losing as many as fifty of his own men.*'[28]

We can see the usual escalation of the casualty figures over time with the near contemporaneous source quoting 10,000 Pompeian dead and the one several centuries later upping it to 50,000 thousand. Even with only 10,000 Pompeians dead their army had been shattered and their leadership scattered (see below). Caesar now had a third clear victory over the Pompeians; to add to the two previous ones of Ilerda and Pharsalus.

Yet once again, victory on the battlefield did not automatically equate to victory in the war. As at Pharsalus, none of the key Pompeian leaders were killed in the battle or the retreat, and Caesar found himself still in hostile territory. For Caesar, the key to this success was to convert it into a wider victory in Africa and the civil war as a whole. In the immediate aftermath of Thapsus, however, Pompeian resistance seemed to continue:

> '*Immediately on his arrival he* [Caesar] *established himself in front of the town of Thapsus. He then took sixty-four elephants, equipped, armed and complete with towers and harness, and these he now drew up in array in front of the town: his object in so doing was to see if* [C.] *Vergilius and the others who were being besieged with him could be induced to abandon their obstinate resistance by the evidence of their comrades' failure. He then addressed a personal appeal to Vergilius inviting him to surrender and reminding him of his own leniency and clemency; but on failing to observe any response he withdrew from the town.*'[29]
>
> '*Thereupon he immediately withdrew from the town, leaving behind the Proconsul* [C. Caninius] *Rebilus in front of Thapsus with three legions.*'[30]

Though the failure of Vergilius to capitulate immediately was a blow, Caesar realized that he could not waste time being caught at a siege, but needed to build on his victory and destroy the Pompeian presence in Africa before they could regroup.

The Endurance of the Pompeians

Naturally, the opposite was true for the Pompeians. For the second time in two years, they had gone into a situation confident of victory and been undone on the battlefield with a total reversal. Again for a second time their grand army of Romans and allies had been destroyed. Yet again though the key Pompeian leaders had survived the battle itself and again found themselves having to retreat to safety to regroup and rebuild. The individual fates of these figures will be covered shortly (see Chapter Eight), but these men knew that they needed to put as much distance between Caesar and themselves as possible in the short term. Again this was made feasible by the battle being fought in Pompeian territory. This allowed them to retreat into either the Numidian interior or the Roman province of North Africa. Thus the fate of the civil war seemingly hung on them escaping Caesar in the short term and regrouping.

History Repeating

Thus we can see that after three months of a 'cat and mouse' campaign in the North African interior where Caesar risked being ground down by the Fabian tactics of the Pompeians, the whole campaign turned on one afternoon and Caesar emerged victorious on the battlefield. In many ways this campaign had echoes of 48 BC, with Caesar roaming around Greece before victory at Pharsalus. Yet there was one key difference here. In 48 BC, Pompeius had clearly determined that he needed to defeat Caesar on the battlefield in order to publicly demonstrate that he had 'saved the Republic' and cement his position as Princeps of Rome.[31]

On this occasion, however, there are no indications that Metellus was expecting to give battle at Thapsus, in fact quite the opposite. If anything the parallel that Metellus may well have been thinking about was the Battle of Dyrrhachium, where Caesar managed to get himself trapped against a coastal city and was besieged for months, before attempting a desperate breakout and being defeated.[32]

It is possible that this very parallel may well have been in Caesar's own mind which spurred him on this occasion to attack Metellus immediately, before the Pompeians had had the chance to complete their siegeworks and seal him behind the Thapsan marshes. As with most of Caesar's actions, it was a gamble, but a calculated one. As at Pharsalus, he was seriously outnumbered, but on this occasion the multiple nations in the army he faced had had a year to integrate their various fighting styles.

However, as at Pharsalus, Caesar had spent time preparing his men to fight in a new manner to negate the Pompeians' strength. In Greece he trained his men to fight in mixed specialist units against Pompeius' cavalry, and on this occasion, he trained them to fight Numidian elephants The *De Bello Africo* draws attention to this fact in the narrative covering Caesar's wanderings in the Numidian interior:

> '*Here, however, was one problem to which he had found an answer; for he had ordered elephants to be brought across from Italy to enable our troops not only to become familiar with them, but also to get to know both the appearance and capabilities of the beast, what part of its body was readily vulnerable to a missile and, when an elephant was accoutred and armoured, what part of its body was still left uncovered and unprotected, so that their missiles should be aimed at that spot. He had also this further object in mind, that his horses would learn by familiarity with these beasts not to be alarmed by their scent, trumpeting or appearance. From this experiment he had profited handsomely: for the troops handled the beasts and came to appreciate their sluggishness; the cavalry hurled dummy javelins at them; and the docility of the beasts had brought the horses to feel at home with them.*'[33]

Thus on both occasions, in Greece and in Africa, Caesar identified the key element that the Pompeians would rely on in battle to give them (or so they thought) the advantage over Caesar's legions. In Greece it was their cavalry and in Africa it was their elephants. On both occasions, Caesar not only identified this Pompeians' strength but trained his men to turn it into a weakness. Thus he went into each battle, confident that he could not only counter, but defeat, the factor that the Pompeians were relying on to bring them victory. Again, as at Pharsalus, once this Pompeian 'advantage' had been neutralised, Caesar was able to capitalise on it more quickly than the Pompeians and convert a successful manoeuvre into outright victory on the battlefield.

Thus it was not a case of Metellus being a poor general, rather, it was that Caesar was the greater strategist and put in more preparation, thought and training before the battle, which gave him the confidence and the flexibility to outmanoeuvre his opponents on the day itself.

Speaking of his opponents, there is some question over just who Caesar was facing at Thapsus that day, centred around the noticeable absence of T. Labienus. As we have seen (see preceding chapters) throughout these three months of campaigning, Caesar's most redoubtable opponent had been his former lieutenant T. Labienus, the man who had (nearly?) beaten him at Ruspina. Yet, despite his presence as co-commander of nearly every battle and skirmish to date, there is notably no mention of Labienus during any of the description of Thapsus.

This interesting omission can be combined with three other pieces of evidence. Firstly, comes the ease with which Labienus escaped from North Africa (see Chapter Eight), Appian's garbled account of him accompanying Pompeius to Spain and the sudden deterioration of the Pompeian tactics. All these raise the suspicion that Labienus was not actually at Thapsus at all, leaving Metellus in sole command, a factor that may well have swung the outcome in Caesar's favour. If this was the case then it clearly points to a falling out between Mettelus and Labienus, prior to the move to Thapsus, with the latter perhaps objecting to the change of tactics that had been working so well. Valerius Maximus does include an interesting clash between the two men earlier in the campaign.[34]

Nevertheless, despite this strategic brilliance for battlefield tactics, Caesar still had difficulties in turning these victories into a winning campaign. Both the Gallic and Civil Wars share similar themes, with Caesar's victories not translating into ending campaigns, and wars dragging on and flaring back up again. Despite beating the Gauls on numerous occasions, there were times when the whole campaign came within an ace of collapsing with the war dragging on for eight years (58–51 BC). This Third Roman Civil War itself was now in its fourth year and showed no sign of abating. Perhaps stung by this (relative) failure in Greece to end the war in 48 BC, he seemingly determined to do so here in Africa, after Thapsus.

Summary – Metellus' Mistake: Caesarian Plan or Opportunist?

Thus after three months of move and counter move in the North African interior, exchanges, battles and victories, the Pompeian army was destroyed in less than a day, and the months of hard work on their part were wasted. As happened in Greece, after finding himself caught in an ongoing stalemate, Caesar chose a bold move to change the momentum of the campaign. By attacking Thapsus and offering Metellus the opportunity of trapping him between the city and the marshes, Caesar was able to tempt him into what in hindsight was clearly a mistake.

Though trapping Caesar at Thapsus was a sound strategic move, the execution was poor, both in terms of splitting his army up and sacrificing the terrain that so suited his own forces, wide open plains for his cavalry and elephants, for a narrow strip between marshes and sea. Once again, Caesar used the terrain to negate his opponents' superiority (as at Pharsalus) and once again he specifically trained his men to negate the Pompeians' strength (on this occasion, their elephants). Again Caesar used his army's speed and greater cohesiveness to best effect, negating his opponents' strengths and reacting the more quickly to win the day.

Metellus, though he had the right idea, clearly left himself vulnerable to a surprise Caesarian attack in those first few days before his siege lines were complete. Whether it was always Caesar's intention to draw Metellus in and then launch a surprise attack or he merely acted out of desperation, is something that he took to his grave, not that he would have admitted the truth to posterity anyway.

Regardless of the motive, Caesar took the opportunity and had his second great victory over a Pompeian army. The most important thing for him now would be to ensure that there would be no need for a third one.

Chapter Eight

Cementing the Victory –
The Destruction of the Pompeian Faction

Caesarian and Pompeian Aims

In the aftermath of his more famous victory at Pharsalus, in 48 BC, it could be argued that Caesar wasted his victory by chasing Pompeius across the Roman East, allowing the Pompeian faction to recover. In truth it is more likely that he was forced to waste his victory by the Pompeians splitting into two; with Pompeius heading east and the rest of the leadership heading west, forcing Caesar to choose.

On the face of it, it could also be said that Caesar faced a similar choice now in the aftermath of his victory at Thapsus. The Pompeian faction was composed of three distinct entities, controlling two territories. The three entities were the hardcore adherents of the Pompeian family, the Senatorial grouping of anti-Caesarians and the Romano-Numidian faction. The two territories they controlled were the Roman province of North Africa and the native Numidian Kingdom. The survivors of Thapsus, which included all the key Pompeian leaders mostly split on these lines with the Pompeians and anti-Caesarians remaining in Roman North Africa and heading north towards its capital Utica, whilst Juba and his allies fled into the Numidian interior.

This split also reflected the likely next actions of these two groupings, with the Pompeians and anti-Caesarians aiming to reach the relative safety of the Roman province, where they had garrisons and ships, before using it as a springboard to leave North Africa and seek safety off the continent and regroup. There can have been little doubt in their mind that North Africa was now lost to the Pompeian cause, and they need to regroup overseas, with Spain being the most obvious destination (with Cn. Pompeius Magnus (jnr) having been dispatched there some months earlier – see Chapter Nine). By contrast Juba could not abandon his kingdom and would have to fight to preserve it. If anything the Pompeians were probably hoping that Juba would slow Caesar down, much as Pharnaces had in the east (See Appendix One).

Thus for the Pompeians and anti-Caesarians, the immediate plan was to seek safety and then plan their escape before Caesar had a chance to catch them. Equally it was clear that Caesar had a narrow window if he was to avoid a repeat of the aftermath of Pharsalus, in which he needed to catch up with the key Pompeian leaders and stop them leaving North Africa. On this occasion he had two additional elements in his favour that he had not had in 48 BC, naval parity (if not superiority) and a native kingdom supporting him (with the Mauri attacking Numidia from the west). Thus we should not be surprised, that Caesar in the aftermath of the Battle of Thapsus had a clear focus on his next actions:

> '*On the following day, after offering sacrifice, he held a parade and in full view of the occupants of the town congratulated his troops, rewarding his entire veteran force and bestowing decorations publicly in front of the dais for conspicuous gallantry and meritorious service. Thereupon he immediately withdrew from the town, leaving behind the Proconsul* [C. Caninius] *Rebilus in front of Thapsus with three legions and Cn. Domitius* [Calvinus] *with two at Thysdra, where* [C.] *Considius* [Longus] *was in command, to continue the blockades of these places; and then, sending M.* [Valerius] *Messalla* [Rufus] *on ahead to Utica with the cavalry, he himself also proceeded with despatch to the same destination.*'[1]

Caesar, therefore, left behind five legions; three to continue the siege of Thapsus and another two to capture a Pompeian stronghold at Thysdrus. We are reminded that despite his victory, Caesar was still in hostile territory and needed to secure his geographical position by eliminating the key Pompeian garrisons. Thus Caesar set off for the obvious target of Utica, the capital of Roman North Africa (Carthage still being a ruin) and the focal point for Pompeian resistance / recovery.

The Collapse of Pompeian North Africa and the Shattering of the Pompeian Faction

As stated, Utica, the largest Roman city in North Africa, with its garrison, commanded by none other than M. Porcius Cato (ostensibly to keep him away from any real fighting) and its port was the obvious choice of refuge for the retreating Pompeians. Naturally leading the retreat were the Romano-Numidian cavalry, which, as the *De Bello Africo* points out encountered expected native resistance:

> '*Meanwhile those horsemen of Scipio's who had escaped from the battle were proceeding in the direction of Utica when they came to the town of Parada. Being refused admittance by the inhabitants, for the news of Caesar's victory had preceded them, they gained possession of the town by force; then, making a pile of faggots in the middle of the market-place and heaping on top all the inhabitants' possessions, they set fire to it and then flung into the flames, alive and bound, the inhabitants of the town themselves, irrespective of rank or age, thereby meting out to them the most cruel of all punishments.*'[2]

Cato too seemingly had issues with the inhabitants of Utica and had to expel a number of key citizens suspected of harbouring Caesarian sympathies, now that news of Thapsus had reached them. He expelled them from the city into a camp in front of the city walls which was subsequently attacked by the returning Pompeian cavalry who, when beaten off by the natives, turned and sacked the city, showing the collapse of discipline in the Pompeian army.

Interestingly we are told that the cavalry then left Utica, having been bought off by both Cato and Faustus Sulla and headed towards Numidia, a reflection of their Numidian composition. Interestingly Faustus Sulla himself chose to abandon Utica (and the anti-Caesarian faction and went with them (along with L. Afranius) to seek refuge in the Numidian interior (and seemingly reach Spain via the longer route). Sulla also appears to have been at Utica throughout the previous months and not with the main Pompeian army. Thus we can see the cracks opening up within the various subsets of the Pompeian faction, with both Sulla and Afranius, hardcore Pompeians, choosing to make for Spain (overland) rather than remain in Utica.

Cato naturally remained and was soon joined by Metellus Scipio and the bulk of the survivors from Thapsus itself. The *De Bello Africo* points out that Cato had undertaken extensive fortifications of the city,[3] yet having expelled a number of citizens and seen the city attacked by the

Romano-Numidian cavalry it was clear that the city would not hold long if the Caesarian forces arrived. This being the case, Scipio and a number of his key Senatorial supporters (Licinius Crassus Damasippus, Manlius Torquatus, and Plaetorius Rustianus) seemingly quickly made plans to take what remained of the Pompeian fleet there and set sail for Spain. Thus, it seemed that Caesar had once again failed to prevent the leader of the Pompeian faction from escaping his grip. One notable absence from this list of escapees was the commander of Utica himself, M. Porcius Cato, who in what was to become one of Rome's most dramatized acts (and latterly that of the Renaissance Europe) famously took his own life. Subsequent historians, writers and dramatists have turned this act into one of supreme self-sacrifice, 'dying for the Republic' rather than live under tyranny:

'As for himself, having made all arrangements with the greatest care and entrusted his children to Lucius Caesar, who at the time was acting as his Quaestor, he retired to bed without arousing any suspicions, there being nothing unusual either about the way he looked or the way he talked; and then, having secretly smuggled a dagger into his bedroom, he accordingly stabbed himself. He had collapsed but was still breathing when his doctor and some members of his household, suspecting something amiss, forced their way into the bedroom and proceeded to staunch and bind up the wound; but with his own hands he tore it open with utter ruthlessness and resolutely made an end of himself.'[4]

'Indeed, such diversity of character carries with it so great significance that suicide may be for one man a duty, for another a crime. Did Marcus Cato find himself in one predicament, and were the others, who surrendered to Caesar in Africa, in another? And yet, perhaps, they would have been condemned, if they had taken their lives; for their mode of life had been less austere and their characters more pliable. But Cato had been endowed by nature with an austerity beyond belief, and he himself had strengthened it by unswerving consistency and had remained ever true to his purpose and fixed resolve; and it was for him to die rather than to look upon the face of a tyrant.'[5]

'Cato, drawing the sword, which he had kept unstained from all bloodshed against the final day – he cried: "Fortune, you have accomplished nothing by resisting all my endeavours. I have fought, till now, for my *country's freedom, and not for my own, I did not strive so doggedly to be free, but only to live among the free. Now, since the affairs of mankind are beyond hope, let Cato be withdrawn to safety." So saying, he inflicted a mortal wound upon his body. After the physicians had bound it up, Cato had less blood and less strength, but no less courage; angered now not only at Caesar but also at himself, he rallied his unarmed hands against his wound, and expelled, rather than dismissed, that noble soul which had been so defiant of all worldly power.'[6]*

Even amongst our few surviving sources, every subsequent retelling of the tale becomes longer, with more details added.[7] Yet we must ask ourselves why he chose this way rather than retreat with Scipio and live to fight another day, as the vast majority of the Pompeian commanders did (or tried to do)? The clear indication is that there was a key split between the Pompeian faction in the immediate aftermath of Thapsus which took place at Utica.

As the subsequent list of Senators who stayed at Utica and sought Caesar's pardon showed, (below) a considerable number had clearly chosen not to continue the fight and to give up and these are most likely to have been the 'anti-Caesarian' faction, who after seeing two major defeats (Pharsalus and Thapsus) had come to the conclusion that Caesar could not be beaten in battle but must be restrained politically. Thus, Utica proved to be the shattering of the grand political alliance that Pompeius had forged. The Pompeians fled for Spain, the anti-Caesarians gave up and the Numidians tried to regroup and fight on.

We will never know the details of the discussions that took place between the various groupings within the Pompeian faction at Utica. It is clear, however, that something significant took place that evening, with Scipio and his adherents taking ship whilst Cato and the others stayed. Thus, Cato could have chosen to take ship and fight on, but clearly wanted to make a grand gesture, which both his friends and enemies ensured would live on. Appian makes it clear that the others had already set sail and that Cato committed suicide on the final evening before Caesar, or at least his advance guard, was due to arrive.[8]

In many ways his death reflected his life, with a failure to fight on and defend the ideals he later came to epitomise. Since his failure to defend Sicily in 49 BC,[9] he had been kept away from any serious fighting by the

Pompeians, commanding first the city of Dyrrhachium and then Utica, being kept on for his political presence and the 'star quality' of his name value, or that of his famous ancestor (M. Porcius Cato 'the Elder'), who had come to epitomise Republican values (whether he actually exhibited them or not in his lifetime). In all honesty none of the subsequent Porciii had come close to living up to the legend of Cato the Elder and that night, having also failed in his political career, Cato the Younger clearly felt that his death might accomplish what his life had not. In that respect, he was spectacularly correct and 2,000 years later, this act is still discussed.

Within the year, Cicero had released a treatise on Cato, as a Republican martyr and hero, though the work is now lost, but its impact forced Caesar himself to produce a counter treatise which he named the Anti-Cato.[10] Thereafter the two men, who once shared similar political aims (see Chapter One), became forever intertwined:

> 'Caesar also hearing of the death of Cato, was heard to say, that he envied Cato's glory, as Cato had envied his; and he gave Cato's estate safe and whole to his children. And certainly it would have been no small part of Caesar's divine achievements, to have caused the safety of Cato.'[11]

In practical terms, however, it made no difference whatsoever and at the approach of the Caesarian advance guard under Valerius Messalla Rufus, the remaining members of the anti-Caesarian faction surrendered Utica and threw themselves on Caesar's mercy, led by none other than L. Iulius Caesar, son of Caesar's cousin and Cato's Quaestor:

> 'After Cato's suicide L. [Iulius] Caesar, intending to turn this incident somehow to his personal advantage, delivered a speech to the assembled people in which he urged them all to open their gates, saying that he set great store by C. [Iulius] Caesar's clemency. Accordingly, the gates were thrown open and he came out from Utica and set forth to meet Caesar. Messalla arrived at Utica in accordance with his instructions and posted guards at all the gates.'[12]

It was not only at Utica where Senatorial resistance to Caesar collapsed; the cities of Usseta and Hadrumetum also surrendered without a fight:

Caesar meanwhile advanced from Thapsus and arrived at Usseta,
where Scipio had kept a large quantity of stores including, amongst
other things, corn, arms and weapons: there was almost the same small
garrison force. Of this arsenal he gained possession on his arrival, and
then came to Hadrumetum. Entering this town without opposition,
he made an inventory of the arms, corn, and money in it, and spared
the lives of Q. Ligarius and C. Considius the son, both of whom were
present at that time. Then, quitting Hadrumetum the same day and
leaving [L.] Livineius Regulus behind there with a legion he hastened
on to Utica.'[13]

Thus, with Caesar victorious at Thapsus, Metellus Scipio fled for Spain, and
a Caesarian fleet off shore, it seems that the other Pompeian commanders
chose to settle with Caesar rather than continue to fight in North Africa.
After all, they could always change sides back to the Pompeian cause after
they had gotten clear of Africa. With a warm welcome guaranteed at Utica,
Caesar made his way to the former Pompeian capital of Roman North
Africa, which his armies had failed to capture in 49 BC (see Chapter Two)
and now received its submission along with the surrender of a number of
Roman Senators. Naturally the *De Bello Africo* presents a list of those who
received Caesar's 'mercy':

'On the way he was met by L. Caesar, who threw himself at his feet and
prayed him for one boon, for one alone, to spare him his life. Caesar readily
granted him this boon; an act which accorded both with his natural
temperament and principles; and in the same way he followed the normal
procedure in sparing the lives of Caecina, C. Ateius, P. Atrius, L. Cella
(both father and son), M. Eppius, M. Aquinus, as well as Cato's son and
the children of Damasippus.'[14]

As can be seen, however, none of these figures could be called senior
Pompeian commanders, more the minnows who had chosen to end
their fight now and save their lives and perhaps live to fight another day.
The most notorious example of this was Cato's son (M. Porcius Cato)
who, though pardoned, joined his brother-in-law in the conspiracy that
led to Caesar's assassination in 44 BC. The Caesarians also captured the
family of Faustus Sulla who had been left behind in the relative safety of

Utica, including his wife (Pompeius' daughter, Pompeia) and his children (Pompeius' grandchildren), who were given safe conduct to Spain.[15]

Thus Caesar had Utica, but neither Metellus nor Cato, both of whom had eluded him in their own ways. However, with the capture of Utica, Caesar now had the majority of the Roman province of North Africa under his control. All that remained was to pick off the remaining Pompeian garrisons, in particular, Thysdra, commanded by the implacable anti-Caesarian C. Considius Longus, and Thapsus itself. As detailed in the *De Bello Africo*, both fell without the need for further fighting as the collapse of Pompeian morale continued:

> '*Considius, who was in command at Thysdra and was accompanied by his household slaves, a bodyguard of gladiators and some Gaetulians, learned of the massacre of his comrades; and being seriously perturbed by the arrival of* [Cn.] *Domitius* [Calvinus] *and his legions, and despairing of saving his life, he abandoned the town, made a secret withdrawal with a handful of his foreign troops and a large sum of money, and beat a hasty retreat to Juba's kingdom. But while he was on the road the Gaetulians who bore him company cut him down in their impatience to loot his treasure, and then made off, as best they could, in various directions.*
>
> *Meanwhile C. Vergilius, who was cut off alike by land and sea, perceived that he was making no progress: that M. Cato had taken his own life at Utica: that the king was a wanderer at large, abandoned by his subjects and held in universal contempt: that Saburra and his troops had been destroyed by Sittius: that Caesar had been received without opposition at Utica; and that out of all that vast army there was nothing left whatever. For his own part, therefore, he accepted the safeguard for himself, and his children offered him by the Proconsul Caninius, who was blockading him, and surrendered himself to the latter with all his effects and the town.*'[16]

Thus, as in 48 BC, the Caesarian forces had overrun the Pompeian territory with no further fighting, with the remaining Pompeians retreating or surrendering. Roman North Africa was now re-joined to the Caesarian Republic and denied to the Pompeians as a power base. Caesar's attention could now be turned to his other North African opponent, King Juba I and the Kingdom of Numidia.

The Collapse of the Numidian Kingdom

Fortunately for Caesar, there was little that he was actually required to do on this front. At some point recently (the exact timings are unclear), the Numidian army of Juba's commander, Saburra, was defeated and routed in an unnamed battle by the Maurian army of P. Sittius. Thus Numidia had a Maurian army marching eastwards, a Gaetulian revolt in the south and now faced a hostile Roman army in the west. Juba's remaining Roman allies had either fled for Spain or had reached an accommodation with Caesar.

That being the case it is hardly surprising that Juba found a frosty reception from his subjects when he retreated in the aftermath of Thapsus. He and the Pompeian commander M. Petreius made for the city of Zama,[17] which he had fortified as a western capital, complete with his treasury and his family. Unfortunately for him, news of both Thapsus and the Maurian victory had reached Zama and the citizens closed their gates and barred his entrance, having no wish to be the target of a Roman attack. Furthermore they sent envoys to Caesar telling him where Juba was and that they would not support him but await Caesar's arrival. Having been thoroughly betrayed by his subjects, Juba and Petreius set off from Zama with a small force of cavalry for a nearby country retreat.

Caesar naturally seized on the news and left Utica the next day to chase Juba down. Furthermore, as he passed through Numidian territory, he let it be known that his famous clemency was available to Numidians as well as Romans, upon which any possible Numidian resistance evaporated:

'He [Caesar] *himself left Utica the following day with his cavalry and proceeded with despatch into the royal territory. Meanwhile in the course of his march there came to Caesar several leaders of the royal forces, who begged him to forgive them. To these suppliants he granted pardon, and then came to Zama. Meanwhile the tidings of his leniency and clemency had spread abroad, with the result that practically all the horsemen in the kingdom came to Caesar at Zama; and there they were set free by him from their fears and the danger which involved them.'*[18]

Thus, Numidia collapsed into Caesar's control, without a shot being fired. The end for Juba and Petreius soon followed. Perceiving that Caesar's cavalry were closing them down and with no obvious route of escape, the two men realized that they only had two options; surrender or death, and both chose the latter.

> 'Meanwhile king Juba, outlawed by all his townships, despaired of saving his life. And so finally, after dining with Petreius, he fought a duel with him with swords, so as to create the impression that both had met a gallant death; and the sword of the stronger man, Juba, easily put an end to Petreius, his weaker adversary. Juba then endeavoured to run himself through the chest with his sword; but not being able to do it, he successfully entreated a slave of his to kill him, and so achieved his purpose.'[19]

Thus, Juba, king of the strongest of the African kingdoms met his fate and the kingdom which had been created by the Romans under Scipio Africanus, was extinguished by the Romans, under Caesar. With it, Caesar now had control of the whole of North Africa. Wasting little time, Caesar abolished the Numidian monarchy and Numidian independence, declaring it a Roman province and left none other than C. Sallustius Crispus (the future historian) as Proconsul. This would not be the last time that civil war campaigns were fought in Africa as the provinces were again caught up in the subsequent civil war campaigns of 44–40 BC. The campaign of 44 BC even saw a Pompeian-sponsored Numidian claimant (Arabio) return and regain Numidia's independence (albeit temporarily, until 40 BC), murdering P. Sittius along the way, another Caesarian conquest which quickly unravelled.

Caesar's Economic Victory

As well as scoring military victories, Caesar translated this success on the battlefield into cold hard cash. Upon taking Utica, as well as finding a number of Pompeian Senators had stayed behind, he also found a group of men referred to as the Three Hundred (see Chapter Three). These men were the merchants and money men who had provided financial support to the Pompeian faction in North Africa and thus formed the economic core at the heart of their opposition. Again it is not known whether they chose to stay behind or were left by Metellus, but the loss of such an influential group of moneymen was another blow to the Pompeian cause. Furthermore Caesar had no wish to let this opportunity go unexploited:

> '*however, for the Roman citizens who were engaged in trade and those members of the Three Hundred who had contributed sums of money to Varus and Scipio, he brought a very detailed accusation against them and dilated at some length upon their crimes, but finally announced that they could come out into the open without fear: their lives at any rate he would spare: their property indeed he would sell, yet on the following condition, that if any man among them personally brought in his own property, he himself would duly register the sale of the property and enter up the money paid under the heading of a fine, so as to enable the man in question to enjoy full security thereafter.*
>
> *For these men, pale with fear and, considering their fate, with little hope of saving their lives, here was an unexpected offer of salvation. Gladly and eagerly they accepted the terms and besought Caesar to fix a lump sum of money to be paid by the entire Three Hundred as a whole. Accordingly, he required them to pay to the Roman People the sum of two hundred million sesterces in six instalments spread over three years; and this they accepted gladly and without a single murmur, expressing their gratitude to Caesar and declaring that this day finally marked for them the start of a new life.*'[20]

Thus Caesar ransomed their lives for a spectacular sum of money (200,000,000 sesterces), not only covering the costs of his campaign, but giving him a handsome profit with which to discharge his army, reward his supporters and fund the rebuilding of his new Caesarian Republic. Furthermore, he was now guaranteed an income for the next three years (if he lived that long). Interestingly, this outcome is starkly contradicted in the later account of Appian: '*Of the 300 he put to death all that he found.*'[21]

As we can see this was done under the banner of fines against those who had taken up arms against the Roman People, rather than sequestering the assets of the defeated. Again this showed a level of political subtlety that had eluded Sulla in the same position forty years earlier when he simply had his opponents and their supporters murdered (proscribed) and stole their estates. On the one hand it may have bolstered his efforts not to look like a tyrant, but on the other it let 300 key men leave Africa, many of whom would have harboured a grudge at the cost of their freedom. Yet this was only the first of such cash injections as he now had the whole Kingdom of Numidia and its riches to exploit.

> 'Meanwhile at Zama Caesar held an auction of the royal property and sold the goods of those who, albeit Roman citizens, had borne arms against the Roman People.'[22]

Leaving Zama in the hands of Sallustius, Caesar returned to Utica and continued the disposal of Numidian assets:

> 'There he sold the property of those who had held military commands under Juba and Petreius and exacted the following payments under the title of fines: from the men of Thapsus, two million sesterces; from their corporation, three million; likewise from the men of Hadrumetum, three million; and from their corporation, five million. But he protected their cities and property from all injury and looting.'[23]

Thus in short order Caesar seized an additional 13,000,000 sesterces in immediate cash, on top of the 200,000,000 that the Roman businessmen were to pay him. Furthermore, those cities who had opposed him that had no ready cash were made to contribute in other economic terms:

> 'As for the inhabitants of Leptis, whose property had been plundered in former years by Juba but had been restored to them after the Senate had appointed arbitrators on receiving a deputation of theirs lodging a formal complaint, Caesar now required them to pay by way of fine three million pounds weight of oil annually, because at the beginning of the war in the course of disagreements among their leaders they had entered into an alliance with Juba, and had assisted him with arms, troops and money. The men of Thysdra, not a well to do community, were fined a certain quantity of corn.'[24]

Thus we can see the economic benefits that Caesar gained from his capture of North Africa and a number of key Pompeian supporters. Equally we can see that the riches of North Africa, which funded the Pompeian resurgence were now denied to the survivors as was the funding of the

'Three Hundred', as long as they kept their word when they reached the safety of Italy.

The Failed Retreat of the Pompeian Faction

Yet, for the Pompeians, there was still considerable scope for things to get worse, and they did. As we have seen, in the aftermath of the Battle of Pharsalus, the key leaders of the Pompeian faction were able to escape both the battle and any subsequent retaliation, due to their control of Greece and more importantly the surrounding seas, facilitating their escape to North Africa.[25] Initially it seemed that the same would occur in the aftermath of Thapsus, with Sulla and Afranius escaping overland and Metellus by sea, both parties aiming to reach Spain. On this occasion, however, Pompeian control of both the land and the sea was contested.

Western Numidia – Unnamed Battle

As we have seen, both Faustus Sulla and Afranius had chosen to leave Utica in the command of a large force of Romano-Numidian cavalry. Rather than take their chances upon the seas, which were contested, they seemed to have calculated that it would be safer to take the longer land route to Spain (across North Africa and then attempt to take the short crossing over the Straits). On the one hand this cavalry force could move quickly and outpace any Caesarian pursuit, but on the other, however, they would need to cross not only (the now) neutral Numidia, but the hostile Maurian territory. However, they presumably saw this as a calculated risk and felt secure with an army of several thousand Romano-Numidian cavalry.

Unfortunately for them, however, blocking their path to freedom was the Maurian army of P. Sittius and a force of several thousand Romani-Numidian cavalry was bound to attract attention:

'[Sittius] *was marching with a small force through Numidia to join Caesar when he happened to fall in with Faustus and Afranius, who were in command of the party, some thousand strong, with which they had plundered Utica and were now making tracks for Spain. And so he promptly laid an ambush by night and attacked them at dawn. A few of the cavalry in their vanguard escaped; but all the rest were either killed or else they surrendered, and Sittius captured alive Afranius as well as Faustus with his wife and children. A few days later some disagreement arose in the army and Faustus and Afranius were killed. As for Pompeia and the children of Faustus, Caesar spared their lives and allowed them to retain all their property.'*[26]

By the time of the later sources, this account had evolved, and it was Caesar himself who ordered the death of Sulla and Afranius, as can be seen in Dio:

'So these were spared; but Afranius and Faustus would not come to him of their own free will, feeling sure of being put to death, but fled to Mauretania, where they were captured by Sittius. Caesar put them to death, as captives, without a trial.'[27]

Thus two important Pompeian leaders were defeated, captured, and then executed. Afranius had been a long time deputy to Pompeius, an ex-Consul of more seniority than Caesar himself and had fought Caesar in three separate campaigns (Spain in 49 BC, Greece in 48 BC and Africa in 46 BC). Sulla was the only surviving son and heir to the former ruler of Rome, L. Cornelius Sulla (the man who had spared Caesar's life) and though only young, was heir to a powerful family patronage (both political and military) not to mention being Pompeius' son-in-law. Thus two key Pompeian leaders were cut down and removed from the equation.

The Battle of Hippo Regius

Worse was to come for the Pompeian faction when the small fleet that had evacuated from Utica ran into a storm off the African coast which drove them into the path of a fleet of Maurian ships, with a short but decisive battle following:

'Meanwhile Scipio, Damasippus, Torquatus and Plaetorius Rustianus were making for Spain aboard some warships; and after a long and very stormy passage they were carried towards Royal Hippo, where P. Sittius had his fleet at that time. Outnumbered as they were by the latter, Scipio's vessels were surrounded and sunk; and Scipio and those I have just named perished aboard them.'[28]

It is interesting that the *De Bello Africo* makes no mention of how Scipio died, in stark contrast to the death of Cato. We only find out from later sources that Scipio too apparently choose suicide over surrender:

> '*Lucius Scipio, the general-in-chief was overtaken by a storm and met a hostile fleet and bore himself bravely until he was overpowered, when he stabbed himself and leaped into the sea.*'[29]
>
> '*Scipio, who had fled from the battle, chanced upon a ship, and set sail for Spain to go to Pompeius. But he was cast ashore in Mauri, and through fear of Sittius made away with himself.*'[30]

Thus, the leader of the Pompeian faction, Pompeius' father-in-law, scion of Rome's two greatest Republican families and the man who was able to oversee the recovery of the Pompeian faction and put an army of over 100,000 troops in the field took his own life on the high seas. Interestingly, despite his own political ancestry and career being greater than that of Cato, today there is none of the *mythos* that has grown up around the suicide of Cato, despite the similarity of both men's demise.

If anything, Metellus chose to continue to fight and fought one last battle before taking his own life. This is due to the fact that Metellus' political career had none of the 'air of noble failure' that surrounded Cato, whose many failings (both political and military) could be ascribed to political integrity, rather than lack of talent. Cato became idealised and his many dubious political manoeuvrings were glossed over, whilst those of Metellus were highlighted, even though both men ended up on the same side.

However, this was not always the case, and by the time of the early Roman Empire, Metellus' actions and reputation were being reconsidered in light of his ending, as can be seen from the following selection of imperial writers and thinkers, including Seneca, with Metellus even being given a pithy last few words:

> '*The same resolution was used by Scipio, who having unsuccessfully defended the cause of Pompeius his son-in-law in Africa, endeavoured to escape into Spain. Understanding that the ship wherein he was sailing was about to be taken by the enemy, he ran himself through; and calling out upon the deck, when Caesar's soldiers asked where the commander*

was, he made answer, "The commander is well", having power only to speak so much as to testify, to his eternal praise, the greatness of his mind.'[31]

'*Certain persons, who were craven in other respects, have equalled in this regard the courage of the bravest. Take, for example, Scipio, the father in law of Cnaeus Pompeius: he was driven back upon the African coast by a headwind and saw his ship in the power of the enemy. He therefore pierced his body with a sword; and when they asked where the commander was, he replied: "All is well with the commander."*

These words brought him up to the level of his ancestors and suffered not the glory which fate gave to the Scipios in Africa to lose its continuity. It was a great deed to conquer Carthage, but a greater deed to conquer death. "All is well with the commander!" Ought a general to die otherwise, especially one of Cato's generals?'[32]

'*Publius Scipio was captured on his ship and added to his honourable death honourable last words.'*[33]

Thus we can see that from the curt dismissal of the *De Bello Africo*, as the Republic faded into the Empire, Metellus' reputation was being reconsidered and found him being added to the pantheon of Republican heroes, an attitude that (unlike Cato) has not lasted to today.[34]

If anything, Metellus' background and success and the way he achieved it (being at the heart of Republican political violence and double dealing) made him a far more ideal candidate for representing the Roman Republic than Cato. It could be argued that both were two sides of the same coin and Cato was the ideal for how people then (and now) wanted to see the Republic, whilst Metellus Scipio was the reality. In any event both men died for the Pompeian cause and could play no further action in the civil wars.

The Survivors

Despite these setbacks, however, several of the key Pompeian leaders were able to escape Africa, the most notable being P. Attius Varus, one of the ruling Pompeian Triumvirate, Caesar's former deputy and long term opponent, T. Labienus, and Pompeius' youngest son, Sextus. Naturally successful escapes make for far less dramatic accounts than unsuccessful ones and there is only one explicit reference to how these men successfully fled Africa:

> '*Then there were those who came to him from Africa, among others his brother Sextus, and Varus, and Labienus with his fleet.*'[35]

Thus there was at least one other Pompeian fleet that avoided the Caesarians and carried a number of key figures to safety. It is a considerable shame that no other details survive amongst our few ancient sources, as the details of the escape of T. Labienus would be of great interest. We had seen that Varus had spent the African campaigns commanding a Pompeian fleet, which seemed to be a speciality of his. Likewise naval operations seem to have been the forte of Sex. Pompeius and whilst we hear nothing of him during these African campaigns, given he was last seen commanding a Pompeian fleet in 48 BC, we can equally imagine he was also a naval commander at the time.

Thus, naval commanders receiving the news of the result of the battle at Thapsus and being able to set off immediately for Spain (see Chapter Nine) does not strike us as surprising. However, T. Labienus is a different matter, as he is the only senior Pompeian commander whom we know to have been present during the fighting with Caesar who survived. It is interesting that the presumption is that Labienus was present at Thapsus, but there is actually no record of him being there. Despite the fact he and Caesar were fighting throughout the three months of the African campaign, the *De Bello Africo* stops mentioning him just before the move to Thapsus.[36] Added to this is Appian's curious statement that:

> '*The elder son of Pompeius, together with Labienus and Scapula, each with his own part of the army, hastened to Spain.*'[37]

This has long been considered an error on the part of Appian, as Labienus clearly didn't leave with Pompeius in January, but was still in Africa in April 46 BC. Yet, given the omissions of the *De Bello Africo* for the Battle of Thapsus itself and the relative ease of Labienus' escape, it does raise the question of whether Labienus was actually present at the Battle of Thapsus itself or had been given other duties, making his escape separately from Metellus the more likely.

If this was the case, then why would Metellus not have present his b commander, and the only man who had successfully matched tactics Caesar on several occasions? Furthermore did this omission affe

Pompeian tactics and their fighting ability and thus the outcome? Whilst this is all speculation, it is an interesting point to consider. Nevertheless, Labienus, the best field commander the Pompeians had, survived the aftermath of Thapsus, where so many of his colleagues did not, and lived to fight another day.

Summary

Thus we can see that despite neither killing nor capturing any of the key Pompeian leaders in his victory at Thapsus, the days afterward saw the deaths of the majority of them, but, interestingly, none at the hands of Caesar himself. Of those leaders only two senior men survived: T. Labienus and P. Attius Varus. Three of the four key Pompeian leaders (see Chapter Three) Metellus Scipio, Cato and Juba had all fallen, leaving only Varus. However, as Varus' powerbase was the backing of the Numidian Kingdom and his alliance with Juba, he was now rendered powerless.

Outside of the ruling Triumvirate, key Pompeian generals, such as Afranius and Petreius had been killed as well as Pompeius' son-in-law, Faustus Sulla. Thus the leadership of the Pompeian faction was drastically culled, and Caesar had clearly enhanced his victory. Two factors soured this, however. The first was the nature of these men's deaths; four suicides (Metellus Scipio, Cato, Petreius and Juba) and two murders at the hands of a mercenary after surrendering (Sulla and Afranius). Thus the key Pompeian leaders gave their supporters the ammunition to turn them into Republican martyrs presenting a challenge to Caesar from the grave; more deaths attributable to his lust for power (as it was portrayed). Furthermore none of the key leaders surrendered, showing that they would not accommodate themselves to Caesar's rule, another example for other members of the oligarchy to follow.

Secondly, however, although none of the surviving two Pompeian leaders in Africa had the status to revive the Pompeian faction, one being a minor official, the other being a former Caesarian general, the problem that Caesar was to face centred on the Pompeian leader who wasn't in \frica, namely the eldest son (and heir) of Pompeius himself (Cnaeus) o by Caesar's actions, now found himself de facto leader of the faction honour bound to avenge his father's death and fight for his cause.

Section V

From the Ashes:
The Continuation of the Civil War

From the Ashes: The Rise of Pompeius Magnus and the Continuation of the Civil War

Caesar Triumphant?

With matters settled in North Africa, both military and economic, Caesar then set his sights on returning to Rome and ensuring that this success was converted into a political settlement, having only briefly been at Rome (for roughly three months) since the beginning of 48 BC. Given that he had only been in Rome for a few months in 49 BC, Caesar had only spent roughly six months in Rome in the last thirteen years, perhaps showing his disdain for the daily political life. The *De Bello Africo* finishes with Caesar's return to Rome and provides us with the dates, along with further evidence of his campaign for further economic gain:

> 'After making these arrangements he went aboard his fleet at Utica on June 13th and arrived two days later at Caralis in Sardinia. There he fined the men of Sulci one hundred thousand sesterces for having harboured [L.] Nasidius and his fleet and assisted him by supplying troops and directed that they should pay as tax one-eighth of their produce instead of one-tenth. He also sold up the property of a few individuals. Then he embarked on June 27th, and leaving Caralis, sailed along the coast. Twenty-seven days later, for bad weather kept holding him up in the various ports, he arrived at the city of Rome.'[1]

Though still not the total master of Rome (see below for Spain and Syria), Caesar had now defeated the Pompeians in two major battles (Pharsalus and Thapsus), destroying two Pompeian armies and seeing the deaths of both leading Pompeian commanders. This military victory had been cemented by undermining the political and economic powerbase of the

Pompeian faction by the pardoning (at a cost) of scores of politicians and businessmen who had previously supported the Pompeian cause.

Yet by doing so, he had allowed scores of his former opponents to return to Rome and Italy. The key to any future political settlement would be to ensure their active, or at least passive, support, once the threat hanging over their lives had been removed and they were back in the comfortable surroundings of Rome. Furthermore, he had still not settled the civil war, which raged once more in both Spain and Syria (see below) clearly diminishing his victories.

In addition to his living enemies in both the Western and Eastern Republic, he had to contend with his dead enemies, having not reconciled any of his key opponents to the Caesarian regime and having to contend with at least three opponents whose impact could not now be countered with military force: Pompeius, 'treacherously' slain by 'perfidious foreigners', and Metellus Scipio and Cato, both choosing to die by their own hand rather than live under Caesarian rule. Finally, there were the murderous legacies of both his uncle (Marius) and the other civil war victor, Sulla, to contend with, who had cemented their rule over Rome with bloodshed.

Thus Caesar had his military victories, the key question he faced was how to use them? In the first instance, he fell back on the tried and tested technique of 'bread and circuses' and advertised his military prowess by throwing the greatest Triumphal celebrations Rome had seen, celebrating Four Triumphs. The first was for his Gallic conquests, which he had not had a chance to have recognized until now, the others were for his victories in Egypt (Ptolemaic Civil War), Asia (Romano-Pontic War) and Africa (Numidia). The latter needed the most political dexterity as he could not officially celebrate a Triumph over civil war opponents but did so over the Numidian King Juba.[2] As Appian points out, however, this last Triumph fooled nobody, especially when Caesar apparently showed images of Metellus and Cato:

'Although he took care not to inscribe any Roman names in his Triumph (as it would have been unseemly in his eyes and base and inauspicious in those of the Roman People to triumph over fellow-citizens), yet all these misfortunes were represented in the processions and the men also by various images and pictures, all except Pompeius, whom alone he did not

венture to exhibit, since he was still greatly regretted by all. The People,
although restrained by fear, groaned over their domestic ills, especially
when they saw the picture of Lucius Scipio, the general-in-chief, wounded
in the breast by his own hand, casting himself into the sea, and Petreius
committing self-destruction at the banquet, and Cato torn apart by
himself like a wild beast.'[3]

As well as the public demonstrations of his military prowess, he supported
this with more tangible (and monetary) benefits for his soldiers and
the People:

'It is said that money to the amount of 60,500 silver talents was borne
in the procession and 2,822 crowns of gold weighing 20,414 pounds,
from which wealth Caesar made apportionments immediately after the
Triumph, paying the army all that he had promised and more. Each
soldier received 5,000 Attic drachmas, each Centurion double, and each
Tribune of Infantry and Prefect of Cavalry fourfold that sum. To each
plebeian citizen also was given an Attic mina.

He gave also various spectacles with horses and music, a combat of foot-
soldiers, 1,000 on each side, and a cavalry fight of 200 on each side. There
was also another combat of horse and foot together. There was a combat
of elephants.'[4]

Thus Caesar paid off the army and the People, elements which at first
seemed the easiest to buy off, yet the People were notoriously fickle and
would support whoever was in favour at the moment and Dio raises
further suspicions about the army:

'Immediately after these events before he crossed into Italy Caesar got rid of
the older men among his soldiers for fear that they might mutiny again.'[5]

As we will see below, despite his victories the civil war continued, and
Caesar's armies would be called on for further campaigns. Nevertheless,
with the army and the People satiated, Caesar turned his immediate
attention to his political position. As can be seen from the below
extract of Dio, the Senate fell over themselves in a superficial display
of obsequiousness.

'*For they* [the Senate] *had voted that sacrifices should be offered for his victory for forty days, and had granted him permission to ride, in the Triumph already voted him, in a chariot drawn by white horses and to be accompanied by all the Lictors who were then with him, and by as many others as he had employed in his first Dictatorship, together with as many more as he had in his second.*

Furthermore, they elected him overseer of every man's conduct (for some such name was given him, as if the title of Censor were not worthy of him) for three years, and Dictator for ten in succession.

They moreover voted that he should sit in the Senate upon the curule chair with the successive Consuls, and should always state his opinion first, that he should give the signal at all the games in the Circus, and that he should have the appointment of the magistrates and whatever honours the People were previously accustomed to assign.

And they decreed that a chariot of his should be placed on the Capitol facing the statue of Jupiter, that his statue in bronze should be mounted upon a likeness of the inhabited world, with an inscription to the effect that he was a demigod, and that his name should be inscribed upon the Capitol in place of that of Catulus on the ground that he had completed this temple after undertaking to call Catulus to account for the building of it.

These are the only measures I have recorded, not because they were the only ones voted, for a great many measures were proposed and of course passed, but because he declined the rest, whereas he accepted these.'[6]

Thus, on the face of it, Caesar had been granted everything he wished for by the Senate, a third annual Dictatorship, with the prospect of another nine to come, along with the powers of a Censor, making him the most powerful Roman since Sulla. Yet Dio goes on to say that Caesar himself bore no illusions about the depth of his support in the Senate:

'*When these decrees had now been passed, he entered Rome, and perceiving that the People were afraid of his power and suspicious of his proud bearing and consequently expected to suffer many terrible evils such as had taken place before, and realizing that it was on this account that they had voted him extravagant honours, through flattery and not through goodwill.*'[7]

This encapsulates the heart of Caesar's problem, victory on the battlefield did not give him a lasting control of the Republic; he was Princeps, not by choice but by default. Furthermore, the Senate was actually less under his control every year. In 49 BC, they were just the rump of his supporters and some neutrals. However, paradoxically, following his victories in 48 BC and now 46 BC, the Senate was filling back up with his former enemies, pardoned by himself in the (vain) hope that they would support him. As Dio points out:

> '*but when he* [Caesar] *induced some of the Tribunes to restore many of those who had been exiled after due trial, and allowed those who had been convicted of bribery in canvassing for office to live in Italy, and furthermore enrolled once more in the Senate some who were unworthy of it, many murmurings of all sorts arose against him.*'[8]

Furthermore, the less time Caesar spent in Rome, the more power the Senate could wield in his absence and the more it would chafe when he was back in Rome and visibly superior to them. Thus the more extravagant honours they bestowed on him, the more it actually worked against him (as many would have hoped for) and the more Caesar stood out not as a Dictator in an emergency, but as a 'tyrant'.

Again Caesar's approach was more practical than tactical. The Dictatorship gave him the power he needed to command Rome's armies and not have to worry about the niceties of ruling by consent and indulging in the Machiavellian world of Republican politics, which as his political career had shown, he was not very adept at anyway. Thus Caesar's grip on the Republic was only wafer thin at best, in an almost inverse ratio to the scale of his victories.

Again this stands in opposition to the plan of his old rival Pompeius, who had planned to rule by 'consent' having 'saved the Republic' from Caesar. By contrast Caesar had clearly seized the Republic and now ruled only by dint of having won on the battlefield. With the ghost of Pompeius now stood the ghosts of Metellus Scipio and Cato. As Cicero's work on Cato (and Caesar's response) showed, Caesar was being held up and judged against his defeated enemies and found wanting, at least amongst the Senatorial oligarchy. Whilst Caesar could temporarily overawe these oligarchs into acquiescence, he lacked a longer term solution.

The error of repeated Dictatorships was compounded in late 46 bc, when Caesar failed to hold the curule elections for the Roman magistrates for the following year, aside from appointing himself sole Consul (as well as Dictator).

> 'Caesar was at that time Dictator, and at length, near the close of the year, he was appointed Consul, after Lepidus, who was Master of the Horse, had convoked the People for this purpose; for Lepidus had become Master of the Horse at that time also, having given himself, while still in the Consulship, that additional title contrary to precedent.'[9]

Thus, Caesar, despite having celebrated four Triumphs to show off his victories, then claimed he needed to be sole Consul and Dictator[10] due to the emergency in Spain and then refused to hold elections for magistrates to run the city and empire as normal. As he then left for Spain shortly afterwards (see below), this left Lepidus in charge of Rome.

This again was sloppy and unnecessarily provocative political practice, showing a tendency towards sole rule and then advertising the fact that he had scorn for the Republican constitution, not only alienating his enemies, but his allies as well. This lack of political touch was further compounded by the arrival of Pharaoh Cleopatra VII, Caesar's lover and her and Caesar's illegitimate (in Roman law) son, Caesarion (Ptolemy XV).

> 'But he [Caesar] incurred the greatest censure from all because of his passion for Cleopatra, not now the passion he had displayed in Egypt (for that was a matter of hearsay), but that which was displayed in Rome itself. For she had come to the city with her husband and settled in Caesar's own house, so that he too derived an ill repute on account of both of them.'[11]

Thus, to add to his acting like the sole ruler of Rome and ignoring the Roman constitution, he now publicly acknowledged his lover, an Egyptian Pharaoh, and their son, also an Egyptian Pharaoh, all of which would add to the poor image the Republican oligarchy had of him. Yet Caesar was seemingly blind to how all this looked and obviously ignored the advice that his supporters would have been giving him. Leaving Lepidus behind to run (and rule) Rome, he set off for Spain in November of 46 bc on his fourth civil war campaign.

The Continuation of the Civil War – the Ghost of Pompeius

This temporary control of the Republic can best be seen by the fact that, despite another major victory on the battlefield, his opponents (though obviously diminished) were not totally defeated and immediately challenged his control of the both the Western and Eastern Republic.

The Assassination of Lucius Iulius Caesar

The first challenge we can see was a minor one in the grand scheme of things, but one with some interesting implications. We have references to the assassination of a Caesar, none other than L. Iulius Caesar, a second cousin of Caesar himself. As we have seen he had been a staunch Pompeian supporter and was with Cato at the end, but became the spokesman for the Senatorial faction in Utica who wished to make peace with Caesar, after which Caesar pardoned him. Yet soon afterwards (possibly in May 46 BC) Caesar was murdered in unknown circumstances. We have two clear references to it and one possible:

> 'but in the case of Lucius Caesar, though the man was related to him and came as a voluntary suppliant, nevertheless, since he had fought against him throughout, he at first bade him stand trial, so that he might seem to have condemned him with some show of legality, and then, as he shrank from putting him to death by his own vote, he postponed the trial for the time being, but afterward killed him secretly.'[12]
>
> 'And it will be found that no Pompeian lost his life except in battle, save only Afranius and Faustus, and the young Lucius Caesar; and it is believed that not even these men were slain by his wish.'[13]
>
> 'For when I heard about L. Caesar the younger, I said to myself: "What will he do for me, his sire?"'[14]

Thus the clearest accusation comes from Dio, who is obviously repeating a charge laid by previous historians, and which was probably circulating at the time, that Caesar ordered the discreet murder of his cousin. Yet such an act was bound to backfire on him politically and Lucius was only ever a minor figure in the Pompeian faction and Caesar could make great use of him, as pardoning one of his own family would grant him significant political capital.

Other than these details we know nothing of the circumstances of his death nor do we even have confirmation that it was in Africa, though that is the presumption. If it was not on Caesar's orders, then there are two possibilities. The first, raised by Suetonius, is that it was Caesarian soldiers, settling scores. The second is that it was by vengeful Pompeians, angered by his desertion of the Pompeian cause (and implicit betrayal of Cato) and seeking a high profile target (due to his name value) for assassination. Both of these options raise clear questions for Caesarian control over the Republic and actually foreshadow the more famous assassination of a Caesar two years later.

The Assassination of Sex. Iulius Caesar and the Revolt of Syria

L. Iulius Caesar was not the only member of the Caesarian family to lose his life in 46 BC, another cousin, Sex. Iulius Caesar, was also murdered and on this occasion the ramifications were much more serious for the Caesarian control of the Republic. Though acknowledged as a young man, Caesar had placed Sex. Iulius Caesar in charge of the key province of Syria in the previous year, following his victory in the Fourth Romano-Pontic War (see Appendix One). The Roman province of Syria was key to controlling the Eastern Republic (having been the rump of the Seleucid Empire and annexed by Pompeius in 63 BC) for a number of reasons.

Firstly, it was the only actual Roman province in the Middle East, the other regions being client kingdoms, and therefore it had the only legionary force. Secondly, the region had been conquered by Pompeius and not only did it owe loyalty to him, but it also supplied a huge contingent to his 'grand army' of 48 BC, which had been collected and led by none other than Metellus Scipio. Thirdly, the province was the bulwark against the only remaining threat in the Middle East to Roman rule, namely the Parthian Empire, who were expected to use Rome's ongoing civil war as a distraction to invade the Near East and rekindle the stalled First Romano-Parthian War.

Thus, control of Syria was vital for Caesar to anchor his newly won control of the Eastern Republic and its allies and thus had to be granted to a trusted kinsman. Yet during Caesar's African campaign, in the early months of 46 BC, Sex. Iulius Caesar was assassinated, and the province rose up in rebellion and declared for the Pompeians once more. At the centre of this revolt is the figure of a man known only as Caecilius Bassus. Both his full name and background are lost to us, and he remains a shadowy figure in the mould of P. Sittius; a military adventurer who used the chaos of the civil wars to rise to prominence.

Both Appian and Dio have detailed accounts of the revolt and the subsequent civil war (most of which falls outside the scope of this volume), but Appian himself admits that he found contrasting stories about Bassus in the sources he used:

> 'The following events took place in Syria and Macedonia about the same time. Caius Caesar, when he passed through Syria, left a legion there, as he was already contemplating an expedition against the Parthians. Caecilius Bassus had charge of it, but the title of commander was held by Sextus Iulius, a young man related to Caesar himself, who was given over to dissipation and who led the legion around everywhere in an indecorous manner. Once when Bassus reproved him, he replied insultingly, and sometime later, when he called Bassus to him and the latter was slow in obeying, he ordered him to be dragged before him. A tumult and blows ensued. The soldiers would not tolerate the indignity and slew Iulius. This act was followed by repentance and fear of Caesar. Accordingly, they took an oath together that they would defend themselves to the death if they were not pardoned and restored to confidence, and they compelled Bassus to take the same oath. They also enlisted and drilled another legion as associates with themselves.
>
> This is one account of Bassus, but Libo says that he belonged to the army of Pompeius and that after the latter's defeat, he became a private citizen in Tyre, where he corrupted certain members of the legion, who slew Sextus and chose Bassus for their leader.'[15]

The question of the timing of this revolt is an interesting one. The *Periochae* of Livy places it before the Battle of Thapsus, which is seemingly confirmed by Dio's version of the Bassan revolt:

> 'moreover, many alarming reports kept coming in from Africa about Caesar, he [Bassus] was no longer content with the existing state of affairs, but began to stir up a rebellion, his aim being either to help the followers of Scipio and Cato and the Pompeians or to win for himself some

political power. But he was discovered by Sextus before he had finished his preparations and explained that he was collecting these troops for the use of Mithridates the Pergamenian in an expedition against Bosporus; his story was believed, and he was released.

So after this he forged a letter, which he pretended had been sent to him by Scipio, on the basis of which he announced that Caesar had been defeated and had perished in Africa and claimed that the governorship of Syria had been assigned to him. He then seized Tyre with the aid of the forces he had got ready, and from there he advanced against the legions of Sextus but was defeated and wounded while attacking him. After this experience, he did not again make an attempt by force upon Sextus, but sent messages to his soldiers, and in some way or other won some of them to himself to such an extent that they murdered Sextus with their own hands.'[16]

Regardless of his origins, the important point was that Sextus was dead and could be of no future use to Caesar (an intriguing point in itself – see Appendix Three) and Syria had fallen to a rebellion and was now held in the name of the Pompeians. With (initially) only one legion, Bassus clearly did not pose a direct threat to Caesar and his control of the Republic.

Yet, beyond these numbers, the more serious aspect was that this rebellion represented the loss of Syria, Rome's only province in the Middle East and one which had been at the centre of support for the Pompeian cause. Clearly this rebellion could spread throughout the Middle and Near East. Furthermore, Syria was the gateway into the Roman East for the Parthian Empire, who were looking at Rome's perceived weakness for an opportunity to exploit it.

An extract from Strabo below shows that Bassus was already using the revolt to grow support amongst allies in the region, all keen to throw off the Roman yoke:

'and he [Bassus] had plenty of allies, I mean the neighbouring chieftains, who possessed strongholds; among these places was Lysias, which is situated above the lake that lies near Apameia, as also Arethusa, belonging to Sampsiceramus and his son Iamblichus, chieftains of the tribe of the Emeseni; and at no great distance, also, were Heliupolis and Chalcis, which latter was subject to Ptolemaeus the son of Mennaeus, who

possessed Massyas and the mountainous country of the Ituraeans. Among the allies of Bassus was also Alchaedamnus, King of the Rhambaeans, who were nomads this side of the Euphrates River; and he was a friend of the Romans, but upon the belief that he was being treated unjustly by the Roman governors he retired to Mesopotamia and then went into the service of Bassus as a mercenary.[17]

Dio also details his military preparations:

'When Sextus was dead, Bassus gained possession of all his army except a few; for the soldiers who had been wintering in Apamea withdrew into Cilicia before his arrival, and although he pursued them, he did not win them over. Returning then to Syria, he took the title of Praetor and fortified Apamea, so as to have it as a base for the war. And he proceeded to enlist the men of military age, not only freemen but slaves as well, to gather money, and to prepare arms.'[18]

'They recruited another legion, and both were drilled together.'[19]

Thus Bassus was able to use Syria to forge together another Romano-native army, composed of both Roman legionaries and native allies to defend the area and expand the rebellion. In doing so he created another quasi-independent region, with himself ruling as its warlord, though he took the title of Praetor, much as we had seen in the First Civil War with Sertorius in Spain (and to a lesser degree M. Marius in Asia). Though in reality ruling as a warlord, Bassus would have used his letter from Metellus Scipio to legitimatize his rule, acting as Propraetor for the Pompeian Roman government. With Metellus dead there was no one to disprove this and the remaining Pompeians would have been happy to continue this fiction.

We are not told when Caesar was informed of the loss of Syria, most likely only after his victory at Thapsus. This must have come as a blow, not only losing a favoured cousin, but seeing his conquest of the Roman east unravel, in less than year (see Appendix One), and his plans for future campaigns undermined. Clearly Caesar would have preferred to take his African army straight to the east to fight the usurper before he could do any further damage. Yet as we have seen the priority was to return to Rome and cement his military victory into a political one (see above).

With matters in Rome settled, however, clearly Caesar would have been itching to get back in the field, but again he was faced by enemies on two sides, forcing him to prioritise. To the West lay Spain, rapidly collapsing to the forces of the two Pompeian brothers and T. Labienus (see below). To the east lay Syria and Bassus. Though he would have been sorely tempted to go east and recover the Eastern Republic, clearly the greater danger lay to the west, with Spain in revolt, a newly conquered Gaul on the verge of it and the Pompeian faction attempting to rise for a third time. Thus Caesar chose Spain as his next theatre of operations.

The Civil War Campaigns in Syria

Naturally this did not mean that Caesar intended to give Bassus a free run at controlling Syria and the Roman Middle East. He dispatched word to his nearest commanders to unseat Bassus and end his rebellion. Rome held three provinces in Asia Minor, the longstanding province of Asia itself (formerly the Kingdom of Pergamum), a more recent conquest, Cilicia, and the newly conquered Bithynia-Pontus, formerly home of the Pontic Empire.

The problem for Caesar was that after his reconquest of the region the previous year, he had made Syria the centrepiece of his control of the Eastern Republic, meaning he had limited forces and commanders elsewhere in the region. The nearest Roman province was that of Cilicia, on the southern coastline of Asia Minor, guarding the entrance into Asia Minor (see Map Three). This was commanded by Q. Cornificius, whom it seems had to take the lead in the matter. This is commented on by Cicero in a letter to Cornificius at the time:

'*Cicero's compliments to his colleague Cornificius. I am exceedingly gratified by your remembrance of me as indicated by your letter. I beg you to retain it, not because I have any doubt of your constancy, but because such is the customary request. We have had news of some disturbances in Syria; and as they are nearer you than me, I am more concerned at them for your sake than for my own. At Rome, though there is the most profound tranquillity, you would prefer to have some salutary business of the right sort on foot. And I hope it will be so, for I see that Caesar is anxious for it. Allow me to inform you that, seizing upon what I venture to call the opportunity of your absence and the greater freedom that it gives me, I am writing with more than usual boldness.'[20]*

Thus, it seems that Cornificius was appointed as Caesarian Propraetor for Syria[21] as well and told to take the lead in recovering the response. Naturally this was easier said than done, especially given that Bassus' forces must have outnumbered Cornificius' own. Despite the surviving sources focusing on the outbreak of the rebellion, they provide far fewer details of the civil war campaigns which followed and mostly dwell on the later years of the warfare (45–44 BC). Only Josephus makes some passing reference to it:

'Caesar's other generals, to avenge the murder, attacked Bassus with all their forces. Antipater, for the sake of his two friends, the deceased, and the surviving Caesar, sent them reinforcements under his sons.'[22]

'thereupon a great war began near Apamea, for Caesar's generals marched against him with a force of cavalry and infantry. Antipater also sent them reinforcements together with his sons, being mindful of the benefits they had received from Caesar and on that account thinking it just to avenge Sextus and exact satisfaction from his murderer.'[23]

All that we can conclude is that the Caesarian campaigns failed and Bassus remained in control of both Syria and the wider region throughout 46 BC, with the war eventually escalating to bring in the Parthian Empire (as Caesar must have feared). These subsequent years of campaigning fall outside the scope of the present volume.[24] Nevertheless, the key element here is that Caesar had lost control of the Middle East, which now opposed him in the name of Pompeius and threatened to unravel his whole masterplan for the Eastern Republic.

The Pompeian Recovery in Spain and the Rise of a New Hope

As we have seen (Chapter Three), the Pompeian faction was not one unified front by 46 BC, but was composed of three major constituent elements, each with its own leader: the family and followers of Pompeius, led by Metellus Scipio; the anti-Caesarian Senatorial faction, led by Cato; and the Romano-Numidian faction led by Attius Varus (and supported by King Juba). Equally as we have seen, although this ruling Triumvirate (and Juba) all survived the Battle of Thapsus itself, three of the four men fell soon afterwards, all by their own hand coincidentally. This just left P. Attius Varus who had the fortune to be in command of the Pompeian navy during the African campaigns and was thus able to make a relatively easy escape and regroup with the rest of the survivors in Spain.

Yet though he was the last surviving commander of the former ruling Triumvirate, this position rested solely on the power of Numidia. With Numidia conquered, Varus had no standing and could not lay claim to the leadership of the surviving faction. In point of fact, the three elements that composed the former Pompeian faction had been reduced to just one: the friends and family of Pompeius, the original Pompeian faction. The anti-Caesarian Senatorial faction had surrendered at Utica and made terms with Caesar (aside from Cato) and the Romano-Numidian faction had been destroyed when Juba and Numidia fell.

Again as detailed earlier, underneath the ruling Triumvirate of the Pompeian faction were two other groupings: the senior military men, such as Afranius, Petreius and Labienus and the next generation of the two Pompeian brothers and Faustus Sulla. Again as we have seen, these too were culled in the aftermath of Thapsus with only Labienus and the Pompeian brothers surviving. Though Labienus had the seniority in rank and the military skills, as a former Caesarian he had no background to lead the faction. Thus it fell to the Pompeian brothers, Cnaeus and Sextus, and Cnaeus in particular, to lead the reduced Pompeian faction in his father's name, with Labienus as their number two.

As we have seen, despite inheriting his father's title of Magnus and inheriting the leadership of the family Pompeius and its adherents, Cnaeus played only a small role in the African campaigns, due to his youth and relative inexperience, having only commanded a fleet during 49–48 BC. As we have seen (Chapter Five), Pompeius led an abortive attack on the Maurian kingdom in early 46 BC, which quickly failed, after which he was 'packed off' to stir up trouble for the Caesarians in Spain. Though this may well have been intended merely to 'get rid of him' from under the feet of the Pompeian commanders in Africa, it had two important consequences; firstly it allowed him to survive the slaughter after Thapsus and thus inherit the leadership of the faction and secondly, he actually succeeded in overturning Caesarian control of

Spain and restoring it to the Pompeian cause, thus creating both a safe haven and a new Pompeian powerbase.

As we have seen, (Chapters Two and Three), Spain was a longstanding Pompeian powerbase, having been re-conquered by Pompeius (Snr) during the First Civil War in the 70s BC. This was reaffirmed by Pompeius seizing control of the province as Consul in 55 BC. Thus, having a thirty year association with the region, he was seen by the cities and tribes of the region as its benefactor. Though the region fell to Caesar in 49 BC, mostly due to the incompetence of the Pompeian commanders (see Chapter Two)[25] as we also saw, the shift of loyalty from the cities and tribes of the region to Caesar was paper thin and only lasted as long as Caesar himself (and his army) was present in Spain. No sooner had Caesar left the province then it rose up in revolt in late 48 BC.[26]

Thus sending the son and heir of the great Pompeius to a region that owed the family loyalty and was unhappy under Caesarian control was an excellent tactical move, even if it was done for other reasons. Pompeius could claim both family loyalty and freedom from Caesarian rule and offer a viable alternative for a province that had longstanding strained relations with (non-Pompeian) rule from Rome.

Spain at the time was composed of three parts; two Roman provinces (Nearer and Farther Spain) and the as yet unconquered regions to the North-West (see Map Three). We do not have an exact timetable for Pompeius' journey to Spain, only that it took place early in 46 BC when Caesar was pinned down in the African interior. Dio presents the best surviving account of the Pompeian campaigns and accompanying events.

'Pompeius put in at the Balearic Isles and took these islands without a battle, except Ebusus, which he gained with difficulty; then, falling sick, he tarried there with his troops. As a result of his delay, the soldiers in Spain, who had learned that Scipio was dead and that Didius was setting sail against them, feared that they would be annihilated before Pompeius could arrive, and so failed to wait for him; but putting at their head Titus Quintius Scapula and Quintus Aponius, both knights, they drove out [C.] Trebonius and led the whole Baetic nation to revolt at the same time.

They had gone thus far when Pompeius, recovering from his illne sailed across to the mainland opposite. He immediately won over ser *cities without resistance, for, being vexed at the commands of their rulers and also reposing no little hope in him because of the memory of his father, they readily received him; and [New] Carthage, which was unwilling to come to terms, he besieged. The followers of Scapula, on learning of this, went there and chose him general with full powers, after which they were most devoted to him and showed the greatest zeal, regarding his successes as the successes of each one of them and his disasters as their own. Consequently their resolution was confirmed by their double purpose of obtaining the successes and avoiding the disasters.*

For Pompeius, too, did what all are accustomed to do in the midst of such turbulent conditions, especially after the desertion of some of the Allobroges whom Juba had taken alive in the war against Curio and had given to him: that is, he granted to the rest every possible favour both in word and in deed. Not only these men, therefore, became more zealous in his behalf, but a number of the opposing side, also, particularly all who had once served under Afranius, came over to him.

Then there were those who came to him from Africa, among others his brother Sextus, and Varus, and Labienus with his fleet. Elated, therefore, by the multitude of his army and by its zeal, he proceeded fearlessly through the country, gaining some cities of their own accord, and others against their will, and seemed to surpass even his father in power.[27]

Thus Pompeius was able to seize the Balearic Islands as a base of operations (and refuge) whilst Metellus and Caesar were fighting each other (Jan–Apr) and then used the Pompeian inspired revolt in Farther Spain as a springboard to invade Spain itself and seize control of the province.

The similarities in the revolt of Scapula and Aponius in Spain and that of Bessus in Syria are striking. The surviving sources draw our attention to their middle ranking origins (Roman knights; the equestrian class) and that all three men organised a revolt seemingly independent of the Pompeian faction itself, but in the name of Pompeius. This is a much overlooked aspect of consideration of the modern cult of Caesar; namely how wafer thin his control of the Roman world was and how easily provinces would revolt against him, despite his overwhelming success on the battlefield.

This also speaks to the success of Pompeius (Snr) in his conquest of the native regions and his embedding of personal loyalty in each location amongst both the elites and the rank and file. Though each region swore loyalty to Caesar when he was physically present (with his army) they soon reverted to supporting the (dead) Pompeius when he left.

Thus Pompeius now had control of the Roman province of Farther Spain and its resources (both legionary and financial), the Baetican tribes and a whole host of other cities and tribes of the region. Several surviving sources comment upon the nature of this new Pompeian army:

'[Pompeius] *collected a new army of Spaniards, Celtiberians, and slaves, and made formidable preparations for war. So great were the forces still remaining which Pompeius had prepared, and which Pompeius himself overlooked and ran away from in his infatuation.*'[28]

'*This great and formidable war had been stirred up by Cnaeus Pompeius, the son of Pompeius Magnus, a young man of great energy in war, and reinforcements flowed in from all parts of the world from among those who still followed his father's great name.*'[29]

'*The army was composed of soldiers from Pharsalus and Africa itself, who had come hither with their leaders, and of Spaniards and Celtiberians, a strong and warlike race. There was also a great number of emancipated slaves in Pompeius' camp, who had all been under discipline for years and were ready to fight with desperation.*'[30]

Thus again, we see a Pompeian army composed of Roman veterans, from Ilerda, Dyrrhachium, Pharsalus and Thapsus, mixed in with native contingents and freed slaves. The *De Bello Hispaniensi* (the pseudo-Caesarian commentary of the subsequent civil war campaign) states that by the time Caesar reached Spain, the Pompeian force was thirteen legions strong (roughly 70,000 men):

'He [Pompeius] *had the eagles and standards of thirteen legions; but among those which he thought afforded him any solid support two were native legions, having deserted from Trebonius; a third had been raised from the local Roman settlers; a fourth was one which was once commanded by Afranius and which Pompeius had brought with him from Africa, while the rest were made up of runaways or auxiliaries. As for light-armed units and cavalry, our troops were in fact far superior both in quality and quantity.*'[31]

Thus in a short period, both Pompeius and the Pompeian faction had put another army of 70,000 men in the field to contest Caesar's control of the Roman world. They had control of Farther Spain and the tribes that dwelt within it, as well as a strong navy and control of the Balearic Islands to defend their flank. Opposing them were the Caesarian controlled province of Nearer Spain and Caesarian controlled North Africa, with an enlarged Maurian Kingdom (which had invaded Spain in 48 BC) and Roman Numidia. Nevertheless it was a strong position that the Pompeians found themselves in by mid-46 BC, as Spain had been used by the Cinnan-Marian faction as a base of operations throughout the 70s BC when fighting the First Civil War. Under the leadership of Q. Sertorius, a Romano-native force had resisted a Roman attempt at reconquest (ironically under the joint command of Pompeius) for nearly a decade, only being overcome by the assassination of its leader.

Snatching Defeat – Caesar and the Ghost of Pompeius

Thus, by the time Caesar left Africa in June 46 BC, he had lost control of two Roman provinces: Farther Spain in the Western Republic and Syria in the Eastern one, somewhat tainting, and undermining, his four Triumphs. Furthermore, he now faced a new Pompeius Magnus, who in the space of six months had gone from being an embarrassment to the leader of the Pompeian Republic and his new rival for control of the Roman Republic and its empire.

The younger Pompeius Magnus is much overlooked in historiography, sandwiched between his more famous father and younger brother (Sextus). This is entirely due to the shortness of his tenure as a leading figure (46–45 BC). However, this does not mean we should underestimate his position at the time. He was the son and heir of Rome's greatest general in living memory (Pompeius Magnus), a Republican martyr who had been cut down whilst resisting Caesar's attempt to overthrow the Republic (at least in Pompeian / anti-Caesarian propaganda).

In many ways, Pompeius' youth and inexperience worked in his favour. By 46 BC he was estimated to be in his late 20s (with a birth date of c.75 BC) and thus as young as his father had been when he achieved his military glory, having been compared to Alexander the Great (Caesar by contrast was now in his 50s). Thus he was the second coming of

Pompeius, a young man who would avenge his father's murder and save the Republic (at least in the anti-Caesarian propaganda). Furthermore, he had none of the stains of Roman politics about him, having been too young to be contaminated with the Republican politics of the 50s BC, from the gang violence to the bribery and corruption that had so tainted Metellus Scipio. Again, this was unlike both Caesar and Pompeius (Snr). He was therefore a blank canvas upon which Caesar's opponents could paint whatever political picture they chose.

In military terms, he was an unknown quantity, having a nondescript naval campaign in 48 BC and a failed African campaign in 46 BC. Yet neither of these campaigns had been supplied with as large a force as he now had. Furthermore, he was not alone, as he had the considerable talents of Caesar's former deputy, T. Labienus to call on, a man who knew Caesar and his tactics well and had come close to defeating or killing Caesar on several occasions during the African campaign (see above).

In many ways, however, Pompeius' rise was as much a political danger to Caesar as a military one. Whilst Republican martyrs may have annoyed Caesar, they didn't directly challenge his rule as they could not form an alternative government. Here was a young man who could. We only have to see the reaction that another young and untainted heir created a few years later when presented as an alternative to the corrupt and murderous politicians of the present. Much as Caesar Octavianus was represented as the future of the Republic (an irony in itself), so the new Pompeius Magnus could be.

Naturally a living and breathing alternative was the last thing that Caesar needed and clearly threatened the loyalty of all the Pompeians and anti-Caesarians he had pardoned, both in Rome and the wider Roman world. As we have seen, loyalty to Caesar across the Roman world had proved to be paper thin, even when his rivals were dead; how much loyalty could he secure when his rival was not only alive, but younger and less bloodied? Thus in many ways, Caesar's political position was more in jeopardy now than it had been at the start of 46 BC, as Metellus Scipio could not be badged as a new hope in the same way as Pompeius Magnus.

The Civil War Campaigns in Spain (46 BC)

Given all this, it is clearly no surprise that Caesar chose to focus on the bigger immediate threat, Pompeius in Spain, rather than secure the longer term strategy of control of the Middle East. Knowing Caesar, he must have considered an immediate attack on Farther Spain from Africa immediately after his Thapsan victory and thus before Pompeius became too embedded in Spain. Yet just as Caesar had other priorities in 48 BC which prevented him from attacking the Pompeians in North Africa immediately after Pharsalus (see Chapter Three), the need to return to Rome and secure his political position must have been impressed upon him, especially with a new focal point of Republican opposition now available.

Thus, once again, Caesar's military strategy was compromised by other imperatives, and it became clear that yet another (a fourth) civil war campaign was needed,[32] putting his dreams of Eastern conquest even further beyond him. Thus, with a return to Rome the imperative, the immediate strategy had to be one of containment, to stop the spread of Pompeian expansion in Spain, whilst he secured his political position and only then could he take up the campaign himself. Just as Pompeius (Snr) had had the need to be seen to have personally defeated the threat to the Republic (Caesar), so now Caesar had to be seen to defeat this new Pompeian threat to his Republic and thus drag the civil war into a fresh generation.

Since C. Trebonius had been defeated and had fled from Farther Spain, immediate command in that region would have fallen to the Governor of Nearer Spain, whose identity is unfortunately not known to us. Between Nearer Spain and Italy itself lay the two provinces of Gaul, which were commanded by two Caesarian 'loyalists': D. Iunius Brutus Albinus in Transalpine Gaul and M. Iunius Brutus in Cisalpine Gaul. As many will have noted, both men were central to the subsequent assassination of Caesar in 44 BC. However, D. Iunius Brutus was not in a position to help the Governor of Nearer Spain due to a Gallic revolt amongst the Bellovaces tribe (in Northern Gaul).[33]

Thus Caesar immediately dispatched one of his African legates, C. Didius, to Spain with reinforcements, as recorded by Dio.[34] These were swiftly followed by Q. Fabius Maximus and Q. Pedius (the latter a nephew of Caesar). As Dio himself comments, these generals were seemingly sent to prevent Pompeius from advancing further rather than to defeat him outright:

> 'For though Caesar also had generals in Spain, namely Quintus Fabius Maximus and Quintus Pedius, yet they did not regard themselves as a match for Pompeius but remained quiet themselves and kept sending urgently for Caesar.'[35]

It is interesting to note the reversal of roles from the Spanish campaigns of just three years earlier, when the Pompeian generals were dispatched to hold Caesar but not defeat him. In all fairness this probably played well with Pompeius' own strategy, allowing him to consolidate his hold on Farther Spain and await the inevitable arrival of Caesar.[36] Thus the battle lines were drawn for a fourth civil war campaign, the second in Spain, as Caesar now had to face the son of his late adversary and a Pompeian faction that had recovered for a third time, both of which would have engendered a significant case of déjà vu in Caesar and must have raised questions of whether he could bring this civil war to an end.

Thus, in November 46 BC, Caesar, having appointed himself sole Consul of Rome as well as Dictator, marched off once more for Spain and a war with the latest Pompeius. These events will be covered in the next volume in the series: *The Battle of Munda (45 BC). Pompey, Labienus and Caesar's Final Battle of the Third Roman Civil War* (forthcoming).

A Gallic Revolt (46 BC)

We only find reference to this revolt in the *Periochae* (summary) of Livy, which is interesting in itself, as none of the surviving pro-Caesarian sources make reference to it. This is probably not an accident, as revolts in Gaul after Caesar had supposedly conquered it undermined the success of Caesar's achievement. In point of fact it is surprising that the Gallic tribes did not take advantage of Caesar's absences (and rumoured defeats) in 48–46 BC to rebel against their recent conquest and shake off the recently imposed Roman rule. The chance survival of a passing reference to such a revolt perhaps indicates that this was actually more prevalent at the time than has been recorded in our surviving record. It seems that this revolt was crushed by D. Iunius Brutus as recorded below:

'Caesar's deputy commander [D. Iunius] *Brutus won a battle in Gaul and defeated the rebellious Bellovaces.'*[37]

Yet, the revolt does have two interesting implications. Firstly, this is clear evidence (if more were needed) that Caesar's control of the Roman world was wafer thin and not as strong as perhaps many today imagine (relying on Caesar the myth rather than the reality). Secondly, it prevented Brutus from being able to assist the unknown governor of Nearer Spain with the Pompeian threat, or defend the route from Spain to Italy, should Pompeius have been successful. Though the revolt was successfully defeated, the ongoing unrest in Spain would have done nothing to reduce the threat of further rebellions of other Gallic tribes across the region.

Summary – Caesar's Dilemma, Pompeius' Legacy

Thus the year ended with Caesar having achieved yet another major victory on the battlefield, but still without a way to end the civil war, which now dragged on into a fifth year. In many ways his position had actually deteriorated. At the start of 46 BC, he had control of the entire Roman world, with the exception of North Africa. By the end of the year he had secured North Africa but had lost Spain and Syria and was again faced with Pompeian held territory at either end of the Mediterranean, just as it had been at the start of the war in 49 BC. He would also have been suffering from déjà vu having to march on Pompeian held Spain again, as he had done some three years earlier. No sooner had one Pompeian army of over 100,000 soldiers been destroyed then another one of 70,000 appeared.

This situation strikes at the very heart of Caesar's problem, he was undoubtedly a superb battlefield general, as Pharsalus and Thapsus demonstrated, but he displayed a marked inability to convert that successfully into a wider victory in the war, which required more political skill than he seemed to possess. Despite the lack of proscriptions in Rome, the seemingly endless series of pardons, and the multiple Triumphs, Caesar could not escape the trap which Pompeius had laid for him back in 49 BC: forcing him into attacking his own state, seemingly simply to defend his own political career.

The Pompeians may have lost on the battlefield, but they still seemed to be winning the political war. Ironically the more successful Caesar was on the battlefield and the more the deaths of his opponents mounted, the more resentment he created. The anti-Caesarians (both declared and hidden) now had a whole pantheon of Republican martyrs to hold as a mirror against Caesar: Pompeius, Cato, Metellus Scipio, Petreius, Afranius, Faustus Sulla, all died by their own hand or were murdered in an un-Roman fashion, opposing Caesar. None surrendered and none were killed honourably on the battlefield.

The revolts in Spain and Syria, orchestrated locally by disaffected Pompeians seemingly pointed to the fact that no matter how many battles he won, Caesar would never be accepted as the Princeps of the Republic. Furthermore he was becoming more politically toxic, not less, with every victory and every office he held, taking him further away from acceptance, not nearer. His own political actions made matters worse, with perpetual Dictatorships, sole Consulships, no curule elections, excessive honours, and transparent Triumphs. His own political powerbase was too narrow, with popular acclaim being no substitute for a Senatorial powerbase, and in fact the more of his enemies he pardoned the more his dominance of the Senate loosened, as his hardcore followers became diluted amongst the returnees.

Thus, though Caesar was Dictator and effective Princeps of Rome, his dominance was always a short term one, propped up by the point of a sword. In many ways Caesar needed the civil war to continue just to keep himself in power and avoid the inevitable resumption of political gravity once the emergency ended. Yet, Caesar himself would not have welcomed this, seeing it as a distraction from fulfilling what he saw as his destiny and leading a Roman army of conquest carving a new eastern empire in emulation of Alexander. Instead he was leading his army to Spain again, to fight another Pompeius, seemingly stuck in a never ending loop.

Yet, as we can see, though the Pompeian faction kept getting back up after being knocked down in a most remarkable fashion, each time they did so, it was with fewer resources and less support. The Pompeian army of 48 BC was massive, supported by the whole Eastern Republic and the client kingdoms within it, along with the majority of the Republican oligarchy. The Pompeian army of 46 BC was potentially just as large, supported by the Kingdom of Numidia, along with substantial support from the Roman political and economic oligarchy. The Pompeian army

Caesar now faced was the smallest yet, supported only by Spanish tribes and the Pompeian family faction.

Thus, each battle and each loss brought more loss of support, both militarily and politically and economically. These were Pyrrhic defeats. Each was accompanied by the loss of more of its leadership, Pompeius in 48 BC, Metellus Scipio and Cato in 46 BC, with the next generation of the faction having to take up the leadership reins. Yet their defeat in this civil war was not inevitable. Caesar, for all his brilliance on the day, had his flaws, flaws which men like Labienus knew well, chiefly his impatience. Furthermore, as we have noted above, Caesar's control of the Republic was a slight one and one which could collapse at any time if given the right encouragement.

Thus, as Caesar set off to face the young Pompeius Magnus in Spain, control of the Republic was still in the balance and either man could end up victorious, with the loser being condemned both by the Romans and subsequent generations. This campaign will be covered in the next volume in this series: *The Battle of Munda (45 BC). Pompey, Labienus and Caesar's Final Battle of the Third Roman Civil War* (forthcoming).

The Fourth Romano-Pontic War (48–47 BC)

As we have seen, Caesar spent the majority of the year 47 BC fighting other wars rather than making a move against the Pompeians in North Africa, giving them vital time to recover and rebuild. The first war he fought was in Egypt, yet another Ptolemaic civil war, from which, despite his usual levels of recklessness, he emerged victorious, giving him virtual control of Ptolemaic Egypt.

As the richest region in the Mediterranean, this would have proved to be an excellent powerbase from which to move on the Pompeians of North Africa (some thousands of miles west). With the Ptolemaic Civil War over by March 47 BC, he would have had plenty of time to do so. Yet instead Caesar marched in totally the opposite direction, north towards Asia Minor.

The reason was the outbreak of the Fourth Romano-Pontic War, which is usually given the misnomer of the 'Pharnacean War', with the usual desire to focus on the individual and not the wider military and political circumstances. The Pontic Empire had been forged by Mithridates VI and at its height (mid-80s BC) ruled from the Black Sea to the Adriatic, eclipsing Rome in the east. Naturally such a challenge was welcomed by the Roman oligarchy and the prospect of commanding the First Romano-Pontic War (88–85 BC) led to the worsening of the First Roman Civil War and was one of the catalysts for the breach between Marius and Sulla and the latter's attack on Rome itself (see Chapter One).

Sulla successfully defeated Mithridates at the Battle of Chaeronea in 86 BC, recovering Greece and Macedon and drove him back into Asia Minor. At the war's height two different Roman armies, each belonging to the two largest civil war factions (the Sullans and the Mario-Cinnans), fought Mithridates, independently from one another. With the need to fight the civil war overriding the need to fight the Pontic War, Sulla made a peace treaty (Dardanus – 85 BC) with Mithridates in 85 BC restoring

Rome's eastern provinces and restricting the Pontic Empire in Asia Minor but leaving it the Black Sea. A second abortive Romano-Pontic War was fought by Sulla's Governor of Asia, L. Licinius Murena, (between 83–81 BC) but ended inconclusively on Sulla's orders.

Naturally, the power of the Pontic Empire and its ally the Armenian Empire attracted the attentions of the Roman oligarchy and even with the First Civil War still raging in the Western Republic (Spain), and without the restraining influence of Sulla himself, a third war broke out in 74 BC over which empire would annex the state of Bithynia in Asia Minor. Whilst the bulk of the fighting was commanded by L. Licinius Lucullus, he was ousted from the command in 67–66 BC by none other than Pompeius Magnus, who eventually carved out a large empire of provinces and client kingdoms for Rome in the east.[1]

The Third Romano-Pontic War was only ended when Mithridates was betrayed by one of his sons (Pharnaces), leading to his suicide. The Pontic Empire was then dismantled by Pompeius, with Pontus proper becoming a Roman province. The northern half of the empire, centred on the Crimea remained an independent Roman client kingdom, ruled by Pharnaces, with Pompeius as his patron. This naturally placed him on Pompeius' side during the Third Civil War. That being the case then it was logical that he contributed forces to Pompeius' eastern army (or navy). The only reference to this in our surviving sources is Eutropius:

> 'Pharnaces, the son of Mithridates the Great, who had assisted Pompeius in Thessaly.'[2]

In the aftermath of the Pompeian defeat at Pharsalus, Pompeius fled eastwards to rebuild his forces and it is not known if there was any direct contact between the two men. Appian states the following:

> 'Cassius sailed to Pharnaces in Pontus to induce him to take up arms against Caesar.'[3]

We know that Cassius, however, failed in his mission, as his fleet defected to Caesar at the Bosphorus (see Chapter Two). Despite owing Pompeius his kingdom, it would be hard to see Pharnaces coming to Pompeius' rescue by attacking Caesar as he passed through Asia Minor. Whilst the rest of Pompeius' client kings in the region failed to support him and sought pardon from Caesar, Pharnaces did not follow suit.

It is not known at what point Pharnaces conceived of his plan to attack the Eastern Republic and recover the lost Pontic homeland. There is no clear timeline in the surviving sources and their accounts are open to many interpretations. The key question we face is when did Pharnaces attack the Roman province of Pontus, before or after the news of Pompeius' murder?

In my view, it was after the report had reached him, so from October onwards. Given the news from Pharsalus, it was likely that Pharnaces had already mobilized his military, to defend his kingdom, if necessary, from Caesar. Caesar's army, however, passed through Asia Minor heading towards Egypt, leaving only a garrison in the Roman province of Asia, commanded by Cn. Domitius Calvinus (Cos. 53 and 40 BC). Furthermore the bulk of native forces of the region had been with Pompeius at Pharsalus and had suffered heavy casualties.

With his patron dead, Caesar tied up in Egypt, and only a garrison in Asia Minor, Pharnaces clearly judged that Rome was weak and, with his ties to his patron dissolved, it was the right time to reconquer Pontus and reconstitute the Pontic Empire. In this he was bolder than the obvious threat to the Eastern Republic, the Parthian Empire, whose war with Rome had been in abeyance since 51 BC.[4]

Dio preserves the best account of the war that followed. Pharnaces launched an immediate attack on the southern and south-eastern coastline of the Black Sea:

> 'he got possession of Colchis without any difficulty, and in the absence of Deiotarus subjugated all Armenia, and part of Cappadocia, and some cities of Pontus that had been assigned to the district of Bithynia.'[5]
> 'Pharnaces, using his victory without delay, and occupying Bithynia and Cappadocia, was aiming to secure the country called Lesser Armenia, and was rousing to revolt all the princes and tetrarchs there.'[6]

Thus huge swathes of Asia Minor fell to the new Pontic Empire, and Rome's enemies were seemingly successful in exploiting the weakness caused by the Third Civil War. Naturally, it fell to the only Roman commander in the region, Domitius Calvinus, to face and defeat Pharnaces. The *De Bello Alexandrino* preserves the best account of this campaign:

'*While these events were taking place in Egypt, king Deiotarus came to Domitius Calvinus, to whom Caesar had assigned the government of Asia and the neighbouring provinces, to beg him not to allow Lesser Armenia, his own kingdom, or Cappadocia, the Kingdom of Ariobarzanes, to be occupied and over-run by Pharnaces: for unless they were liberated from this scourge, he could not carry out his instructions and pay out the money he had promised to Caesar. As Domitius not only considered the money to be indispensable for defraying military expenses, but also decided it was a shameful affront to the Roman People and to the triumphant C. Caesar as well as a slight to himself that the kingdoms of their allies and friends should be seized by a foreign king, he forthwith sent a deputation to Pharnaces, bidding him withdraw from Armenia and Cappadocia and not assail the rights and majesty of the Roman People by resorting to civil war. In the belief that this warning would have greater force if he approached closer to that area with an army, he set out for his legions; then, taking with him one of the three, the Thirty-Sixth, he sent to Caesar in Egypt the two which the latter had called for in his despatch. One of these two did not arrive in time for the Alexandrian War, as it was sent by the overland route through Syria. Cn. Domitius reinforced the Thirty-Sixth legion with two from Deiotarus, which the latter had had for several years, having built them up on our system of discipline and armament; he also added to it 100 horsemen, and took a like number from Ariobarzanes. He sent P. Sestius to C. Plaetorius, the Quaestor, with instructions to bring the legion which had been formed from the hastily improvised forces in Pontus; and Quintus Patisius to Cilicia to muster auxiliary troops. All these forces speedily assembled at Comana according to the orders of Domitius.*'[7]

Thus we can see the weakened nature of the Roman defences in the east, with Domitius only having one legion left, having dispatched two more to Caesar in Egypt. Consequently, he had to hastily form a second legion from a garrison in Pontus and received two more from the Galatians, supplemented by forces from Cappadocia. Whilst Domitius was building his scratch army, diplomacy between the two continued, with Pharnaces withdrawing from Cappadocia, but still holding on to Lesser Armenia, once part of Pontus.[8]

'Meantime the envoys brought back this reply from Pharnaces: "he had withdrawn from Cappadocia, but had recovered Lesser Armenia, which he ought to possess by due right of inheritance from his father. In short, the issue touching that kingdom should be kept open for Caesar's decision; for he was ready to do what Caesar should decide." Now Cn. Domitius observed that he had withdrawn from Cappadocia not from free choice but of necessity, since he could defend Armenia next door to his own kingdom more easily than the more distant Cappadocia, and also because he had supposed that Domitius would bring up all three legions; and that when he heard that two of those legions had been sent to Caesar, this had heightened his rash resolve to stay on in Armenia. Consequently Domitius proceeded to insist that Pharnaces should withdraw from that kingdom also: "as far as legal right went, there was no difference between Cappadocia and Armenia, nor had he any right to demand that the question should be left open pending Caesar's arrival; a matter was 'open' when it remained just as it had been." Having given him this reply Domitius set out for Armenia with the forces I have recorded above and began by marching along the higher ground. From Comana in Pontus there is, in fact, a lofty, wooded ridge which extends into Lesser Armenia and forms the boundary between Cappadocia and Armenia. This route, as he saw, offered definite advantages, namely that on the higher ground no sudden enemy attack could develop, and that, as Cappadocia adjoined this ridge, it was likely to assist him by affording an abundance of supplies."[9]

Meanwhile Pharnaces sent several embassies to Domitius to discuss peace and to take princely gifts for Domitius. All these he firmly rejected and replied to the envoys that as far as he was concerned nothing should take precedence over the prestige of the Roman People and the recovery of the kingdoms of its allies. Then, after completing an uninterrupted succession of long marches, he began to approach Nicopolis, a town in Lesser Armenia which is actually situated in the plain, though it is hemmed in on two sides by high mountains at a fairish distance. Here he pitched camp roughly seven miles from Nicopolis. From this camp he had to traverse a narrow and confined defile; and for this reason Pharnaces arrayed the pick of his infantry and practically all his cavalry in an ambush, giving orders, moreover, that a large number of cattle should be pastured at various points within this gorge, and that the peasants and burghers should go about openly in that area. His object in so doing was *that, if Domitius should pass through that defile as a friend, he might have no suspicions of an ambush, as he would observe both men and beasts moving about the countryside, as if friends were in the offing; while if he should come in no friendly spirit, treating it as enemy territory, his troops might become scattered in the process of plundering and so be cut down piecemeal.*

While making these dispositions he still constantly continued sending delegations to Domitius to talk of peace and friendship, as he believed that by these self-same tactics Domitius could the more readily be duped. But on the other hand Domitius' hopes of peace afforded him a motive for tarrying in the camp, where he was. Consequently, as Pharnaces had now lost his immediate opportunity and was afraid that his ambush might be discovered, he recalled his troops to camp. On the next day Domitius advanced nearer Nicopolis and pitched his camp over against the town. While our troops were fortifying it, Pharnaces drew up his line of battle according to his own established custom. This, in fact, was formed with its front as a single straight line, with each of the wings reinforced by three supporting lines; and on the same principle support lines were also posted in the centre, while in the two spaces, on the right hand and on the left, single ranks were drawn up. Having once begun the task of fortifying his camp, Domitius completed it, with part of his forces posted in front of the rampart.'[10]

Thus, Domitius set out for Lesser Armenia, where Pharnaces had chosen his battleground.

Battle of Nicopolis (48 BC)

'The following night Pharnaces intercepted some couriers who were carrying despatches to Domitius concerning the situation at Alexandria. From them he learned that Caesar was in a very dangerous position, and that an urgent request was being made to Domitius that he should send Caesar reinforcements as soon as possible and himself advance through Syria closer to Alexandria. On learning this, Pharnaces saw himself virtually victorious if he could spin out the time, as he thought that Domitius must speedily withdraw. Accordingly, from that side of the town which he saw offered our men the easiest and most favourable

line of approach to do battle, he carried two straight trenches, four feet deep and spaced not so very far apart, as far as the point beyond which he had decided not to advance his own battle line. Between these trenches he consistently drew up his line, while posting all his cavalry on the flanks outside the trench; for otherwise they could not be of any use, and they far outnumbered our cavalry.

Domitius, however, was more disturbed by Caesar's peril than by his own; and as he thought that he would not be safe in withdrawing, if he made a fresh attempt to secure the terms he had rejected or if he withdrew for no good reason, he deployed his army from its nearby camp into battle formation. He posted the Thirty-Sixth legion on the right wing and the Pontic one on the left, while the legions of Deiotarus he concentrated in the centre, leaving them, however, a very narrow frontage and posting his remaining cohorts behind them in support. The lines being thus arrayed on either side, they proceeded to battle.

The signal to attack was given almost simultaneously on both sides then came the charge, with hotly contested and fluctuating fighting. Thus the Thirty-Sixth legion launched an attack on the king's cavalry outside the trench and fought so successful an action that it advanced up to the walls of the town, crossed the trench, and attacked the enemy in rear. The Pontic legion, however, on the other flank, drew back a little from the enemy, and attempted, moreover, to go round or cross the trench, so as to attack the enemy's exposed flank; but in the actual crossing of the trench it was pinned down and overwhelmed. The legions of Deiotarus, indeed, offered scarcely any resistance to the attack. Consequently the king's forces, victorious on their own right wing and in the centre of the line, now turned upon the Thirty-Sixth legion. The latter, nevertheless, bore up bravely under the victors' attack and, though surrounded by large enemy forces, yet with consummate presence of mind formed a circle and so made a fighting withdrawal to the foothills, where Pharnaces was loth to pursue it owing to the hilly nature of the ground. And so, with the Pontic legion an almost total loss and a large proportion of the troops of Deiotarus killed, the Thirty-Sixth legion retired to higher ground with losses not exceeding 250 men. There fell in that battle not a few Roman knights, brilliant and distinguished men. After sustaining this defeat Domitius none the less collected the remnants of his scattered army and withdrew by safe routes through Cappadocia into Asia.'[11]

Thus the only Roman army in Asia Minor had been defeated, with three of its four legions destroyed (roughly 15,000 men). As the *De Bello Alexandrino* makes clear, however, this defeat was down to the poor quality of the legions that Pharnaces faced, with the new Roman legion and the two Galatian ones collapsing, but the veteran Roman one being initially successful. Nevertheless, the Roman and native forces had been defeated, giving Pharnaces the opportunity to reconquer Pontus proper:

> *'Elated by this success and confident that his wishes for Caesar's defeat would be granted, Pharnaces seized Pontus with all his forces. There he played the role of victor and utterly ruthless tyrant and, promising himself his father's fortune though with a happier ending, he took many towns by storm, plundered the property of Roman and Pontic citizens, and decreed for those who in respect of youth and beauty had anything to commend them such punishments as proved more pitiful than death. Thus he held unchallenged sway over Pontus, boasting that he had recovered the kingdom of his father.'*[12]

Thus, as Caesar sat in Alexandria, caught in the midst of the Ptolemaic Civil War, Asia Minor was being overrun by the revived Pontic Empire, with the clear fear being that the Parthian Empire would soon exploit this and overrun the Middle East. Cicero summed up the news when it reached Rome: *'when such disaster has been sustained in Asia'*.[13]

Caesar's Dilemma – Pharnaces, Pompeians and Parthians

Having successfully concluded the Ptolemaic Civil War by around March 47 BC, and with his 'candidate' on the throne (Cleopatra VII), Caesar now turned his attention to his next move. In many ways, Caesar was rather isolated in Egypt, cut off from the rest of the Caesarian Republic. To the west lay Roman North Africa, now the heartland of the recovering Pompeian faction (with Cyrene between them as a buffer). To the immediate north lay Roman Syria (and Judea), still under Caesarian control, but to the north of that lay the Pontic Empire and to the east the Parthian Empire; enemies on three sides.

Though he needed to eliminate the Pompeians to cement his control of the Republic, Caesar correctly calculated that the near and present danger were the enemies in the east. Left unchecked, Pharnaces would keep expanding this new empire, attacking the undefended Roman provinces of Asia and Cilicia. He could then move either south into Syria or retrace his father's steps westwards into Greece. The unknown quantity in this equation were the Parthians, who had recently been repulsed from an attack on Syria (52–51 BC). Whilst their King (Orodes II) rightly judged that another attack would be foolish while Caesar and his legions were just in Egypt, if Caesar moved westwards towards Africa and Pharnaces threatened Syria himself, they would have to act.

Thus if Caesar did move on the Pompeians in North Africa, Rome's whole eastern empire could be overrun. Combined with this was the political calculation that an extension to the Roman Civil War would ensure that the emergency situation continued and along with it, the need for his supreme power. So Caesar set off for Asia Minor and war with Pharnaces, leaving the Pompeians more time to regroup and rebuild their army.

Pharnaces himself, however, was suffering from a severe case of irony. The previous war had ended when he revolted against his father whilst based in the Crimean province of Pontus. Now that he had reconquered much of Asia Minor (his father's kingdom), he found that he too had been revolted against, this time by the man he left as Governor of the Crimea:

'Meanwhile, learning that Asander, whom he had left as governor of Bosporus, had revolted, he gave up advancing any farther. For Asander, as soon as word was brought that Pharnaces was moving far away from him, and it seemed likely that however prosperous he might be temporarily, he would not fare well later on, rose against him, thinking thus to do a favour to the Romans and to receive the sovereignty of Bosporus from them.'[14]

Thus, he was restrained from advancing further and, if we are to believe Dio, was preparing to return to the Crimea to battle the usurper. This plan had to be abandoned when Caesar marched his legions from Egypt towards Asia Minor. Naturally with his position deteriorating, Pharnaces chose to negotiate with Caesar, which is recorded in the De Bello Alexandrino.[15] Clearly, such negotiations were never going to succeed. Pharnaces had invaded and conquered Roman territory, defeated a Roman commander in battle and committed atrocities against the Roman civilians in the territories he conquered. Furthermore, Caesar needed a victory, to make a statement, both to the former Pompeian supporting rulers of the Near and Middle East and to the Parthians themselves. Thus Caesar determined on a battle, and the site was that of a previous Romano-Pontic battle in 67 BC, which had been a major victory for Mithridates.

Battle of Zela (47 BC)

Again the *De Bello Alexandrino* contains an excellent and contemporaneous account (possibly first hand) of the battle which followed:

> 'Zela is a town situated in Pontus, with adequate natural defences, considering its position in a plain: for its battlements are reared upon a hillock, a natural one for all its artificial appearance, whose summit is loftier than all the terrain surrounding it. Encircling this town are many considerable hills, intersected by valleys; and one of these, a very lofty one, which enjoys no little fame in those parts thanks to the victory of Mithridates, and the misfortune of Triarius and defeat of our army, is all but linked to the town by tracks along the higher ground, and is little more than three miles distant from Zela. Here Pharnaces repaired the ancient works of his father's once prosperous camp and occupied the position with his entire forces.
>
> Caesar pitched his camp five miles distant from the enemy; and as he now saw that that valley by which the king's camp was protected would, if its width separated them, equally afford protection to a camp of his own, provided only that the enemy did not anticipate him in capturing the ground in question, which was much nearer the king's camp, he ordered materials for a rampart to be carted within the entrenchments. This was speedily collected. The following night he left camp at the fourth watch with all his legions in light order and the heavy baggage left behind in camp, and surprised the enemy at dawn by capturing that very position where Mithridates once fought his successful action against Triarius. To this spot he ordered the slaves to bring from the camp all the accumulated material for the rampart, so that none of his troops should quit their work of fortification, since the intervening valley which separated the enemy's

camp from the emplacements which Caesar had begun was not more than a mile wide.

On suddenly observing this situation at dawn, Pharnaces drew up all his forces in front of his camp. In view of the highly uneven character of the intervening ground Caesar supposed that it was the king's normal military practice more than anything that occasioned this deployment; or else his object was to delay Caesar's own work of fortification, through the necessity of keeping more men standing to arms; or again it might be intended as a display of confidence on the king's part, to shew that it was not on fortification so much as on armed force that Pharnaces relied to defend his position. Accordingly, Caesar was not deterred from keeping the remainder of his army engaged on the work of fortification, deploying only the front line in front of the palisade. Pharnaces, however, took it into his head to engage.

Whether it was the lucky associations of the spot that drove him to take this course, or whether it was his scrupulous observance of omens, to which, as we afterwards heard, he gave careful heed, that so prompted him; or maybe it was the small number of our troops which, according to his information, were standing to arms (for he had supposed that that vast gang of slaves which transported the material for the rampart, as though it was their daily employment, was in fact composed of troops); or maybe even it was his confidence in that veteran army of his, which, as his envoys boasted, had fought and conquered upon twenty two battle-fields, coupled with a contempt for our army, which he knew had been routed by himself when Domitius led it: anyway, having decided to engage, he began the descent down the steep ravine. For some little time Caesar laughed contemptuously at this empty bravado on the part of the king, and at his troops packed closely on ground which no enemy in his senses would be likely to set foot on; while in the meantime Pharnaces with his forces in battle array proceeded to climb the steep hillside confronting him at the same steady pace at which he had descended the sheer ravine.

This incredible foolhardiness or confidence on the part of the king disconcerted Caesar, who was not expecting it and was caught unprepared. Simultaneously he recalled the troops from their work of fortification, ordered them to stand to arms, deployed his legions to meet the attack, and formed line of battle; and the sudden excitement to which all this gave rise occasioned considerable panic among our troops. Disorganised as our men were, and as yet in no regular formation, the king's chariots armed with scythes threw them into confusion; but these chariots were speedily overwhelmed by a mass of missiles. In their wake came the enemy line: the battle cry was raised, and the conflict joined, our men being greatly helped by the nature of the ground but above all by the blessing of the immortal gods. For just as the gods play a part in all the chance vicissitudes of war, so above all do they do so in those where human strategy has proved quite powerless to avail.

Heavy and bitter hand-to-hand fighting took place; and it was on the right wing, where the veteran Sixth legion was posted, that the first seeds of victory were sown. As the enemy were being thrust back down the slope on this wing, so too on the left wing and in the centre, much more slowly, but thanks nevertheless to the same divine assistance, the entire forces of the king were being crushed. The ease with which they had climbed the uneven ground was now matched by the speed with which, once dislodged from their footing, the unevenness of the ground enabled them to be driven back. Consequently, after sustaining many casualties, some killed, some knocked out by their comrades' falling on top of them, those whose nimbleness did enable them to escape none the less threw away their arms; and so, after crossing the valley, they could not make any effective stand from the higher ground, unarmed as they now were. Our men, on the contrary, elated by their victory, did not hesitate to climb the uneven ground, and storm the entrenchments. Moreover, despite the resistance of those enemy cohorts which Pharnaces had left to guard his camp, they promptly won possession of it.

With his entire forces either killed or captured Pharnaces took to flight with a few horsemen; and had not our storming of his camp afforded him a freer opportunity for flight, he would have been brought alive into Caesar's hands.'[16]

Thus, Caesar and his battle hardened Roman legions were too strong for the Pontic army and he had the victory he needed. He then apparently cemented this battle in popular Roman (and modern) culture, summing it up with the phrase '*veni, vid vici*' (I came, I saw, I conquered).

Pharnaces survived the battle and fled to Sinope where he was forced to surrender, ironically to Domitius Calvinus:

'*He was beaten and fled to Sinope with 1,000 cavalry. Caesar was too busy to follow him but sent Domitius against him. He surrendered Sinope to Domitius, who agreed to let him go away with his cavalry. He killed his horses, though his men were extremely dissatisfied at this, then took ship and fled to the Bosphorus. Here he collected a force of Scythians and Sarmatians and captured Theodosia and Panticapaeum. His enemy, Asander, attacked him again, and his men were defeated for want of horses, and because they were not accustomed to fighting on foot. Pharnaces alone fought valiantly until he died of his wounds, being then fifty years of age and having been king of Bosphorus fifteen years.*'[17]

The Battle of Zela brought about the end of the Fourth Romano-Pontic War and the end to the briefly revived Pontic Empire. Following Pharnaces' death, the usurper Asander and the Caesarian sponsored candidate Mithridates II (another son of Mithridates VI) fought for the throne, with Asander emerging successful and ruling until c.17 BC, having married Pharnaces' daughter to legitimise his rule. From this point onwards, however, the Bosphoran Kingdom remained a loyal Roman client kingdom (until it was overrun by migrating tribes in the fourth or fifth centuries AD) but never again attempted to restore the Pontic Empire.

Naturally, after his victory Caesar was able to restore Roman control over the conquered regions of Asia Minor and then set off for Italy and Rome, where he had not been since the winter of 49/48 BC to cement his political position and then use Italy as a launch pad for an invasion of North Africa. Though his victory had destroyed the revived Pontic Empire and sent a warning to the Parthian Empire, it gave the Pompeian faction vital time to regroup and rebuild, ready to challenge Caesar once more for control of the Roman Republic.

Appendix II

Who's Who in the
Third Roman Civil War (47–46 BC)

Given the continuous narrative of Caesar and the number of other surviving sources that comment on this period, we know the identities of a large number of Roman politicians and officers that were taking part in the conflict, in both major and minor roles. That being the case, the following is a brief 'Who's Who' of those involved in the various campaigns of 48 BC, along with their subsequent fates.

The Main Protagonists

C. Iulius Caesar (Cos. 59, 48, 46, 45 BC)   Killed 44 BC
Nephew of the great C. Marius, who was a leading general in the First Civil War and son-in-law of L. Cornelius Cinna, who ruled Rome between 87–84 BC. Came to notice in Roman politics in the 60s championing the Marian cause against the ruling Sullan faction, but still only a minor figure. Won the Consulship for 59 BC as an agent of Pompeius (and latterly Crassus) and was rewarded with a command in Gaul. Defied expectations by launching a war of conquest, backed by Pompeius and Crassus. Formed a fresh alliance with Pompeius and Crassus, whilst still being the junior member, remained in Gaul throughout the 50s BC. Identified by Pompeius as the last obstacle to his dominance in Rome and manipulated into invading Italy as an 'enemy of the state'.

Defeated at Dyrrhachium, he regrouped and won a major victory at the subsequent Battle of Pharsalus. Neither this victory, nor the subsequent murder of Pompeius brought the war to a conclusion and he fought further battles of Thapsus in 46 BC and Munda in 45 BC. Despite the Pompeians still holding regions of Spain and Syria, he was preparing a major war of conquest against the Parthian Empire when he was famously murdered in the Senate, by a large group of Senators, composed of former enemies and many of his own officers, to prevent him becoming sole ruler of Rome.

Q. Caecilius Metellus Pius Scipio Nasica   (Cos. 52 BC)   Suicide 46 BC
Scion of two of Rome's leading families, became Pompeius' father-in-law and then fellow Consul in 52 BC and de facto deputy. Sent to the Eastern Republic in 49 BC to raise an army, he returned to Greece in early 48 BC to fight Caesar's officers but too late to take part in the Battle of Dyrrhachium. He fought a significant part in the subsequent Battle of Pharsalus and retreated to North Africa in its aftermath, becoming commander of the Pompeian forces following Pompeius' murder in Egypt. Rebuilding these forces, he faced Caesar in the African campaigns of early 46 BC and attempted to trap him at the city of Thapsus. Was defeated in the subsequent battle when Caesar launched a surprise attack on (his divided) forces. Successfully escaped the battle, reaching Utica and then setting sail for Spain. Intercepted by the Maurian navy, he lost the subsequent battle but committed suicide rather than be captured.

Notable Leading Figures

M. Aemilius Lepidus   (Cos. 46 and 42 BC)   Died 13/12 BC
Son of a First Civil War general and a supporter of Caesar. Left in charge of Rome by Caesar during 49 BC. Proposed Caesar as Dictator that year. Appointed as Governor of Spain in 48 BC and quelled the rebellions, ensuring stability until 47 BC, when he was recalled, becoming Caesar's consular colleague for 46 BC and Master of the Horse.

Became one of the main leaders of the faction after Caesar's death but politically outmanoeuvred by M. Antonius and Caesar Octavianus after the Battles of Philippi in 42 BC. Left alive by Octavianus (Augustus) as Pontifex Maximus (Chief Priest). Died of natural causes in 13/12 BC.

L. Afranius   (Cos. 60 BC)   Killed 46 BC
A long serving Pompeian commander, having fought under Pompeius during the First Civil War and then in the Eastern Wars. Elected as Consul under Pompeius' patronage (the year before Caesar). Commanded Pompeius' legions in Spain in 49 BC but was defeated by Caesar. Captured and pardoned, he immediately returned to fighting for Pompeius, being at both Dyrrhachium and Pharsalus. Fought Caesar for a third time, in the North African campaign, and retreated to Utica in the aftermath of Thapsus. Along with Faustus Sulla he retreated across North Africa with

a cavalry force but was defeated by Sittius in battle and was murdered soon afterwards by Sittius' forces.

M. Antonius   (Tr. 49, Cos. 44, 34, 31 BC)   Suicide 30 BC

One of the two Tribunes who fled to Caesar at the beginning of 49 BC. Received an extraordinary Propraetorian command (which technically he could not hold as a serving Tribune). Held command in Italy during 49 BC and led the defence of Brundisium in early 48 BC. Took command of the Caesarian relief army which crossed into Illyria in early 48. Present at the Battles of Dyrrhachium and Pharsalus. Was Caesar's deputy during his Dictatorship of 48/47 BC but fell from favour, before being appointed Consul for 44 BC. Became one of the leaders of the Caesarian faction following Caesar's murder in 44 BC. Seized control of the Republic as one of the Second Triumvirate and took control of the Eastern Republic. Took command of the Second Romano-Parthian War and attempted to carve out his own familial empire in the east. Defeated by Caesar Octavianus at the Battle of Actium in 31 BC. Committed suicide following Octavianus' invasion of Egypt.

P. Attius Varus   (Pr. c.53 BC)   Killed 45 BC

Pompeian commander. Briefly fought Caesar's men in Italy before withdrawing. Seized command of Roman Africa and defeated the Caesarian invasion (with Numidian help). Created a Pompeian stronghold and quasi-independent fiefdom in North Africa. Became one of the Pompeian faction leaders in the aftermath of Pharsalus. Commanded a portion of the Pompeian fleet. Retreated from Africa to Spain after the defeat at Thapsus. Killed during the final battle of Munda.

Caecilius Bassus   Killed 42 BC?

Pompeian commander who fled to Syria in the aftermath of Pharsalus. Led the revolt against the Caesarian control of the province in 46 BC, killing Sex. Iulius Caesar. Fought an ongoing Civil War against the Caesarian commanders. He retained control of the province until 42 BC when his forces merged with those of the anti-Caesarian faction of Brutus and Cassius. Disappears from the surviving record but may have died at the Battle of Philippi along with Cassius.

Cn. Calpurnius Piso Frugi   (Cos. 23 BC)
Pompeian commander who fought against Caesar in Spain and retreated to North Africa in the aftermath of Caesar's victory, serving under Afranius and Juba. Commanded a force of Numidian cavalry in the campaigns against Caesar. Pardoned in the aftermath of Thapsus he fought with Brutus and Cassius at Philippi and was pardoned by Octavianus. Served as Consul alongside Augustus in 23 BC when the Princeps fell ill and would have had a leading role in the subsequent chaos had Augustus died.

C. Cassius Longinus   (Pr. 44 BC)   Killed 42 BC
Former supporter of Crassus who took over the defence of the Roman East in the aftermath of the Battle of Carrhae. Pompeian naval commander in 48 BC who led an abortive attack on Sicily. Took his navy to the east in the aftermath of Pharsalus, but rather than defeat Caesar as he crossed the Bosphorus, his fleet defected, providing Caesar with an effective navy, and quickening his pursuit of Pompeius. Famously was one of the co-leaders of the conspiracy that murdered Caesar in 44 BC and co-leaders of the 'Republican' faction in the subsequent civil war. Killed in 42 BC after the Battle of Philippi.

Q. Cassius Longinus   (Tr. 49 BC)   Died 47 BC
One of the two Tribunes who fled to Caesar at the beginning of 49 BC. Became Caesarian Governor of Further Spain but ruled tyrannically, sparking off a rebellion and his replacement. Died in early 47 BC in a shipwreck.

M. Claudius Marcellus Aeserninus   (Cos. 22 BC)
Caesarian Quaestor in Spain, who led the rebellion against Q. Cassius in 48 BC. Surrendered his force to the Caesarian Governor, Lepidus and was pardoned.

P. Cornelius Dolabella   (Cos. 44 BC)   Suicide 43 BC
Caesarian legate in charge of the Adriatic fleet in 49 BC, defeated by the Pompeians and withdrew. Clashed with M. Antonius, as Tribune in 47 BC but took Caesar's place in the Consulship of 44 BC and command of the proposed Parthian War. Clashed with C. Trebonius and C. Cassius in the east, committed suicide in Syria in 43 BC.

P. Cornelius Scipio Pomponianus Sallustio[1]   (Cos 35 BC)
Minor member of the Scipio family. Supported Caesar in 47–46 BC and used by him, a figurehead for the army invading North Africa. Disappears from the surviving narratives after the Thapsan campaign, though may be the Scipio who reached the Consulate in 35 BC.

C. Considius Longus   (Pr. 50s)   Killed 46 BC
Promagistrate in Africa in 50 BC. Returned there as a Pompeian commander in 49 BC and helped govern the province until 46 BC. Pompeian commander of the Hadrumetum garrison during Caesar's invasion who refused to change sides. Later commander of Thysdra. Fled the city in the aftermath of the Battle of Thapsus but was murdered by his Gaetulian soldiers.

F. Cornelius Sulla   Killed 46 BC
Son and heir of the late Dictator, and son-in-law of Pompeius. Held command of Pompeian forces in Macedonia in 48 BC and fought Domitius Calvinus. Withdrew to Africa after the defeat at Pharsalus. Seemed to remain in Utica with Cato during the African campaign and retreated across North Africa with a cavalry force in the aftermath of Thapsus. Defeated by Sittius in battle, he was murdered soon afterwards by Sittius' forces.

P. Cornelius Sulla   (Cos. 65 BC)   Died 45 BC
Nephew of the late Dictator, and brother-in-law of Pompeius, but a Caesarian commander. Fought in both the Battles of Dyrrhachium and Pharsalus. Sent by Caesar to Italy to ferry troops to Sicily for an Invasion of Africa but faced mutinous legions. Died, presumably of natural causes, in 45 BC.

Q. Cornificius   (Pr. 45 BC)   Killed 42 BC
Caesarian Governor of Illyria, who resecured the province for the Caesarian faction defeating the Pompeian commander M. Octavius. Became Governor in Cilicia after Caesar's eastern campaigns and probably led the civil war campaigns against Bassus in 46 BC. Later became Caesarian Governor of Africa but was proscribed by the Triumvirate. Killed in battle with his Triumviral successor during the Civil War of 42 BC.

C. Didius   Killed 45 BC
Caesarian commander sent to Spain in 46 BC in the aftermath of the Thapsan campaign. Defeated the Pompeian fleet in naval battle in 45 BC. Sent Caesar Pompeius Magnus' head after the Battle of Munda but was killed in the aftermath of the battle fighting the Lusitanians.

Cn. Domitius Calvinus   (Cos. 53 and 40 BC)
Caesarian commander dispatched to face Metellus Scipio in 48 BC and later took part in the Battle of Pharsalus. Became Governor of Asia but was defeated by Pharnaces II later in 48 BC. Served with Caesar in North Africa in 46 BC. He became an ally of Octavianus, following Caesar's murder and remained a key member of Octavianus' circle of supporters. His date of death is unknown.

Q. Fabius Maximus   (Cos. 45 BC)   Died 45 BC
A member of the most famous branch of the Fabian clan. A Caesarian general who was sent to Spain by Caesar in 46 BC to check Pompeius and fought at the Battle of Munda in 45 BC. Made Suffect Consul later that year and celebrated a Triumph for his campaign in Spain. Died on the last day of office, presumably of natural causes, though had shown no signs of ill health beforehand.

Q. Fufius Calenus   (Cos. 47 BC)   Died 40 BC
Caesarian commander in Spain and Greece. Commanded the Caesarian forces which recovered Greece in the aftermath of Pharsalus. Became Consul in 47 BC and joined M. Antonius in the aftermath of Caesar's murder. Died of (presumed) natural causes, in 40 BC, whilst commanding forces in Transalpine Gaul against Caesar Octavianus.

A. Gabinius   (Cos. 58 BC)   Died 47 BC
Former Pompeian commander, who sided with Caesar, after being discarded by Pompeius. Took command of Caesarian forces in Illyria but was heavily defeated by the Illyrian tribes in late 48 BC. He survived the battle, but died soon afterwards, possibly in early 47 BC.

L. Iulius Caesar   (Cos. 64 BC)

Cousin of Caesar, and uncle of the Antonius brothers, who fought with Caesar in Gaul and returned to Rome in 49 BC. Made Prefect of the City by Antonius to deal with the violence caused by the warring Tribunes. Following Caesar's murder, he attempted to prevent the collapse of the Caesarian faction, proscribed by the Triumvirate but survived. Fate unknown after 40 BC. Probable father of the L. Iulius Caesar who fought with the Pompeians.

L. Iulius Caesar   (Q. Pre-50 BC)   Killed 46 BC

Pompeian supporter, though he was a cousin of Caesar, and his father was a close Caesarian supporter. Served as a Pompeian envoy in Italy in 49 BC. Became Proquaestor to Cato in North Africa in 46 BC and led the surrender of the anti-Caesarian faction in the aftermath of Thapsus. Murdered soon afterwards, possibly by vengeful Pompeians.

Sex. Iulius Caesar   Killed 46 BC

Cousin of Caesar and one of his junior officers in Spain. Appointed Governor of Syria in 47 BC, he was murdered in a Pompeian sponsored revolt in 46 BC, organized by Caecilius Bassus.

D. Iunius Brutus Albinus   (Pr. 45 BC)   Killed 43 BC

Caesarian commander placed in charge of the naval siege of Massilia in 49 BC. Governor of Transalpine Gaul in 46 BC where he faced a native rebellion at the same time as the Pompeian revolt in Spain. Went on to hold a Praetorship in 45 BC. Was one of the leading conspirators who murdered Caesar in 44 BC. Took up command in Cisalpine Gaul where he fought against M. Antonius in 43 BC, but was forced to flee when his army mutinied. Captured and murdered by a Gallic chief.

M. Iunius Brutus   (Pr. 44 BC)   Suicide 42 BC

Scion from a family that claimed to be descended from the Brutii who helped (perhaps inadvertently) to found the Republic. Rumoured to be the bastard son of Caesar himself. Supported Pompeius in 48 BC and was present at the Battle of Pharsalus and reconciled with Caesar after the battle. Governor of Cisalpine Gaul in 46 BC at the time of the Pompeian revolt in Spain. Famously was one of the co-leaders of the conspiracy that murdered Caesar in 44 BC and co-leaders of the 'Republican' faction in the subsequent civil war. Committed suicide in 42 BC after the Battle of Philippi.

T. Labienus   (Pr. c.59 BC)   Killed 45 BC

Senior Caesarian commander in Gaul but defected to join Pompeius when Caesar invaded Italy. Became a senior Pompeian commander, fighting at both Dyrrhachium and Pharsalus. Having regrouped in Africa in the aftermath of Pharsalus, he successfully fought Caesar at the Battle of Ruspina in 46 BC and had several other clashes with him during the subsequent campaigns. Withdrew to Spain in the aftermath of Thapsus and found himself as deputy leader of the Pompeian faction (supporting Pompeius Magnus). Killed in the Battle of Munda. His son became a Parthian client who conquered Asia Minor in 40 BC.

L. Manlius Torquatus   (Pr. 49 BC)   Killed 46 BC

Pompeian commander, who commanded the Pompeian forces attacked by Caesar during the final battle of Dyrrhachium and seems to have played a key role in the victory. He retreated to North Africa after the Battle of Pharsalus but died in the aftermath of the Battle of Thapsus, after being captured; either executed or by his own hand.

L. Nonius Asprenas   (Pr. 47?, Cos. 36 BC)

Caesarian commander in charge of the rearguard at the Battle of Thapsus. Defeated the Pompeian garrison. Continued to serve under Caesar in Spain in 45 BC. Supported Octavianus in the period of the Triumvirate and reached the Consulship. Death is unrecorded.

M. Octavius

Pompeian naval commander in Illyria, who helped to defeat the Caesarian forces there in 49 BC. Defeated by Cornificius in 48 BC in the aftermath of Pharsalus. Continued his naval command in Africa in 47–46 BC. Subsequent career and fate unknown.

Q. Pedius   (Cos. 43 BC)   Died 43 BC

Caesarian commander, who served in Gaul and was a nephew of Caesar. Crushed Milo's rebellion in 48 BC. Caesarian general who was sent to Spain by Caesar in 46 BC to check Pompeius. Returned to Rome in 45 BC and celebrated a Triumph for his campaigns. Named an heir in Caesar's will, along with his cousin Caesar Octavianus. Supported the Triumvirate and made Consul in 43 BC along with Octavianus but died in office, presumably of natural causes (though the death clearly benefited Octavianus).

M. Petreius   Killed 46 BC
Fought in both the First and Second Civil Wars. Pompeian commander in Spain. Defeated by Caesar, he re-joined Pompeius in Greece. Retreated to North Africa after the Battle of Pharsalus, where he served as a commander, fighting Caesar at the Battle of Ruspina. Survived the Battle of Thapsus and retreated into Numidia with King Juba, but when being closed down by Caesar, chose suicide (dying in a duel with Juba).

Cn. Pompeius 'Magnus'   Killed 45 BC
Eldest of the two sons of Pompeius Magnus and thus his political inheritor. Commanded a Pompeian fleet in 48 BC. Relocated to North Africa in the aftermath of both Pharsalus and his father's murder. Excluded from command due to his youth, he launched a failed attack on the Caesarian supporting Maurian Kingdom in 46 BC. With the deaths of the majority of Pompeian factional leaders after Thapsus, along with T. Labienus, he became the head of the Pompeian faction and commanded the Pompeian forces at the Battle of Munda in 45 BC, but was killed in the aftermath.

Sex. Pompeius   Killed 35 BC
Youngest of the two sons of Pompeius Magnus and an accomplished naval commander. He became joint leader of the Pompeian faction after the Battle of Thapsus and faced Caesar in Spain at the Battle of Munda in 45 BC. Becoming sole leader after the murder of his elder brother, he again took to the sea and opposed first Caesar and then the Caesarian Triumvirate, seizing control of Sicily. Fought civil war campaigns against Caesar Octavianus and was ultimately defeated, before fleeing east to fight civil war campaigns against Antonius' forces. Captured and murdered in 35 BC by the Antonine general M. Titius.

M. Porcius Cato   (Pr. 54 BC)   Suicide 46 BC

More commonly known today as Cato the Younger. Contemporary of Caesar who opposed the various Duumvirs during the 60s and 50s. Pompeian supporter in the civil war. Commander in Sicily in 49 BC but withdrew rather than defend the island. Kept away from further military commands, withdrew to Africa after the defeat at Pharsalus. Famously committed suicide after the defeat at Thapsus rather than compromise with Caesar.

M. Porcius Cato   Killed 42 BC

Son of Cato (the Younger), surrendered to Caesar at Utica in 46 BC. Brother-in-law of Brutus, he was part of the conspiracy that led to Caesar's assassination in 44 BC. Fought with Brutus and Cassius in Greece and was killed during the Battle of Philippi.

C. Sallustius Crispus   (Pr. 46 BC)

Caesarian commander, who held a junior command in Illyria in 49 BC but was defeated by Pompeian forces. Nearly killed in a mutiny by the Caesarian legions in 47 BC. Organized supplies for Caesar, whilst he was cornered in Ruspina. In the aftermath of Thapsus, he became Governor of the New African province created by Caesar. Later became a noted historian.

P. Sittius   Killed 44 BC

Minor Roman politician who fled Rome after the Second Civil War and found himself in the employ of the Mauri, rising to command an element of their army or a mercenary force. Jointly led the Maurian attack on Numidia in 46 BC, diverting Juba from helping the Pompeians fight Caesar. Defeated the Pompeian force of Faustus Sulla and Afranius after Thapsus and likely ordered their murders. Killed in 44 BC by the Pompeian sponsored Numidian prince, Arabio.

L. Trebellius   (Tr. 47 BC)

Tribune who opposed his colleague Dolabella and his populist legislation, initially on his own and later in conjunction with M. Antonius. Possibly an Aedile in 44 BC, he can be found serving with Antonius in 43 BC before disappearing from the surviving record.

C. Trebonius   (Cos. 45 BC)   Killed 43 BC
Caesarian commander, who had served with him in Gaul and was placed in charge of the siege of Massilia. As Praetor in 48 BC, opposed Caelius' measure on debt alleviation. Served in Spain as a Provincial Governor. Driven out of the province in 46 BC by a Pompeian revolt. Became Consul in 45 BC and was one of the conspirators in the murder of Caesar in 44 BC. Took up command in Asia where he fought against P. Cornelius Dolabella in 43 BC but was captured and murdered.

P. Vatinius   (Cos. 47 BC)
Caesarian commander in charge of the defence of Brundisium in 49 and 48 BC. He campaigned in Illyria during 47 BC and defeated the Pompeian commander M. Octavius, recovering the province for the Caesarians. Was rewarded with a Consulship in late 47 BC.

Non Romans

Bocchus II   (King of the Mauri 49–33 BC)   Died 33 BC
Bogud   (King of the Mauri 49–31 BC)   Killed 31 BC
Joint Kings of the Maurian Kingdom in North Africa. Supported Caesar in opposition to their rivals in Numidia. They were preparing to act as a Caesarian base for an attack on Numidia and Pompeian Africa from the west when a revolt broke out in Caesarian Spain. Bogud led Maurian forces into Spain to assist the Caesarians against the rebels. In the subsequent civil war between Antonius and Octavianus the two brothers took opposing sides, with Bogud being deposed and dying during the prelude to the Battle of Actium.

Cleopatra VII   (Ptolemaic Pharaoh 51–30 BC)   Suicide 30 BC
Pharaoh of Ptolemaic Egypt, placed upon the throne as a puppet (and lover) by Caesar. Mother to Caesar's only natural son (Caesarion – Ptolemy XV).

Juba I   (King of Numidia c. 85–46 BC)   Suicide 46 BC
King of Numidia. Threw his whole support behind Pompeius. Defeated the Caesarian invasion of North Africa in 49 BC and butchered the survivors. Continued to support the Pompeian faction in the aftermath

of Pharsalus and helped them to rebuild. Marched the Numidian Army to face Caesar at Ruspina but had to divert back to face Sittius' invasion and thus was unable to take part in the Battle of Thapsus in 46 bc and fled in the aftermath. Died in a suicide pact with the Roman commander M. Petreius, being finished off by a slave. The Numidian monarchy and the country independence fell with him.

Pharnaces II   (Bosphoran King c. 97–47 bc)   Killed 47 bc
Son of the legendary Mithridates VI of Pontus, he nevertheless betrayed his father during the Third Romano-Pontic War, leading to his suicide, and received the northern part of the Pontic Empire, the Crimean Kingdom of the Bosphorus) in return. A client of Pompeius, he used the chaos of the civil war to invade Rome's Eastern Republic in 48 bc (perhaps with Pompeian encouragement). Defeated by Caesar in 47 bc, he fled back to his kingdom but was betrayed and killed by a subordinate.

Ptolemy XIII   (Ptolemaic Pharaoh 51–47 bc)   Killed 47 bc
One of the heirs of Ptolemy XII, who engaged in a civil war with his sister (Cleopatra VII). Ordered the murder of Pompeius, and his supporters, in an ill thought out bid to ingratiate himself with Caesar, a ploy which backfired spectacularly. When Caesar ruled in favour of his sister, he took up arms and was defeated by Caesar in early 47 bc, dying in the aftermath.

Ptolemy XIV   (Ptolemaic Pharaoh 47–44 bc)   Killed 44 bc
Nominal co-ruler of Ptolemaic Egypt with his sister Cleopatra. Died suspiciously in the aftermath of Caesar's assassination and was replaced by Cleopatra's (and Caesar's) son Caesarion (Ptolemy XV).

Saburra   Killed 46 bc
Numidian General left in charge of the war against the Mauri and P. Sittius in Western Numidia. Defeated in battle by Sittius, around the time of the Battle of Thapsus and killed.

Lesser Figures

Allienus   (Pr. 49 BC)
Caesarian commander in Sicily in 46 BC. Later served under Trebonius in the east before defecting to C. Cassius.

Q. Aponius
Pompeian supporter in Spain, who led the Pompeian revolt in 46 BC.

Q. Aquila
Caesarian naval commander in Africa in 46 BC. Took part in the Battles of Leptis and Hadrumetum. Led the naval blockade of Hadrumetum.

M. Aquinus
Pompeian supporter who surrendered to Caesar at Utica in 46 BC.

C. Ateius
Pompeian supporter who surrendered to Caesar at Utica in 46 BC.

P. Atrius
Pompeian supporter who surrendered to Caesar at Utica in 46 BC.

Caecina
Pompeian supporter who surrendered to Caesar at Utica in 46 BC.

C. Caninius Rebilus   (Cos. 45 BC)
Caesarian commander, present at the Battle of Thapsus and left in charge of the subsequent siege.

L. Cella and L. Cella
Pompeian supporters who surrendered to Caesar at Utica in 46 BC.

L. Cispius
Caesarian naval commander in Africa in 46 BC. Took part in the Battles of Leptis and Hadrumetum. Led the naval blockade of Thapsus.

C. Considius
Son of the Pompeian commander (see above), surrendered to Caesar at Utica in 46 BC.

P. Cornelius
Pompeian commander of Sarsura, killed defending the city from Caesar.

M. Eppius   (Q. pre 52 BC)
Pompeian supporter who surrendered to Caesar at Utica in 46 BC.

C. Hostilius Saserna
Caesarian commander placed in charge of the Leptis garrison in 46 BC.

P. Hostilius Saserna
Caesarian commander placed in charge of the Ruspina garrison in 46 BC.

Q. Ligarius
Pompeian supporter who surrendered to Caesar at Utica in 46 BC.

L. Livineius Regulus
Caesarian commander placed in charge of the Hadrumetum garrison in 46 BC.

C. Messius   (Aed.)
Caesarian commander placed in charge of the garrison of Acylla in 46 BC.

L. Nasidius
Pompeian naval commander who fought at the Battle of Massilia in 49 BC and commanded a fleet off Africa and Sardinia in 47 and 46 BC. Usually conflated with a Q. Nasidius who served under Sex. Pompeius and M. Antonius, but there is no evidence to support this.

Pacideius and Pacideius

Two Roman cavalry commanders who supported Labienus at the Battle of Ruspina in 46 BC. One was later seriously injured at the Battle of Tegea.

(Q.) Pompeius Rufus

A Pompeian commander who survived the massacre in the immediate aftermath of the Battle of Thapsus. Cannot be soundly identified with any known Pompeius Rufus, though may well have been the Tribune of 52 BC.[2]

T. Quintius Scapula

Pompeian supporter in Spain, who led the Pompeian revolt in 46 BC.

(Q.?) Tullius Rufus

A Pompeian commander killed in the massacre in the immediate aftermath of the Battle of Thapsus.

M. Valerius Messalla Rufus   (Cos. 53 BC)

A Caesarian commander, probably present at the Battle of Thapsus, sent on to Utica in the aftermath.

C. Vergilius   (Pr. 62 BC)

Pompeian commander of the garrison at Thapsus. Surrendered soon after the Battle with the collapse of Pompeian North Africa.

Appendix III

The Family of Iulius Caesar and the Third Civil War

One element that has emerged from this work is the role played by the various close family members of C. Iulius Caesar, a subject which has never received sufficient attention. Roman politics was family based and Caesar's own rise to power was considerably aided by the connections made by various marriages. The greatest of these was his aunt Iulia's marriage to the leading Roman general and politician C. Marius, whose demise along with his immediate family in the First Civil War left Caesar able to take up the mantle of his late uncle and tap into that vein of political support.

As well as the marriages of the generation before him, Caesar's own marriage and that of his offspring played an important part in his career. Significantly Caesar married the daughter of Rome's ruler in the mid-80s; L. Cornelius Cinna, (Cornelia) perhaps cementing the Marian-Cinnan factional alliance that dominated Rome during the first decade of the First Civil War. His next marriage saw an interesting reversal as he married into the opposite faction of the Civil War by marrying Pompeia, daughter of Q. Pompeius Rufus (son of Sulla's Consular colleague and close ally) and Sulla's own daughter. His final wife was a step down in political terms, Calpurnia, daughter of L. Calpurnius Piso Caesoninus, who actually succeeded Caesar as Consul in 58 BC, which despite a decent political lineage brought few connections.

Despite all these marriages, Caesar suffered from the fact that he only had one legitimate child, a daughter Iulia, (from Cornelia), who famously married Cn. Pompeius Magnus (59–54 BC), making him Caesar's son-in-law and making the Battle of Thapsus a clash between Pompeius' fathers-in-law.

Yet equally as famous is the fact that Caesar had no legitimate son of his own, with Caesarion (Ptolemy XV) naturally not recognized as legitimate in Roman law, no matter who his mother was. Any student of Roman history knows that into this void stepped C. Octavius, son of Caesar's niece, who was adopted in Caesar's will as his son, becoming C. Iulius Caesar Octavianus, who by skilful political manoeuvrings (and the generalship of his friend Agrippa) became uncontested Princeps of Rome, and ushered in the end of the Republic, by evolution not revolution.

Yet the rise of Octavius had created the image that Caesar had no other relatives to rely on, unlike the large family faction of Pompeius, with connections to the Metelli, Scipiones, Crassi and Sullani. As we have seen, however, this is a false impression and Caesar relied on the support of at least three relatives, and the opposition of another, all of whom could have played a prominent part in the Caesarian Republic, had both they, and Caesar lived, perhaps reducing the role that Octavius came to occupy.

L. Iulius Caesar (Cos. 64 BC)   Died. c. 40 BC

The most senior of Caesar' family to support him was his cousin Lucius, who rose to the rank of Consul before him, in 64 BC and unlike Caesar was himself the son of a Consul (90 BC). Thus in terms of precedent, Lucius was actually the more senior man in the Iulii Caesarones family. As was common he served as a Legate under his cousin during the Gallic Wars and equally supported him during the early civil war campaigns, primarily in Rome itself, lending political support. By contrast his son joined with Pompeius, though the details behind this family rift have not survived. In the aftermath of Caesar's assassination he remained a key member of the Senate but fell foul of the Triumvirate that took charge of the Caesarian faction and was proscribed though later pardoned. He is believed to have died c. 40 BC.

A staunch supporter of his cousin, he represented the senior branch of the family and could be relied upon for political support in the Senate, and was a similar age to Caesar, so a contemporary and never a successor.

L. Iulius Caesar   Murdered 46 BC

Son of the above Consul, he was famously the only member of the immediate Caesar family who opposed Caesar, siding with Pompeius. As mentioned above the reason for the split with his second cousin and his father has not been passed down to us. Initially he served as an emissary for Pompeius in Italy in 49 BC on tokenistic peace talks with Caesar. He later served as a junior commander in the Pompeian navy in 49 and 48 BC. Following the Pompeian recovery in Africa in 47 BC, we find him acting as Proquaestor to Cato in Utica. He was present at Cato's famous suicide, having elected to stay behind in Utica and make terms with his cousin. Pardoned by Caesar, he was murdered shortly afterwards, potentially by either side.

It is interesting to speculate upon the role Lucius would have played in the Caesarian Republic, had he lived. His Pompeian allegiance and connection to Cato would have made him acceptable to the anti-Caesarian elements of the Senate and he represented the latest generation of the linear family of Caesar, though his exact birth date was unknown. Clearly suspected by the Caesarian faction for his previous affinities, it is worth speculating on the role he would have played had Caesar lived, or more importantly in the aftermath of his death.

Sex. Iulius Caesar   Murdered 46 BC

Another young Caesar who would have played a significant role in the Caesarian Republic was Sex. Iulius Caesar, who also represented the younger generation of the family, but with none of the Pompeian / Catonic taint (as the Caesarians would have seen it). Sextus was clearly a rising star of the family, descended from the Consul of 91 BC (most likely grandson), he accompanied Caesar in his campaigns, serving as a Military Tribune in Spain in 49 BC and a Legate in the Fourth Romano-Pontic War. It is not known if he served with Caesar in Greece in 48 or in Egypt later that year.

What is certain is that Caesar was grooming him for a senior role within his Republic, having been appointed as Governor of the crucial province of Syria, charged with maintaining stability of the newly conquered Eastern Republic and defending it from any Parthian advances. He clearly would have had a role in the proposed Caesarian invasion of Parthia, and it is worth speculating on how much further he could have gone. Young, of the linear Caesar family, dedicated to his cousin and with considerable military experience, had he lived would Caesar's will have nominated him to inherit instead of the younger, more distantly related and inexperienced Octavius?

As it was, any such future was ended in 46 BC when he too was murdered, this time in a Pompeian inspired revolt by his own men, encouraged by the adventurer Caecilius Bassus who took up command in Syria in the name of Metellus Scipio and the Pompeians. Thus Caesar not only lost a commander and a province, but a cousin and potential successor.

Q. Pedius   (Cos. 43 BC)   Died 43 BC

The fourth and final family member was a not part of Caesar's immediate family, but was Caesar' own nephew, son of his sister Iulia. He too served with his uncle during the Gallic wars and later the civil wars. Elected as Praetor for 48 BC, he commanded operations against the Pompeian inspired uprising in Italy that year by Milo. Presumably in Italy over the 47–46 period, he was sent by Caesar as one of his advance commanders to stem the Pompeian uprising in Spain in mid-46 BC. He fought with Caesar during the Spanish campaigns of 45 BC and was awarded a Triumph on his return to Rome.

Named as one of Caesar's heirs in his will, became Suffect Consul in 43 BC along with his cousin and Caesar's newly adopted son, Octavianus Caesar on the deaths of the serving Consuls during the civil war campaigns of that year, having been chosen specifically by Octavianus to be his colleague. Passed the Lex Pedia condemning Caesar's assassins but died (perhaps conveniently) before the arrival of the newly formed Triumvirate of Caesarian commanders, removing another heir of Caesar from the equation.

Summary

Thus we can see that not only was Caesar supported by members of his family during the civil war, but that the double murders of the younger Caesars in 46 BC (Lucius and Sextus) robbed Caesar of the next generation of the family who could have supported him in cementing his rule of the Republic and actually would have been viable candidates to succeed him, in the event of his death. Their early removal forced Caesar to turn to a more distant and untested candidate (Octavius). On such vagaries, the history of the world rests.

Appendix IV

How Many Civil Wars?[1]

As readers will note I have deliberately chosen to include the provocative sub-title of the Third Roman Civil War for this series of books. This deliberately challenges the cosy status quo that has emerged in modern historiography of the Roman civil war period, and which ignores a fundamental question for anyone studying this era of Roman history; namely when is a civil war not a civil war? The short answer seems to be when it is a rebellion, revolt or even a conspiracy. There seems to have developed a very narrow and illogical definition of when a Roman army fighting a Roman army constitutes a civil war and when one does not.

Thus we have the absurdity of a Consul marching his army on Rome itself in 88 and 87 BC constituting a civil war, while a Proconsul acting in exactly the same way just ten years later (in 77 BC) does not.

Throughout my various works I have sought to challenge this cosy and somewhat lazy consensus that has emerged, first by lengthening the duration of the First Civil War from its traditional 88–82 BC to 91–70 BC, which allows us to include the Lepidian, Sertorian and Marian campaigns, where again Roman fought Roman, as sequels to the events of the 80s BC.[2] Under this schema, the war only ended in 70 BC (with the last military) campaign being fought in 71 BC, with the Consulships of Pompeius and Crassus and their political reform and general amnesty. This approach owes more to Appian, with his work on the civil wars covering 133–31 BC than to Florus, with each campaign being a separate war.

All too often modern historiography ignores this question and seems to follow the Florine route and wants to separate these various conflicts into nice self-contained wars. This is not just a problem with Roman history. Modern historiography seems to demand that civil wars be clearly defined between two opposing sides each with a different ideological standpoint.

Thus, English history only has one Civil War (1642–1651) with two clearly defined sides, each with separate ideological stand points (monarchy vs parliament) and even clearly defined costumes). Yet this war was at least the seventh fought between the English in the last thousand years. We have the civil war between Stephen and Matilda for the crowns of England and Normandy (1135–1153), the two civil wars fought between Kings John and Henry III and their rebellious nobles (1215–1217 and 1264–1267), another in the reign of Edward II (1321–1322) and the two wars fought for the English crown between the various branches of the Plantagenet dynasty between 1399 to 1403 and 1455 to 1487 (the latter of which is dubbed the War of the Roses).

Thus, English history has at least seven civil wars in the last thousand years yet only one makes the cut as an 'official' civil war. The obvious question is why are the others ignored and downgraded into non-civil wars each with a meaningless title (Baron Wars, Wars of the Roses)? Is it because they do not fit into a nice ideological framework or an unwillingness to acknowledge that societies collapse more often than we would like to admit?

If we look at history, we can discern two broad types of civil war. One is the 'modern' version where we have a clash between two clear sides, each with an ideological standpoint, usually centred on a question of governance. Thus, we have the classic English, American, Spanish and Chinese Civil Wars. Yet the second type is where there is a complete breakdown of government, and a society collapses into anarchy with various competing warlords emerging and fighting for supremacy. These types can most commonly be seen in modern Africa.

Returning to Rome, which type of civil wars can we see? All too often modern historians want them to be the clear cut ideological civil wars, between *optimates* and *populares* (terms which have been grossly distorted). Thus, our two official civil wars of the period – Sulla vs Marius and Caesar vs Pompeius – are often painted in these terms. Yet having reviewed these events, such terms are meaningless. The various protagonists did not go to war over differing views of how to govern, but turned to their armies to defend their own positions from the attacks of their enemies. The events of the 80s and 40s both snowballed out of everyone's control with the Republican system collapsing and leading to periods of anarchy where various Roman generals fought for supremacy amongst themselves until a victorious individual emerged who could rebuild central authority and calm the bloodshed i.e. dominate without looking like they were doing so; Pompeius and Crassus in 71–70 BC and Octavianus in 30–27 BC.

Thus, modern Roman historiography leaves us with a Florine-like patchwork of different wars:

Social War	(91–88 BC)
First Civil War	(88–81 BC)
Sertorian Rebellion	(81–72 BC)
Lepidian Revolt	(78–77 BC)
Catiline Conspiracy	(63–62 BC)
Second Civil War	(49–31 BC)

The clear danger of following such an approach of course is that it shifts focus away from the underlying causes of these conflicts and onto the individuals and thus blurs the line between symptom and cause. Should we be focusing on Sulla, Lepidus, Catilina, Caesar, or the underlying issues that were at work behind them? Clearly having read this volume, the reader will understand that focussing on the individuals at the expense of the wider picture is not a method I chose to pursue. Not one of these men woke up one morning and thought that they would like to march their army against their own state simply to gain power for themselves, but the Republican politics had forced them to believe that they had no alternative and that what they were doing was for the benefit of the Republic.

Ultimately as these events proved, the Republican system did not provide a robust enough framework to keep the various tensions between the Senatorial oligarchy from spilling over into violence and civil war. Various attempts were made to modify the Republic; be it Triumvirate (official or unofficial), or sole rule (subtle or obvious). The one version that emerged victorious from this period was sole rule; one figure guiding and overseeing the smooth running of the Republic and acting as arbiter to keep the others in check. Yet this too was flawed and laid the foundations for the role of Emperor, first on a hereditary basis and then merit or armed force.

Yet, if we are to reject the Florine version of the wars in this period, what are we to replace it with? Do we simply follow the Appianic version and state that the whole of this period was one giant civil war, or do we reject the notion of a civil war in a society such as Rome altogether? I have and will continue to argue that within this period of Roman history there were distinct periods of civil wars, when the clashes and tensions within the Republican system boiled over into full blown military conflict and in two out of the three cases, total system wide (and empire wide collapse).

Civil war within a country is one thing, but civil war in a society that had a full-blown empire is another matter altogether and magnified the chaos and fighting on a Mediterranean wide level. As we have seen in two out of three cases, Rome's empire became a battleground for the various parties of the civil war and led to the extinction of several independent kingdoms, who became too closely associated with a losing side (namely Numidia and Egypt).

Having rejected the modern Florine notion of multiple separate wars, I would like to offer up a fresh scheme for the civil wars within this period, if only to stimulate further debate on a subject that can never have a right answer.

The First Civil War 91–70 BC

All too often, discussions of the First Civil War ignore the fact that Italy had been riven by civil warfare for three years with two rebel factions fighting the Republican government. This is the very reason that Sulla had an army of battle hardened veterans in Italy within marching distance of Rome and citizen distribution was at the heart of the political manoeuvring which led to Sulla's loss of command. Thus, the war that broke out in 91 BC between the various societies that made up the Roman system, must be classed as a civil war, with neighbour fighting neighbour and, if we are to believe the more dramatic sources, brother fighting brother.

Thus, the First Civil War period saw a number of different phases, which were not neatly separate conflicts but were all intertwined. The war in Italy led to the Consular attack on Rome in 88 BC, both of which mixed together to spark off the war of 87 BC. There then followed a lull whilst at least two different Roman armies separately fought off a foreign invasion. When that invasion had been dealt with then all sides engaged in a fight for supremacy which brought about another lull as Sulla consolidated his control of Italy and the western empire. Some regions were forcibly reunited (Sicily, Africa) whilst others (Spain and Gaul) were managed through negotiation between warlords. Yet the faction that lost Italy soon stoked a rebellion in Spain where the civil war continued (mixed in with a native rebellion, as it had done in Italy) for another nine years. Whilst the civil war continued in the Western Republic (Spain), other elements of the faction that lost Italy spearheaded another foreign invasion of Rome's empire, again blurring the lines between civil war and foreign war.

Thus, we can see that during this period there were no neat delineations between civil war, native rebellion and foreign wars, but all became inexorably interlinked in one great collapse of the Republican system. It is also not a coincidence that the largest slave rebellion in Roman history happened during this period of chaos, when a certain slave named Spartacus took advantage of the devastation in Italy, disaffection with Rome and overseas wars to launch his rebellion.

By 71 BC there emerged another lull when the fighting ended in Spain, Italy and Asia. Yet it required the actions of Pompeius and Crassus, who chose to unite Rome (rather than continue the division and personally benefit from it). Their Consulship did not only set an example that two oligarchs could work in a peaceful manner, especially if they cooperated by the constitutional settlement, they removed a number of tension points (though some would say reintroduced them) and saw a very public recall of all Romans who had been exiled during the previous twenty years of tumult. Thus, it can be argued that this lull became a definitive endpoint.

The Second Civil War 63–62 BC

That the events of 63/62 BC constitute a civil war should not be difficult to argue. Although the ancient sources and modern histography choose to focus on events in Rome, the key facts are that there were widescale rebellions against Rome throughout Italy and native rebellions in Gaul (again mixing the two) and two Romano-Italian armies fought one another in a set piece battle. That there was only one set piece battle, and that it was over relatively quickly should not disqualify this from being classed as a civil war. In fact, the surviving sources paint a picture of wider military action across Italy, but we only have the barest of detail for it. Had we fuller sources for this fighting then we would be able to see the true scale of the civil war in Italy.

The other argument is that if this was a civil war, was it a continuation of the first war and thus can we extend the First Civil War down to 62 BC?

As we have reviewed, the causes of this conflict did have their roots in the first war, be they disgruntled Sullan politicians and veterans, or displaced Italian communities. Yet I would argue that it was a separate conflict from that of 91–70 BC and that the years 69–64 BC were not merely a lull in the first war, but that the Pompeian-Crassan Consulships did end the First Civil War. That a war can be finished but still leave matters unsettled can be seen frequently throughout history; most recently in the First and Second World Wars (at least in Europe). So, although the Second Civil War had its roots in the First, they were, I believe, separate conflicts. This can also be seen by the fact that the New Republic reconstituted out of the ashes of the First Civil War did not collapse as it had done in 91–70 or 49–27 BC.

The Third Civil War 49–27 BC

This is perhaps the most uncontentious of the three, with it being widely accepted that the events between the crossing of the Rubicon in 49 BC and the victory of Octavianus constitute another period of one civil war which again saw a total collapse of the Republican system the emergence of various factions and warlords. It saw too the blurring between civil war and foreign war, again most easily seen in the east with the attack of the Parthian Empire being spearheaded by Roman generals. This period also saw lulls in the fighting between the various overlapping conflicts. There was no certainty that Octavianus' victory at Actium in 31 BC would be the final major battle of the war, any more than the Battle of Pharsalus in 48 BC or Philippi in 42 BC.

If there is one contentious issue, then it must be the end date of this civil war. It clearly did not conclude with the battle of Actium in 31 BC as Antonius still fought on with his defence of Egypt, which only fell in 30 BC. Yet as we have explored above, winning a campaign did not bring about victory, especially in a civil war; it was winning the peace. This is where both Sulla and Caesar failed when they had military control of the Republic. Roman civil wars did not seem to end when one side was victorious in battle, as new opponents soon emerged. Roman Civil Wars only ended when everyone agreed that there was no further need to fight and that the imbalances in the Republican system that they had believed were there, had been righted. For that reason, I would argue that the Third

Civil War did not end until the First Constitutional Settlement of the newly renamed Augustus in 27 BC; with the intervening years 30–27 BC being merely a lull in the fighting. Thus, Republican politics was both the cause of the civil wars and the solution (however temporary).

Bibliography

Abbott, F. (1917). 'Titus Labienus', *Classical Journal* 13, 4–13.

Amela, L. (2003). *Cneo Pompeyo Magno. El defensor de la República Romana* (Madrid: Signifer Libros).

——. (2008). 'The Campaign of Quintus Fufius Calenus in Greece During the Year 48 B.C. and the City of Megara. The Consequences of the War'. *Athenaeum* 96, 279–291.

Anders. A. (2015). 'The Face of Roman Skirmishing', *Historia* 64, 263–300.

Anderson. E. (2013). 'Publius Sittius and Caesar's Revenge', *History Today* 63.9

Appel, H. (2012). 'Pompeius Magnus: his Third Consulate and the senatus consultum ultimum', *Biuletyn Polskiej Misji Historycznej* 7, 341–360.

Badian, E. (1974). 'The Attempt to Try Caesar,' in J. Evans (ed.), *Polis and Imperium: Studies in Honour of Edward Togo Salmon* (Toronto: Edgar Kent Inc.), 145–166.

——. (1996). 'Tribuni Plebis and Res Publica', in J. Linderski (ed.) *Imperium Sine Fine* (Stuttgart: Franz Steiner Verlag Wiesbaden GmbH), 187–214.

Ballesteros Pastor, L. (2017). 'Pharnaces II and His Title "King of Kings"', *Ancient West & East* 16, 297–303.

Balsdon, J. (1957). 'The Veracity of Caesar', *Greece & Rome* 4, 19–28.

Barrett, A. (1972). 'Catullus 52 and the Consulship of Vatinius', *Transactions and Proceedings of the American Philological Association* 103, 23–38.

Bartsch, S. (1997). *Ideology in Cold Blood. A Reading of Lucan's Civil War* (Cambridge MA: Harvard University Press).

Batstone, W. & Damon, C. (2006). *Caesar's Civil War* (Oxford: Oxford University Press).

Bell, A. (1994). 'Fact and "Exemplum" in Accounts of the Deaths of Pompey and Caesar', *Latomus* 53, 824–836.

Beneker, J. (2011). 'The Crossing of the Rubicon and the Outbreak of Civil War in Cicero, Lucan, Plutarch and Suetonius', *Phoenix* 65, 74–99.

Berdowski, P. (2012). 'Cn. Pompeius, the son of Pompey the Great: an embarrassing ally in the African War? (48–46 BC)', *Palamedes* 7, 117–142.

Bexley, E. (2009). 'Replacing Rome: Geographic and Political Centrality in Lucan's Pharsalia', *Classical Philology* 104, 459–475.

Billows, R. (1982). 'The Last of the Scipios', *American Journal of Ancient History* 7, 53–68.

——. (2008). *Julius Caesar: The Colossus of Rome* (London: Routledge).

Boak, A. (1918). 'The Extraordinary Commands from 80 to 48 BC: A Study in the Origins of the Principate', *American Historical Review* 24, 1–25.

Broughton, T. (1951/2). *The Magistrates of the Roman Republic Volume I & 2* (New York: American Philological Association).

——. (1960). *Supplement to the Magistrates of the Roman Republic* (New York: American Philological Association).

——. (1986). *Supplement to the Magistrates of the Roman Republic* (New York: American Philological Association).

——. (1989). 'M. Aemilius Lepidus: His Youthful Career', in R. Curtis (ed.). *Studia Pompeiana & Classica in Honour of Wilhelmina F. Jashemski, vol. II:* (New York: A. D. Caratzas), 13–23

Brown, R. (1999). 'Two Caesarian Battle-Descriptions: A Study in Contrast', *Classical Journal* 94, 329–357.

Brunt, P. (1971). *Social Conflicts in the Roman Republic* (London: W.W. Norton).

——. (1988). *The Fall of the Roman Republic* (Oxford: Oxford University Press).

Canfora, L. (2007). *Julius Caesar: The Life and Times of the People's Dictator* (Edinburgh: Edinburgh University Press).

Chrystal, P. (2019). *Rome: Republic into Empire: The Civil Wars of the First Century* BC (Barnsley: Pen & Sword History).

Collins, H. (1953). 'The Decline and Fall of Pompey the Great', *Greece & Rome* 22, 98–106.

Cornwell, H. (2014). 'The Construction of One's Enemies in Civil War (49–30 BC)', *Hermathena* 196/197, 41–68.

Coşkun, A. (2019). 'The Course of Pharnakes II's Pontic and Bosphoran Campaigns in 48/47 BC', *Phoenix* 73, 86–113.

Coulter, C. (1952). 'Pollio's History of the Civil War', *Classical Weekly* 46, 33–36.

Damon, C. (1994). 'Caesar's Practical Prose', *Classical Journal* 89, 183–195.

Drogula, F. (2019). *Cato the Younger: Life and Death at the End of the Roman Republic* (Oxford: Oxford University Press).

Duncan, M. (2017). *The Storm Before the Storm: The Beginning of the End of the Roman Republic* (London: PublicAffairs).

Eden, P. (1962). 'Caesar's Style: Inheritance versus Intelligence', *Glotta* 40, 74–117.

Ehrhardt, C. (1995). 'Crossing the Rubicon', *Antichthon* 29, 37–41.

Epstein, D. (1987). *Personal Enmity in Roman Politics 218–43 BC* (London: Routledge).

Evans, R. (2004). 'Caesar's use of the Tribuni Plebis', *Questioning Reputations* (Pretoria), 65–92.

——. (2016). 'Pompey's Three Consulships: The End of Electoral Competition in the Late Roman Republic', *Acta Classica* 59, 80–100.

Ezov, A. (1996). 'The "Missing Dimension" of C. Julius Caesar', *Historia* 45, 64–94.

Fentress E. (1982). 'Tribe and Faction: The Case of the Gaetuli', *Mélanges de l'École Française de Rome Antiquité*, 94, 325–334.

Fezzi, L. (2019). *Crossing the Rubicon: Caesar's Decision and the Fate of Rome* (London: Yale University Press).

Field, N. (2009). *Warlords of Republican Rome: Caesar Versus Pompey* (Barnsley: Pen & Sword Books).

Flower, H. (2010). *Roman Republics* (Princeton: Princeton University Press).

Frank, T. (1907). 'Caesar at the Rubicon', *Classical Quarterly* 1, 223–225.

Fuller, J. (1965). *Julius Caesar: Man, Soldier, and Tyrant* (London: Eyre and Spottiswoode).

Gelzer, M. (1980). *Caesar: Politician and Statesman* (London: Harvard University Press).

Gerrish, J. (2019). *Sallust's Histories and Triumviral Historiography. Confronting the End of History* (London: Routledge).

Golden, G. (2013). *Crisis Management during the Roman Republic: The Role of Political Institutions in Emergencies* (Cambridge: Cambridge University Press).

Goldsworthy, A. (2006). *Caesar: Life of a Colossus* (Yale: Yale University Press).

——. (2023). *Caesar's Civil War: 49–44 BC* (London: Osprey Publishing).

Goodman, R & Soni. J. (2012). *Rome's Last Citizen. The Life and Legacy of Cato, Mortal Enemy of Caesar* (New York: Thomas Dunne Books).

Gray, E. (1979). 'The Consular Elections held in 65 BC', *Antichthon* 13, 56–65.

Greenhalgh, P. (1980). *Pompey. The Roman Alexander* (London: Littlehampton Book Services Limited).

——. (1981). *Pompey. The Republican Prince* (London: Littlehampton Book Services Limited).

Grillo, L. (2012). *The Art of Caesar's Bellum Civile: Literature, Ideology, and Community* (Cambridge: Cambridge University Press).

Gruen. E. (1974). *The Last Generation of the Roman Republic* (Berkeley: University of California Press).

Haley, S. (1985). 'The Five Wives of Pompey the Great', *Greece & Rome* 32, 49–59.

Hayne, L. (1996). 'Caesar and Lentulus Crus', *Acta Classica* 39, 72–76.

Hillman, T. (1996). 'Pompeius ad Parthos?' *Klio* 78, 380–399.

Holland, T. (2003). *Rubicon: The Triumph and Tragedy of the Roman Republic* (London: Little Brown UK).

Holliday, V. (1969). *Pompey in Cicero's Correspondence and Lucan's Civil War* (Hague: De Gruyter Mouton).

Holzapfel, L. (1904). 'Die Anfänge des Bürgerkrieges zwischen Cäsar und Pompejus', *Klio* 4 327–382.

Isayev, E. (2007). 'Unruly Youth? The Myth of Generation Conflict in Late Republican Rome', *Historia* 56, 1–13.

Jal, P. (1962). 'Le rôle des Barbares dans les guerres civiles de Rome, de Sylla à Vespasien', *Latomus* 21, pp. 8–48.

——. (1963*). La guerre civile à Rome* (Paris: Presses Universitaires de France).

Jameson, S. (1970). 'The Intended Date of Caesar's Return from Gaul', *Latomus* 29, 638–660.

Jones, C. (1970). 'Cicero's Cato', *Rheinisches Museum für Philologie* 113, 188–196.

Keaveney, A. (2007). *The Army in the Roman Revolution* (London: Routledge).

Knight, D. (1968). 'Pompey's Concern with Pre-eminence After 60 BC', *Latomus* 27, 878–883.

Konrad, C. (1996). 'Notes on Roman Also Rans', in J. Linderski (ed.). *Imperium Sine Fine: T. Robert S. Broughton and the Roman Republic* (Stuttgart: Franz Steiner Verlag Wiesbaden GmbH), 103–143.

Lange, C. (2018). *Triumphs in the Age of Civil War: The Late Republic and the Adaptability of Triumphal Tradition* (London: Bloomsbury Academic).

Lange, C. & Scott, A. (2020). *Cassius Dio: The Impact of Violence, War, and Civil War* (Leiden).

Lange, C. & Vervaet, F. (2019) *The Historiography of Late Republican Civil War* (Leiden: Brill).

Lazenby, J. (1959). 'The Conference of Luca and the Gallic War; A Study in Roman Politics 57–55 BC', *Latomus* 18, 63–76.

Leach, J. (1978). *Pompey the Great* (London: Routledge).

Linderski, J. (1996). 'Q. Scipio Imperator', in J. Linderski (ed.). *Imperium Sine Fine: T. Robert S. Broughton and the Roman Republic* (Stuttgart: Franz Steiner Verlag Wiesbaden GmbH), 145–185.

Lintott, A. (1968). *Violence in Republican Rome* (Oxford: Oxford University Press).

——. (1971). 'Lucan and the History of the Civil War', *Classical Quarterly* 21, 488–505.

——. (1974). 'Cicero and Milo', *Journal of Roman Studies* 64, 62–78.

——. (1999). *The Constitution of the Roman Republic* (Oxford: Oxford University Press).

Long, G. (1864). *The Decline of the Roman Republic Volumes 1–5* (London: Bell and Dalby).

López Barja de Quiroga, P. (2019). 'The Bellum Civile Pompeianum: The War of Words', *Classical Quarterly* 69, 700–714.

Lord, L. (1938). 'The Date of Julius Caesar's Departure from Alexandria', *Journal of Roman Studies* 28, 19–40.

Lounsbury, R. (1976). 'History and Motive in Book Seven of Lucan's Pharsalia', *Hermes*, 104, 210–239.

MacKay, L. (1952). 'Pharsalus and the Roman Fate', *Phoenix* 6, 147–150.

Marin, P. (2009). *Blood in the Forum. The Struggle for the Roman Republic* (London: Continuum).

Masters, J. (1992). *Poetry and Civil War in Lucan's Bellum Civile* (Cambridge: Cambridge University Press).

Meier, C. (1995). *Caesar. A Biography* (London: Basic Books).

Meyer, E. (1919). *Caesars Monarchie und das Prinzipat des Pompejus* (Stuttgart: J.G. Cotta'sche Buchhandlung).

Melchior, A. (2009). 'What Would Pompey Do? Exempla and Pompeian Failure in the "Bellum Africum"', *Classical Journal* 104, 241–257.

Miączewska, A. (2014). 'Quintus Fufius Calenus: a Forgotten Career', *Hermathena* 196/197, 163–204.

Millar, F. (1994). 'Popular Politics at Rome in the Late Republic', in I. Malkin & Z. Rubinsohn (eds.) *Leaders and Masses in the Roman World: Studies in Honor of Zvi Yavetz* (Leiden: Brill), 91–113.

Morgan, L. (1997). 'Levi Quidem de re...': Julius Caesar as Tyrant and Pedant', *Journal of Roman Studies* 87, 23–40.

——. (2000). 'The Autopsy of C. Asinius Pollio', *Journal of Roman Studies* 90, 51–69.

Morrell, K. (2017). *Pompey, Cato, and the Governance of the Roman Empire* (Oxford: Oxford University Press).

Morstein-Marx, R. (2007). 'Caesar's Alleged Fear of Prosecution and His "Ratio Absentis" in the Approach to the Civil War', *Historia* 56, 159–178.

Niccolini, G. (1934). *I fasti dei tribuni della plebe* (Milan: Dott. Antonio Giuffrè).

Osgood, J. (2015). 'Ending Civil War at Rome: Rhetoric and Reality, 88 BC-197 AD', *American Historical Review* 120, 1683–1695.

Peaks, M. (1903). 'Caesar's Movements, January 21 to February 14, 49 BC', *Classical Review* 18, 346–349.

Peer, A. (2015). *Julius Caesar's Bellum Civile and the Composition of a New Reality* (London: Routledge).

Pelling, C. (1973). 'Pharsalus', *Historia* 22, 249–259.

Pina Polo, F. (2019). 'Losers in the Civil War between Caesarians and Pompeians. Punishment and Survival', in K-J Hölkeskamp & H. Beck (eds.) *Verlierer und Aussteiger in der Konkurrenz unter Anwesenden. Agonalität in der Politischen Kultur des Antiken Rom*, 147–168.

Pocock, L. (1959). 'What Made Pompeius Fight in 49 BC?', *Greece & Rome* 6, 68–81.

Postgate, J. (1905). 'Pharsalia Nostra', *Classical Review* 19, 257–260.

Powell, A & Welch, K. (2002). *Sextus Pompeius* (London: Classical Press of Wales).

Pucci Ben Zeev, M. (1996). 'When was the title "Dictator perpetuus" given to Caesar?' *L'antiquité classique* 65, 251–253.

Raaflaub, K. (2003). 'Caesar the Liberator? Factional Politics, Civil War, and Ideology.' In F. Cairns & E. Fantham (eds.). *Caesar Against Liberty? Perspectives on his Autocracy*. (Cambridge: Cambridge University Press). 35–67.

Rambaud, M. (1955). 'Le Soleil de Pharsale', *Historia* 3, 346-378.

Rawson, E. (1978). 'The Identity Problems of Q. Cornificius', *Classical Quarterly* 28, 188–201.

Reubel, J. (1994). *Caesar and the Crisis of the Roman Aristocracy. A Civil War Reader* (Oklahoma: University of Oklahoma Press).

Ridley, R. (1981). 'The Extraordinary Commands of the Late Republic: A Matter of Definition', *Historia* 30, 280–297.

——. (1983). 'Pompey's Commands in the 50s: How Cumulative?' *Rheinisches Museum für Philologie* 126, 136–148.

——. (2000). 'The Dictator's Mistake: Caesar's Escape from Sulla', *Historia* 49, 211–229.

——. (2004). 'Attacking the World with Five Cohorts; Caesar in January 49', *Ancient Society* 34, 127–152.

Riggsby, A. (2006). *Caesar in Gaul and Rome: War in Words* (Austin: University of Texas Press).

Rondholz, A. (2009). 'Crossing the Rubicon: A Historiographical Study', *Mnemosyne* 62, 432–450.

Rossi, A. (2000). 'The Camp of Pompey: Strategy of Representation in Caesar's Bellum Civile', *Classical Journal* 95, 239–256.

Rowe, G. (1967). 'Dramatic Structures in Caesar's Bellum Civile', *Transactions of the American Philological Association* 98, 399–414

Ryan, F. (1994). 'The Quaestorship of Favonius and the Tribunate of Metellus Scipio', *Athenaeum* 82, 505–521.

Sabin, P. (2000). 'The Face of Roman Battle', *Journal of Roman Studies* 90, 1–17.

Sage, E. (1920). 'The Senatus Consultum Ultimum', *Classical Weekly* 13, 185–189.

Sampson. G. (2005). *A re-examination of the office of the Tribunate of the Plebs in the Roman Republic (494–23 BC)* (Unpublished Thesis).

——. (2008). *The Defeat of Rome. Crassus, Carrhae and the Invasion of the East* (Barnsley: Pen & Sword Military).

——. (2010). *The Crisis of Rome. The Jugurthine and Northern Wars and the Rise of Marius* (Barnsley: Pen & Sword Military).

——. (2013). *The Collapse of Rome, Marius, Sulla, and The First Civil War 91–70 BC* (Barnsley: Pen & Sword Military).

——. (2017). *Rome, Blood, and Politics. Reform, Murder and Popular Politics in the Late Republic 146–70 BC* (Barnsley: Pen & Sword History).

——. (2019). *Rome, Blood, and Power: Reform, Murder and Popular Politics in the Late Republic 70–27 BC* (Barnsley: Pen & Sword History).

——. (2020). *Rome and Parthia: Empires at War: Ventidius, Antony and the Second Romano-Parthian War, 40–20 BC* (Barnsley: Pen & Sword Military).

——. (2021). *Rome's Great Eastern War: Lucullus, Pompey, and the Conquest of the East, 74–62 BC* (Barnsley: Pen & Sword Military).

——. (2022). *The Battle of Dyrrhachium (48 BC). Caesar, Pompey, and the Early Campaigns of the Third Roman Civil War* (Barnsley: Pen & Sword Military).

——. (2023). *The Battle of Pharsalus (48 BC). Caesar, Pompey, and their Final Clash in the Third Roman Civil War* (Barnsley: Pen & Sword Military).

——. (Forthcoming). *The Battle of Munda (45 BC)*. *Pompey, Labienus and Caesar's Final Battle of the Third Roman Civil War* (Barnsley: Pen & Sword Books).

Seager, R. (1979). *Pompey. A Political Biography* (Oxford: Wiley-Blackwell).

Shackleton-Bailey, D. (1960). 'The Roman Nobility in the Second Civil War', *Classical Quarterly* 10, 253–26.

Simmons, D. (2011). *From Obscurity to Fame and Back Again: The Caecilii Metelli in the Roman Republic* (Unpublished Thesis).

Sirianni, F. (1979). Caesar's Decision to Cross the Rubicon', *L'Antiquité Classique* 48, 636–638.

——. (1993). 'Caesar's Peace Overtures to Pompey', *L'Antiquité Classique* 62 (1993), 219–237.

Southern, P. (2002). *Pompey the Great* (Stroud: The History Press: Ltd).

Stanton, G. (2003). 'Why Did Caesar Cross the Rubicon?', *Historia* 52, 67–94.

Stem, S. (1999). *Cicero and the Legacy of Cato Uticensis* (Unpublished Thesis).

——. (2005). 'The First Eloquent Stoic: Cicero on Cato the Younger', *Classical Journal* 101, 37–49.

Stevenson, T. (2015). 'Appian on the Pharsalus Campaign: Civil Wars 2.48–91.' in K. Welch (ed.), *Appian's Roman History. Empire and Civil War* (Swansea: Classical Press of Wales), 257–275.

Sumner, G. (1977). 'The Pompeii in their Families', *American Journal of Ancient History* 2, 8–25.

Syme, R. (1938). 'The Allegiance of Labienus', *Journal of Roman Studies* 28, 113–125.

——. (1939). *The Roman Revolution* (Oxford: Oxford University Press).

——. (1963). 'Ten Tribunes', *Journal of Roman Studies* 53, 55–60.

Taylor, L. (1941). 'Caesar's Early Career', *Classical Philology* 36, 113–132.

——. (1957). 'The Rise of Julius Caesar', *Greece & Rome*, 4, 10–18.

——. (1949). *Party Politics in the Age of Caesar* (Berkeley: University of California Press).

Townsend. P. (1940). 'The Oil Tribute of Africa at the Time of Julius Caesar', *Classical Philology* 35, 274–283.

Treggiari, S. (1969). 'Pompeius' freedman biographer again.' *Classical Review* 19, 264–266.

Tucker, R. (1988). 'What Actually Happened at the Rubicon?' *Historia* 37, 245–248.

Tyrrell, W. (1972). 'Labienus' Departure from Caesar in January 49 BC', *Historia* 21, 424–440.

van Ooteghem, J. (1954). *Pompee le Grand. Batisseur d' Empire* (Bruxelles: Palais Des Académies).

Veith, G. (1920). *Der Feldzug von Dyrrhachium zwischen Caesar und Pompeius* (Wien: L.W. Seidel und Sohn).

Vervaet, F. (2006). 'The Official Position of Cn. Pompeius in 49 and 48 BC', *Latomus* 65, 928–953.

von Fritz, K. (1942). 'Pompey's Policy before and after the Outbreak of the Civil War of 49 BC', *Transactions and Proceedings of the American Philological Association* 73, 145–180.

von Ravensburg, A. (1961). *Burgerkrieg Zwischen Casar Und Pompejus, Im Jahre 50/49 V. Chr. Und Die Kampfe Dei Dyrrhachium Und Pharsalus*.

Watts, E. (2019). *Mortal Republic: How Rome Fell into Tyranny* (London: Basic Books).

Welch, K. (1995). 'Antony, Fulvia, and the Ghost of Clodius in 47 BC', *Greece & Rome* 42, 182–201.

——. (1998). *Julius Caesar as Artful Reporter: The War Commentaries as Political* (London: Classical Press of Wales).

——. (2012). *Magnus Pius. Sextus Pompeius and the Transformation of the Roman Republic* (Swansea: Classical Press of Wales).

Westall, R. (2013). 'The Relationship of Appian to Pollio.' *Analecta Romana Instituti Danici* 38, 7–34.

——. (2015). 'The Sources for the Civil Wars of Appian of Alexandria', in K. Welch (ed.). *Appian's Roman History. Empire and Civil War* (Swansea: Classical Press of Wales), 125–167.

——. (2016). 'The Sources of Cassius Dio for the Roman Civil Wars of 49–30 BC', in C. Lange and J. Madsen (eds.) *Cassius Dio. Greek Intellectual and Roman Politician* (Leiden: Brill), 51–75.

——. (2017). *Caesar's Civil War. Historical Reality and Fabrication* (Leiden: Brill).

Wiseman, T. (1996). 'Crossing the Rubicon, and Other Dramas', *Scripta Classica Israelica* 15, 152–158.

——. (2010). 'The Two-Headed State: How Romans Explained Civil War', in B. W. Breed, C. Damon, & A. Rossi (eds.). *Citizens of Discord. Rome and its Civil Wars* (Oxford: Oxford University Press). 25–44.

Wylie, G. (1989). 'Why Did Labienus Defect from Caesar in 49 BC?', *Ancient History Bulletin* 3, 123–127.

——. (1992). 'The Road to Pharsalus', *Latomus* 51, 557–565.

Yarrow, L. (2006). *Historiography at the End of the Republic: Provincial Perspectives on Roman Rule* (Oxford: Oxford University Press).

Yates, D. (2011). 'The Role of Cato the Younger in Caesar's "Bellum Civile"', *Classical World* 104, 161–174.

Yavetz, Z. (1971). 'Caesar, Caesarism, and the Historians', *Journal of Contemporary History* 6, 184–201

Notes

Chapter One

1. See G. Sampson. (2022). *The Battle of Dyrrhachium (48 BC). Caesar, Pompey, and the Early Campaigns of the Third Roman Civil War* (Barnsley) & (2023). *The Battle of Pharsalus (48 BC): Caesar, Pompey, and their Final Clash in the Third Roman Civil War* (Barnsley).
2. See G. Sampson (2018). *Rome. Blood and Politics. Reform, Murder and Popular Politics in the late Roman Republic 133–70 BC.* (Barnsley)
3. Ibid
4. See G. Sampson (2010). *The Crisis of Rome. The Jugurthine and Northern Wars and the Rise of Marius* (Barnsley).
5. See G. Sampson. (2013). *The Collapse of Rome, Marius, Sulla, and The First Civil War 91–70 BC* (Barnsley).
6. Ibid.
7. See G. Sampson (2019). *Rome. Blood and Power. Reform, Murder and Popular Politics in the late Roman Republic 70–27 BC.* (Barnsley).
8. See R. Ridley. (2000). 'The Dictator's Mistake: Caesar's Escape from Sulla', *Historia* 49, pp.211–229.
9. See E. Gray. (1979). 'The Consular Elections held in 65 BC', *Antichthon* 13, pp.56–65.
10. See G. Sampson (2021). *Rome's Great Eastern War: Lucullus, Pompey, and the Conquest of the East, 74–62 BC* (Barnsley).
11. See G. Sampson. (2008). *The Defeat of Rome. Crassus, Carrhae and the Invasion of the East* (Barnsley).
12. See S. Haley. (1985). 'The Five Wives of Pompey the Great', *Greece & Rome* 32, pp.49–59.

Chapter Two

1. See G. Sampson (2022 & 2023) respectively.
2. Named after the Second Romano-Punic War Roman general; Q. Fabius Maximus Verrucosus, who successfully contained Hannibal, during his invasion of Italy, by avoiding battle.
3. T. Broughton. (1952). *The Magistrates of the Roman Republic* 2, p. 283.

Chapter Three

1. See G, Sampson (2023).
2. See G. Sampson (2022) & (2023).
3. See G. Sampson (2013).
4. Liv. *Per* 113.1
5. Vell. 2.54.2
6. Plut. *Cat.* 57

7. Dio. 42.57.1–3
8. See J. Linderski. (1996). 'Q. Scipio Imperator', in J. Linderski (ed.). *Imperium Sine Fine: T. Robert S. Broughton and the Roman Republic* (Stuttgart), pp.145–185.
9. See. T. Broughton. (1952), 2, p.189 & G. Niccolini (1934), pp.279–281.
10. See C. Konrad, (1996). 'Notes on Roman Also Rans', in J. Linderski (ed.). *Imperium Sine Fine: T. Robert S. Broughton and the Roman Republic* (Stuttgart), pp.123–141.
11. See K. Morrell. (2017). *Pompey, Cato, and the Governance of the Roman Empire* (Oxford).
12. See G. Sampson (2020).
13. See F. Abbott. (1917). 'Titus Labienus', *Classical Journal* 13, pp.4–13, R. Syme. (1938). 'The Allegiance of Labienus', *Journal of Roman Studies* 28, pp.113–125, W. Tyrrell. (1972). 'Labienus' Departure from Caesar in January 49 BC', *Historia* 21, pp.424–440, G. Wylie. (1989). 'Why Did Labienus Defect From Caesar in 49 BC?', *Ancient History Bulletin* 3, 123–127.
14. See G. Sampson (202).
15. Sall. *Cat.* 59.6
16. See A. Powell & K. Welch. (2002). *Sextus Pompeius* (London), K. Welch. (2012). *Magnus Pius. Sextus* Pompeius and the Transformation of the Roman Republic (Swansea).
17. *De. Bell. Afr.* 87
18. Ibid. 90
19. Appian mention them in passing. App. *BC.* 2.100
20. See Plut. *Caes.* 11.6

Chapter Four
1. See G. Sampson (2022).
2. *De. Bell. Alex.* 43
3. App. *Ill.* 12
4. Ibid. 27
5. App. *Ill.* 28
6. See also Cic. *Att.* 11.16.1
7. *De. Bell. Alex.* 44
8. Ibid. 45–47
9. See L. Amela. (2008). 'The Campaign of Quintus Fufius Calenus in Greece During the Year 48 B.C. and the City of Megara. The Consequences of the War'. *Athenaeum* 96, pp.279–291.
10. Dio. 42.14.1
11. Ibid. 42.14.3
12. See G. Sampson (2023).
13. Dio. 43.1.2
14. Ibid. 43.29
15. See G. Sampson (2023).
16. Dio 42.56.3
17. *De Bell. Afr.* 98, Also see a reference to Nasidius in *De. Bell. Afr.* 64
18. See G. Sampson (2022).
19. Dio. 42.27.3–4
20. Ibid
21. As Metellus Scipio's own record showed, this could, however, be a side effect of a 'natural' adoption.
22. Plut. *Ant.* 9.1

23. Plut. *Ant.* 9.1, Cic. *Phil.* 2.99
24. Dio. 42.30.2–3
25. See L. Lord. (1938). 'The Date of Julius Caesar's Departure from Alexandria', *Journal of Roman Studies* 28, pp.19–40.
26. Dio. 42.30.1
27. Ibid. 42.31.1–3
28. Dio. 42.32.3
29. Plut. *Ant.* 9.2
30. Liv. *Per.* 113.5
31. Dio. 42.33.1–3
32. Ibid. 42.30.1
33. *De. Bell. Alex.* 65.2
34. Cic. *Att.* 11.21.2
35. Ibid. 22.2
36. Dio. 42.56.4

Chapter Five

1. Dio. 42.33.1–3
2. See A. Miączewska. (2014). 'Quintus Fufius Calenus: a Forgotten Career', *Hermathena* 196/197, pp.163–204 & A. Barrett. (1972). 'Catullus 52 and the Consulship of Vatinius', *Transactions and Proceedings of the American Philological Association* 103, pp.23–38.
3. See G. Niccolini. (1934). *I fasti dei tribuni della plebe* (Milan), pp.341–343 and T. Broughton. (1952). 2, p.296.
4. Dio. 42.51.3
5. Ibid. 42.51.1–3
6. Suet. *Iul.* 38.2
7. Dio 42.52.1–2. Plut. *Caes.* 51 names them as a Galba and a Cosconius
8. App. *BC.* 2.92
9. Ibid
10. Dio. 42.52.3
11. Dio. 42.52–54, App. *BC.* 2.93–94, Plut. *Caes.* 51, Suet. *Caes.* 40.1, Front. 1.9.4
12. See G. Sampson (2022).
13. Cic. *Div.* 2.52
14. T. Broughton. (1960), p.20. See R. Billows. (1982). 'The Last of the Scipios', *American Journal of Ancient History* 7, pp.53–68.
15. Plut. *Caes.* 52.4–5, Suet. *Caes.* 59
16. App. *BC.* 2.95
17. *De. Bell. Afr.* 3
18. Ibid
19. *De. Bell. Afr.* 5
20. The *De Bello Africo* (5) states that 'the rest of Caesar's forces failed to arrive to reinforce him'.
21. *De. Bell. Afr.* 6
22. Caes. *BC.* 2.38. Also see P. Townsend. (1940). 'The Oil Tribute of Africa at the Time of Julius Caesar', *Classical Philology* 35, pp.274–283.
23. *De. Bell. Afr.* 7
24. Ibid

25. *De. Bell. Afr.* 9–11
26. Ibid. 12
27. *De. Bell. Afr.* 19
28. Ibid. 13–15
29. *De. Bell. Afr.* 17
30. Ibid. 18
31. App. *BC.* 2.95
32. Dio. 43.2
33. Plut. *Caes.* 52.9
34. *De. Bell. Afr.* 18
35. Ibid. 20
36. *De. Bell. Afr.* 23
37. P. Berdowski. (2012). 'Cn. Pompeius, the son of Pompey the Great: an embarrassing ally in the African War? (48–46 BC)', *Palamedes* 7, pp.117–142.
38. Sall. *Cat.* 21
39. Cic. *Fam.* 5.17
40. Cic. *Sull.* 56
41. See E. Anderson. (2013). 'Publius Sittius and Caesar's Revenge', *History Today* 63.9.
42. *De. Bell. Afr.* 25, also see Dio. 43.3.1–4 and App. *BC.* 2.96 (who doesn't mention Sittius by name)
43. *De. Bell. Afr.* 25
44. Dio. 43.3.1
45. Ibid. 43.3.4

Chapter Six
1. Appian. *BC.* 2.96
2. *De. Bell. Afr.* 24
3. Appian. *BC.* 2.96
4. *De. Bell. Afr.* 29
5. Ibid
6. *De. Bell. Afr.* 28
7. Ibid. 34
8. *De. Bell. Afr.* 36
9. Ibid. 37
10. *De. Bell. Afr.* 38
11. Ibid. 39
12. *De. Bell. Afr.* 39–40
13. Ibid. 40
14. *De. Bell. Afr.* 40
15. Ibid. 41
16. *De. Bell. Afr.* 42
17. Ibid. 43
18. *De. Bell. Afr.* 48
19. Ibid. 49
20. *De. Bell. Afr.* 50
21. Ibid. 51
22. *De. Bell. Afr.* 52

23. Ibid. 55. See E. Fentress (1982). 'Tribe and Faction: The Case of the Gaetuli', *Mélanges de l'École Française de Rome Antiquité*, *94*, pp.325–334.
24. *De. Bell. Afr.* 59
25. Ibid. 60
26. *De. Bell. Afr.* 61
27. Ibid. 61
28. Ibid
29. *De. Bell. Afr.* 63
30. Ibid. 64
31. *De. Bell. Afr.* 65–66
32. Ibid. 67
33. *De. Bell. Afr.* 67
34. Ibid.
35. *De. Bell. Afr.* 69
36. Ibid
37. *De. Bell. Afr.* 70
38. Ibid
39. *De. Bell. Afr.* 71
40. Ibid. 74
41. *De. Bell. Afr.* 74
42. Ibid. 75
43. *De. Bell. Afr.* 76
44. Ibid. 77
45. *De. Bell. Afr.* 79

Chapter Seven
1. Dio.43.4.5
2. *De. Bell. Afr.* 79
3. Dio. 43.7.1
4. Ibid.43.7.2
5. *De. Bell. Afr.* 79
6. Ibid.
7. *De. Bell. Afr.* 80–81
8. Dio. 43.7–8
9. Plut. *Caes.* 53
10. *De. Bell. Afr.* 81
11. Dio. 43.8.2
12. Plut. *Caes.* 53.2
13. App. *BC.* 2.97
14. *De. Bell. Afr.* 80
15. Ibid. 82
16. Dio. 43.8.2
17. *De. Bell. Afr.* 83
18. Flor 2.13.67
19. *De. Bell. Afr.* 85
20. Ibid. 85
21. Ibid.
22. *De. Bell. Afr.* 86

23. See Flor. 2.13.67 who has Juba in the initial battle.
24. Dio. 43.8.3–4
25. Ibid. 9.1
26. Plut. *Caes.* 53.3–4
27. *De. Bell. Afr.* 86
28. Plut. *Caes.* 53.4
29. *De. Bell. Afr.* 86
30. Ibid
31. See G. Sampson (2022) and (2023).
32. Ibid.
33. *De. Bell. Afr.* 72
34. Val. Max. 8.14.5

Chapter Eight
1. *De. Bell. Afr.* 86
2. Ibid. 87
3. *De. Bell. Afr.* 88
4. Ibid
5. Cic. *De Off.* 1.112
6. Sen. Ep. 24.6–8
7. Especially see Plut. *Cato.* 59–73
8. App. *BC.* 2.98
9. See G. Sampson (2022).
10. Dio. 43.13.4. See C. Jones. (1970). 'Cicero's Cato', *Rheinisches Museum für Philologie* 113, pp.188–196, S. Stem. (2005). 'The First Eloquent Stoic: Cicero on Cato the Younger', *Classical Journal* 101, pp.37–49, D. Yates, (2011). 'The Role of Cato the Younger in Caesar's "Bellum Civile"', *Classical World* 104, pp.161–174.
11. Val. Max. 5.1.10
12. *De. Bell. Afr.* 88
13. Ibid. 89
14. Ibid.
15. App. *BC.* 2.100
16. *De Bell. Afr.* 93
17. It is not clear if this was the same Zama as the Battle of 202 BC.
18. *De. Bell. Afr.* 92
19. Ibid. 94
20. *De. Bell. Afr.* 90
21. App. *BC.* 2.100
22. Ibid. 97
23. Ibid
24. Ibid
25. See F. Pina Polo. (2019). 'Losers in the Civil War between Caesarians and Pompeians. Punishment and Survival', in K-J Hölkeskamp & H. Beck (eds.) Verlierer und Aussteiger in der Konkurrenz unter Anwesenden. *Agonalität in der Politischen Kultur des Antiken Rom*, pp.147–168.
26. *De. Bell. Afr.* 95
27. Dio. 43.12.2
28. *De. Bell. Afr.* 96

29. App. *BC*. 2.100
30. Dio. 43.9.5, Plut. *Caes.* 54
31. Val. Max. 3.2.13
32. Sen. 24.9–10, Also see *Suas.* 6.2 & 7.8
33. Liv. *Per.* 114
34. See R. Goodman & J. Soni. (2012). *Rome's Last Citizen. The Life and Legacy of Cato, Mortal Enemy* of Caesar (New York). F. Drogula. (2019). *Cato the Younger: Life and Death at the End of the Roman Republic* (Oxford).
35. Dio. 43.30.4
36. *De Bell. Afr.* 78
37. App. *BC.* 2.87

Chapter Nine
1. *De Bell. Afr.* 98
2. See C. Lange. (2018). *Triumphs in the Age of Civil War: The Late Republic and the Adaptability of* Triumphal *Tradition* (London).
3. App. *BC.* 2.101
4. Ibid. 2.102
5. Dio. 43.14.1
6. Ibid. 14.3–7
7. Dio. 43.15.1
8. Ibid. 43.27.2
9. Dio. 43.33.1
10. Sulla may have held both simultaneously, but it is more likely he took the Consulship after the Dictatorship
11. Ibid. 43.27.3
12. Dio. 43.12.3
13. Suet. *Caes.* 75.3
14. Cic. *Fam.* 9.7, dated to May 46 BC
15. App. *BC.* 3.77. Also see App. *BC.* 4.58, Dio, 47.26.4–7, Strab. 16.752, Joseph. *BJ.* 1.216, & *AJ.*14.268, Liv. *Per.* 114.
16. Dio. 47.26.4–7
17. Strab. 16.752–753
18. Dio. 42.27.1–2
19. App. *BC.* 4.58
20. Cic. *Fam.* 12.17
21. See T. Broughton. (1952). 2, p. 297
22. Joseph. *BJ.* 1.216–217
23. Joseph. AJ. 14.268–269
24. See G. Sampson. (Forthcoming). *The Battle of Munda (45 BC). Pompey, Labienus and Caesar's Final Battle of the Third Roman Civil War* (Barnsley).
25. See G. Sampson (2022).
26. Ibid
27. Dio. 43.29–30
28. App. *BC.* 2.87
29. Vell. 55.2–3
30. App. *BC.* 103
31. *De. Bell. Hisp.* 7.4

32. Spain in 49 BC, Greece in 48 BC and Africa in 46 BC.
33. In the region of modern Belgium.
34. Dio. 43.14.2
35. Dio. 43.31.1
36. See Dio. 43.31.2 for a pro-Caesarian view of Pompeius' strategy.
37. Liv. *Per.* 114.

Appendix One
1. See. G. Sampson (2021).
2. Eutrop. 6.22
3. App. *BC.* 2.87
4. See G. Sampson (2008).
5. Dio. 42.45.3
6. Plut. *Caes.* 50.1
7. *De. Bell. Alex.* 34
8. A. Coşkun. (2019). 'The Course of Pharnakes II's Pontic and Bosphoran Campaigns in 48/47 BC', *Phoenix* 73, pp. 86–113.
9. Ibid. 35
10. *De. Bell. Alex.* 36–37
11. Ibid. 38–40
12. *De. Bell. Alex.* 41
13. Cic. *Att.* 11.16.1
14. Dio. 42.46.4
15. *De. Bell. Alex.* 69–72
16. Ibid. 72–77
17. App. *Mith.* 120

Appendix Two
1. T. Broughton. (1960). p20.
2. See G. Sumner (1977). 'The Pompeii in their Families', *American Journal of Ancient History* 2, pp.8–25.

Appendix Four
1. This is a variation of the appendix found in G. Sampson (2019), pp.307–313.
2. See G. Sampson (2013).

Index